MW00440780

"As Wilt argues with vigour,
But if people fight together [
accessible, publicly owned,
not free—well, we might just be on a fast track to winning the world
we need."

—AVI LEWIS, filmmaker and co-founder of The Leap

"Will electric cars and ride-sharing platforms solve climate change?
For James Wilt, these supposedly eco-friendly innovations are the
latest in a long history of profit-driven threats to public transit. Wilt
debunks the hype surrounding electric, autonomous vehicles and
makes the case for a decarbonized future that guarantees mobility for
everyone."

—SHELAGH PIZEY-ALLEN, executive director of TTCriders

"In 2020, we stand at a critical juncture: will we democratize and
decarbonize mass transit systems—or will we allow private electric
vehicles to dominate our streets? In this lucid, accessible, and
sharply argued book, James Wilt presents an inspiring vision of
mobility justice for transit workers, riders, and broader communities.
In the process, he deftly critiques the twin paradigms of automobility
and austerity, which threaten to dismantle public transit in the
United States, Canada, and beyond."

—THEA RIOFRANCOS, co-author of *A Planet to Win:
Why We Need a Green New Deal*

"James Wilt's new book blows open the false promises and dead
ends of individualized, tech-savvy, platform-based solutions to our
collective need to get around. In their place Wilt recovers a demand
of public transit for all, with the needs of groups like the disabled and
the health of our planetary systems driving his case. If you're looking
for a radical orientation to the problems of transit, get this book."

—ALEX BIRNEL, Texas voting rights advocate and
community organizer

"Wilt cuts through the narratives of Silicon Valley billionaires and
lays bare the equity problems with ride-hailing services, electric cars,
and autonomous vehicles, while making the essential case that only a
massive reinvestment in public transit with democratic, community
control can achieve a future of transportation that is inclusive and
sustainable. A must-read for anyone who cares about building a
transport system that truly serves everyone while addressing the
climate crisis."

—PARIS MARX, freelance writer and editor of *Radical Urbanist*

Do Androids Dream of Electric Cars?

Do Androids Dream of Electric Cars?
© 2020 James Wilt

First published in 2020 by
Between the Lines
401 Richmond Street West
Studio 281
Toronto, Ontario M5V 3A8
Canada
1-800-718-7201
www.btlbooks.com

Every reasonable effort has been made to identify copyright holders. Between the Lines would be pleased to have any errors or omissions brought to its attention.

Cataloguing in Publication information available from
Library and Archives Canada
ISBN 9781771134484

Text design by DEEVE
Cover design by Danesh Mohiuddin
Printed in Canada

We acknowledge for their financial support of our publishing activities: the Government of Canada; the Canada Council for the Arts; and the Government of Ontario through the Ontario Arts Council, the Ontario Book Publishers Tax Credit program, and Ontario Creates.

Do Androids Dream of Electric Cars?

Public Transit in the Age of
Google, Uber, and Elon Musk

James Wilt

Between the Lines
Toronto

In memory of Larry J. Hanley (1956–2019), international president of the Amalgamated Transit Union

Contents

The slow bleed

Transit doesn't require years more testing, thousands of engineers, and tens of billions of dollars more in investments to perfect; we know that buses, trains, and streetcars work, as they have for over a century.

WAKANDA TRANSIT

We once dreamed of a world without cars. Early science fiction is littered with futuristic promises of public transportation. *When the Sleeper Wakes* by H.G. Wells, published in 1899, featured rapidly moving sidewalks with seats, kiosks, and "an innumerable and wonderfully diversified multitude of people." Stanley G. Weinbaum's 1935 "The Worlds of If" speculated about a crowded but friendly "trans-oceanic rocket." In Ray Bradbury's 1950s classic *Fahrenheit 451*, protagonist Guy Montag rode a "silent air-propelled train [that] slid soundlessly down its lubricated flue in the earth and let him out ... onto the cream tiled escalator rising to the suburb."[1]

As the twentieth century wore on, depictions of transportation veered toward the privatized, with the flying cars, jetpacks, and speeders in *The Jetsons* and *Star Wars* capturing the public imagination. Yet the curious presence of public transit lingered, mostly as convenient prop: the backdrop of action movies like *Speed* and *Mission: Impossible*, or a locale for somewhat inconvenient or bizarre meetings, meditations, or getaways. *Stranger Than Fiction's* Harold Crick reads a fateful manuscript on the night bus until it pulls into the depot. Clementine and Joel have an awkwardly adorable meeting on the Long Island Rail Road in *Eternal Sunshine of the Spotless Mind*. Peter Parker rescues New York subway riders in *Spider-Man 2*. In those films, public transit is an almost unfortunate reality of society, with participants finding joy amid the grime and crowdedness.

But in 2018, a startlingly sympathetic Hollywood depiction of public transportation came in the form of a Marvel blockbuster, *Black Panther*. Celebrated for many reasons—it was the first top-tier superhero movie with a Black director and nearly all-Black cast—the film featured soaring shots of fictional Wakanda's capital that included sophisticated maglev trains and streetcars. The movie triggered a torrent of think pieces about its immaculate mobility systems, with headlines including "The Attainable Wonders of Wakandan Transit," "Black Panther's Wakanda Is a Transportation Utopia with a Dash of Reality," and "'Black Panther' Succeeds as Urban Utopia: There Are No Cars in Wakanda."[2]

That was no accident. Director Ryan Coogler was explicitly inspired by Oakland and San Francisco's Bay Area Rapid Transit (BART) system when envisioning Golden City's transportation network.[3] Sure, viewers weren't privy to relevant details like scheduling or fare payments (or anything about what life is like in a society ruled by a "benevolent dictator" like T'Challa).[4] But Janette Sadik-Khan, former commissioner of the New York State Department of Transportation, still tweeted that it was "one of the first movies to get urbanism right, with a transit-friendly, walkable Wakanda."[5]

Sadly, that vision came crashing down as soon as you left the movie theatre. One Twitter user, who tagged New York's Metropolitan Transportation Authority in their post, mused: "There's nothing quite like experiencing a technologically advanced Wakanda only to come back to reality and experience a broken ass transit system underground in between stations overheating with no service." Others complained about the notoriously dilapidated transit network in Washington, DC, a system so underfunded that it's now auctioning off the naming rights to its new subway stations.[6] One user recommended the Washington Metropolitan Area Transit Authority "send a delegation to Wakanda to check out their transit system," while another tweeted: "The first thing Wakanda should do for the world is fix WMATA."[7]

Such a rude awakening, from theatre to train, encapsulates the unfortunate reality facing riders in almost every city in North America. Public transportation is in seriously bad shape. Ridership numbers are far from the only way to evaluate the transit crisis—but they're a fine place to start. The decline started in 2015, after an all-time ridership record the year prior.[8] Between 2014 and 2017, total ridership in the United States fell by a startling 6 percent.[9] Bus ridership plummeted by over 14 percent.[10] A shocking 31 of the country's 35 largest transit systems lost ridership between 2016 and 2017.[11]

Even New York City—by far the largest transit system in the U.S., so big that it's often excluded from national averages because it skews the data—experienced sizable losses after several years of sustained increases. Between 2016 and 2017, the city's subway ridership dropped by almost 30 million rides, while buses lost 35 million rides.[12] Chicago, Washington, DC, and Philadelphia all experienced declines.[13] "I think it needs to be considered an emergency," said renowned transit planner Jarrett Walker.[14] And these trends continued into 2019.[15]

Canada has somewhat bucked the trend; most remarkably, Vancouver's ridership increased 7.1 percent in 2018, reiterating its role as one transit leader in North America.[16] But most cities in North America are in serious trouble.

POLICY BIAS

This isn't a new crisis. Public transit has been systematically neglected in favour of the private automobile for decades.

Around three-quarters of Americans have driven to work since 1990, with transit use flatlining at around 10 percent.[17] In Canada, about two-thirds of commuters drive to work, with 25 percent of Toronto residents and 23 percent of Montrealers using transit.[18] But in the European Union's 72 largest cities, an average of 49 percent of people use transit to get to work, and it's as high as 74 percent in Vienna.[19]

Such usage isn't due to some innate Europeanness that North Americans are unable to access. In fact, many of the cities that we think of as the most progressive on this front were themselves once dominated by cars. It was mass struggle in Amsterdam in the 1960s and 1970s that forced politicians to turn against car-centric design and introduce widespread cycle paths.[20] The transit geographies of Europe are the result of specific policy decisions to promote non-automotive means of transportation: options that governments on this side of the Atlantic have consciously refused or undermined. As a result, transit and active transportation are still technically options in North American cities—but they're by no means reliable, efficient, or affordable.

Much of the blame for the recent ridership decline has been placed on the rapid growth of ride-hailing services (also known as transportation network companies, or TNCs) such as Uber and Lyft.[21] Such companies certainly add to congestion and poach affluent riders from transit routes. But they only represent the tip of an iceberg formed by decades of city planning and highway construction that premised the private automobile as the ideal form of transportation and administered austerity on transit agencies. Between 2010 and 2019, the U.S. added 1,200 miles of new transit infrastructure—and 28,500 miles of new roadway.[22]

A study by New York City's TransitCenter found that private car trips are rapidly replacing transit rides, with 2018 serving as a record year for per capita mileage.[23] Companies like Uber and Lyft are playing a part—but the researchers concluded it's still mostly people driving their own private vehicles that's taking away ridership from transit. As TransitCenter's director of research Steven Higashide put it to *Government Technology*: "None of this is to discount the role that TNCs are playing. But we do think it's important for cities to keep in mind that it really comes down to these basic questions of, does transit deliver a competitive travel plan or not? And for the most part, if it doesn't, you're still seeing people buying private vehicles."

The situation is worsening in many communities. Not because public transportation is outdated, unwanted, or too costly. It's that the very concept of a new generation of automobiles—first a proliferation of personal electric vehicles, then ride-hailing services like Uber and Lyft, and eventually autonomous vehicles (AVs) of some form or another—are being wielded by austerity-minded politicians as reasons to not invest in public transportation. These "three revolutions" in transportation are widely proclaimed as the inevitable way of the future, and they're sapping our ability to plan transit for the public good.

In late 2019, a commissioner for Michigan's Macomb County argued that Detroit's transit system should be replaced by ride-hailing subsidies for low-income residents (everyone else would pay full rate).[24] A referendum in Nashville to approve an ambitious $5.4 billion transit plan was defeated by a Koch brothers–backed opposition; one city councillor suggested that residents should vote against the proposal because "driverless buses will be ready in 12 months."[25]

Marta Viciedo, director of Miami's Urban Impact Lab, told me that many decisions in South Florida are being made on the promise of autonomous vehicles; city leadership used it to recently justify highway extensions. In late 2019, Ontario's Conservative government cancelled $1 billion in funding for a light rail system in Hamilton; earlier that year, it became the first province to allow autonomous vehicle testing without a human driver at the wheel and committed $40 million to an auto sector plan that would help develop autonomous vehicle infrastructure.[26] A prolonged bias toward privatized transportation is finding new justification.

Worsening transit service leads to stagnating or declining ridership, which in turn is used to justify more service cuts. Jarrett Walker, author of the indispensable *Human Transit: How Clearer Thinking about Public Transit Can Enrich Our Communities and Our Lives*, identifies seven demands that riders require before relying on public transportation:

> It takes me *where* I want to go.
> It takes me *when* I want to go.
> It is a good use of my *time*.
> It is a good use of my *money*.
> It *respects* me in the level of safety, comfort, and amenity it provides.
> I can *trust* it.
> It gives me *freedom* to change my plans.[27]

But few politicians ride the bus, meaning they rarely have to think about these needs. "Politicians don't use transit," Vince Puhakka of Toronto's TTCriders told me. "They can afford to take Uber home from their restaurant. It's a form of elite projection. They think everyone can do what they do."

Elected officials are thus quick to blame ridership losses on a host of other factors: low gasoline prices, Uber and Lyft, telecommuting, lack of congestion pricing or carbon taxes. But loss of transit ridership is ultimately caused by the sustained failure of governments to fund and prioritize service in a way that fulfills those seven rider demands and creates an actual alternative to automobility. (I use *automobility* to refer to the driving of all personal vehicles including cars, SUVs, pickup trucks, and minivans, as well as the broader political and cultural biases that justify its continuance.) The main culprit is austerity, unleashed most intensely on low-income communities.

If transit is funded by governments at all, it tends to be big infrastructure projects: new rail lines, stations, or upgrades. Every politician loves a ribbon cutting. Certain types of transit modes (usually rail) and sheer distance of track become fetishized as intrinsically beneficial, without much consideration of quality of service.[28] Such capital spending is important, of course; many communities do need new rail lines. There is also an estimated $90 billion backlog of public transit modernization needs in the United States.[29]

In some major cities, conditions have become beyond absurd. In 2016, a Twitter account and website called IsMetroOnFire.com tracked which subway lines in Washington, DC, were literally on fire, as well as constant delays and multi-day shutdowns due to deferred maintenance.[30]

With only a few exceptions, federal governments in the U.S. and Canada have never meaningfully funded operating costs of running transit, leaving many transit agencies with functional infrastructure but without the means to run it at full capacity. You can't operate buses without drivers. Ride-hailing and talk of imminent autonomous vehicles provide a convenient distraction to these realities.

The irony is that many improvements to public transportation can be both simple and affordable. Dedicated bus lanes

"The main threat of autonomous vehicles is a political threat. We know that autonomous vehicles, if they ever arrive, may be decades away. Yet a lot of elected officials and a lot of other decision makers sometimes talk about them as if they're going to be here tomorrow, as if that means we should just rip up traditional transit systems. The bigger threat is not that the technology somehow disrupts transit. It's that in many cases it empowers politicians who are always looking for some reason to cut public transit."

—STEVEN HIGASHIDE, TransitCenter, New York City

with traffic signal priority can have immediate impacts on reliability and efficiency of transit—and require only a few buckets of paint and new traffic light hardware. Other changes, like all-door boarding and off-board fare payment, can reduce the amount of time it takes riders to get on a vehicle.

Big infrastructure projects such as rail line repairs and a new fleet of electric buses, or service improvements like free public transit and hiring more drivers, may require more planning and money. But ultimately, no more than what's currently shelled out on automobility, especially when its impacts on climate, public health, and poverty are accounted for. The austerity that transit is subjected to is by no means consistent; governments massively subsidize fossil fuels and automobile usage both directly and indirectly. But as the late transit expert Paul Mees argued, we don't need to wait for sprawled communities to miraculously densify before providing quality public transportation: the answer is consistent funding, public ownership, and common-sense planning by people who actually ride transit.[31]

What is required for transit to succeed is real, unwavering political commitment and funding, fought for by transit workers and riders. Seattle, for example—which has emphasized cooperation between rail and buses, consistent off-peak service, and several incentives to buy monthly passes (including transit passes considered a job benefit)—has bucked the trend to great success. Ridership there has increased by 50 percent since the early 2000s.[32] After years of plummeting usage, transit systems in New York City and Washington, DC, saw recent upticks in usage following significant investments in system maintenance and upgrades.[33]

Communities that prioritize transit service in funding and planning see increased usage.[34] Recognition of that reality is what companies like Uber and Lyft are siphoning. They capitalize on real flaws and criticisms of public transportation with convenient apps and tens of billions in venture capital funds to make it seem like they're offering a revolutionary service that renders transit obsolete.

New tricks like Netflix-inspired transportation subscription services or heavily subsidized arrangements with small towns to provide "transit" with ride-hailing vehicles mask a simple truth: that all companies like Uber and Lyft bring to the table is an elite taxi service that has successfully evaded regulations, suppressed wages to record-low levels, and downloaded most costs onto drivers.

The allure of the venture-capital-backed services is convincing many policymakers that the solution to transportation woes is far *more* private vehicles—and in turn, an abandonment or even outright opposition to public transit. Once allowed into a city, these firms become exceedingly difficult to regulate.[35]

There's also no guarantee such firms will stick around. In late 2019 the car-sharing service Car2Go, owned by Daimler of Mercedes-Benz fame, announced it was pulling out of North America due to "the volatile state of the global mobility landscape." Other ridiculous experiments like Uber's $200 per trip helicopter service between Wall Street and JFK airport reiterate that such companies don't care about improving service for all, only profiteering off the whims of the rich.[36] Relying on such fickle private companies is no way to plan a transportation system.[37]

A war for streets and communities is currently under way. It's the same war that created automotive dominance and sprawled, racially segregated regions in the first place. Doubling down on such commodification with the "three revolutions" of next-generation vehicles including electric, ride-hailing, and autonomous vehicles will likely lead to greater emissions, worsened inequality, more sprawl and dangerous streets, and even less accessibility for seniors, people with disabilities, and women, trans, and gender non-conforming people. Conditions are also moving quickly in this direction. But it's not inevitable. Communities can fight back—and force politicians to build better public transportation, as part of a much greater struggle against the forces of inequality and oppression.

"We have to recognize that the status quo of policy neglect is one of the things that's leading to lower transit ridership in recent years," Higashide told me. "It's going to take concerted action to turn it around. But we've seen it happen in enough places to know that it's possible."

Public transportation is usually, and correctly, imagined as buses, light rail, streetcars, and subways operating in a large city. But it also means intercity buses and passenger rail, minivans and minibuses, and paratransit for people with disabilities. The key aspects for the purposes of this book are that the vehicles and systems are publicly owned, driven by professional and preferably unionized workers, and operating for socially beneficial purposes—not private profits. Such a vision can encompass the largest city to the smallest town.

In many parts of the world, public transit is a fully functional part of society.[38] Yonah Freemark, founder of the U.S. transit blog the *Transport Politic*, stresses that he doesn't think there is any reason to think transit doesn't have a future. "If you look at conditions outside of the United States," he told me, "the situation is far more optimistic, and ridership has maintained or grown in most major cities. And that's because of significant additional investments they've made and improvements in services provided. Those have resulted in basically people wanting to use the services. I see no reason to think that wouldn't be the same in the U.S. and those trends wouldn't continue."

That doesn't mean that cities like Seattle or Vienna are perfect in how they approach transit. Even the best services can be enmeshed in politics of privatization and gentrification. But we can learn from the successes of such places, while we struggle against the forces of private capital accumulation and commodification that distort the public mandate of transit.

FOOD FOR THE STRUGGLE

This book provides some of the information necessary to resist the incursions of more (and new) automobiles in our cities and towns—and to advocate for more free, reliable, accessible, and pleasurable public transportation. It touches on cycling and pedestrian infrastructure along the way: after all, every transit user starts or ends their journey on foot, bike, or mobility aid like wheelchair or scooter. But as Paul Mees argued: "Unless public transport is so convenient that it offers real competition to the car, then schemes to promote walking and cycling, and restrain car use, will founder."[39] My priority is to make a strong case for transit in the face of next-generation automobiles, with the expectation that such struggles will greatly improve the experiences of cyclists and pedestrians. Measures like lowering speed limits and reducing street space dedicated to automobiles will increase safety for everyone, and allow for more square footage and funding to be devoted to sidewalks, cycle tracks, and transitways.

To make that case, this book is divided into three parts. Part one, Depot, briefly examines the history of automobility in North America, the rapid privatization of transportation, and the political economy of the "three revolutions." It is the failures of transit in many places that have allowed public support for next-generation automobility to take hold. Part two, Departure, is broken up into seven subject-based chapters: climate and environment, economic and racial inequality, safety and congestion, genuine accessibility for marginalized people, data privacy and surveillance, rural and intercity service, and labour unions. In each, the supposed benefits of next-generation automobility are explored, as well as their potential limitations. Then, the often-serious flaws of public transportation are acknowledged, before moving on to the incredible potential to improve such modes with proper funding and democratic planning. These short subject-based chapters are not exhaustive; they are principally intended to provide basic information to counter claims of next-generation automobility.

Part three, Destination, concludes with descriptions of how public transit systems should be funded and planned.

I interviewed forty-eight experts for this book, including community activists, academics, transit planners, authors, and journalists. Some of the most exciting work around transit politics is happening in other countries, including in the Global South. However, my focus here is on the U.S., with additional interviews and examples from Canada. Of large countries, the two nations feature among the highest per capita emissions in the world, more than double the global average.[40] Much of that pollution comes from transportation. Other countries have much to teach us about public transportation, but this project's focus is on the problems that face North America and how its communities can fight back.[41]

ASSUMPTIONS

Before we begin, allow me to clearly articulate six of the book's fundamental assumptions.

1. Transportation systems must be publicly owned, operated, and planned to succeed. The aim of private firms—manufacturers, ride-hailing services, or autonomous vehicle aspirants—isn't to genuinely improve the ability for everyone to get around. It's to dominate the market share and maximize profits. Privatization of transportation almost always leads to higher fares, worsened service, unexpected stoppages, and fragmentation of networks. Private companies are also much harder to gather information about, effectively regulate, or hold to account.[42] A central assumption is that truly public transportation remains the best system to guarantee accessibility, affordability, and reliability. And that despite its failures, we—transit riders, potential riders, and workers, and all of us who have to sell our labour power to survive—must fight to make it the best that it can be. The ultimate goal of radical transit politics should be fully democratized control, with riders having legitimate power over decisions. That said, current but often problematic systems of state ownership keep democratization within the realm of possibility.

2. Everyone has a "right to the city." This idea, advocated for by the likes of French philosopher Henri Lefebvre and British geographer David Harvey, conceptualizes the city as a key site of struggle against the manifestations of capitalist production and state power. Many social movements are grounded in the right to the city, including universal access to quality housing, good food, and free transit. It's not just about securing vastly improved public housing and services, however, but an ongoing quest to "make and remake ourselves and our cities," as Harvey put it in his famous 2003 essay.[43] This book's overarching critique is grounded in the argument that such privately owned modes violate the right to the city for many residents. Conversely, public transit holds the potential for a greatly expanded sense of right to the city, practically (being able to use a bus to get to an appointment or grocery store) as well as politically (having true power over decision-making). Despite its name, this right extends to towns and rural areas.

3. The book is anchored in American sociologist Mimi Sheller's paradigm of "mobility justice," which views urban and regional transportation as one part of a set of struggles that range from micro issues such as disability and gender to transnational issues such as climate change and migration policy.[44] Sheller identified a "triple crisis" of mobility: the climate crisis, urbanization crisis (automobility, poverty, evictions), and refugee crisis. All are unfolding in territories with brutal legacies of chattel slavery and colonial genocide; militarized border walls, rampant gentrification, and mass incarceration are only the latest updates. Sheller told me, "If you're not aware of the broader geographical and spatial patterns of social injustices, you're probably just going to make them worse." Transit access remains horrifically poor for many Indigenous and Black communities, worsened by racist policing and security—and we must work to undo this ongoing oppression. Struggles must also be anchored in explicit class terms. Automotive dominance is an outcome of prioritizing private capital accumulation over mobility rights. Many policymakers emerge from, or have ties to, powerful capitalist interests. These affiliations impact for whom cities and regions are built. Public transit agencies themselves often reproduce racist, exclusionary, and classist politics—but transit history is also marked by instances of riders fighting back to build a better society.

4. Improving transit to the point of it serving as a dominant mode for a majority of the population will require the phasing out of private automobiles. Street space is a zero-sum game: every additional car, SUV, truck, or minivan on the road adds to congestion and slows other modes down. For the benefits of buses and trains to be maximized, car traffic must be reduced: dedicated transit lanes, traffic signal priority, lower speed limits for private automobiles, and outright bans from certain parts of the city. These policies will undoubtedly provoke anger from many drivers, which is why they must be paired with greatly reduced or free fares and improved service to low-income and low-density areas. Automobility means that a driver can get to any part of a city or region, at any time of day, in a reasonable span. Cities serve that desire by paving every street to every house.[45] While transit can't perfectly replicate this—transfers, for instance, may be required on many routes—with proper funding, it can offer many of the same benefits. Public transportation must be funded as oppositional to automobility. We can either have continued automotive dominance or great transit. It's one or the other.

5. Catastrophic climate change is already here—and it's about to get far, far worse. A devastating 2018 report by the UN Intergovernmental Panel on Climate Change (IPCC) warned that the world has to slash greenhouse gas emissions by 45 percent by 2030 and achieve zero emissions by 2050 in order to keep average temperatures under 1.5°C of warming from pre-fossil-fuel times.[46] That will require a radical transformation of society, including a wartime-like buildout of renewable electricity generation and electrification of transportation and heating and cooling of buildings. We don't have time to waste or mistakes to risk. Boosters of next-generation automobility promote personal electric vehicles as a solution to climate change. But there's a great deal of uncertainty about timelines, driver preferences, behavioural psychology, and whether ride-hailing and autonomous vehicles will be fully electrified. The only mode of transportation that we can guarantee will roll out as planned is the century-old technologies of public transportation. Fledgling environmental movements like the Sunrise Movement and Extinction Rebellion have communicated well the dire urgency facing society, but have so far rarely engaged with the threats of automobility. Transit, along with housing, are key climate policies, and we must organize with that in mind.

6. Transit is a powerful and multifaceted issue to organize around. Riders are often centrally located in bus stops and train stations, where they can be approached to have a conversation, sign a petition, or be invited to an organizing meeting. Transit offers an opportunity to build power around an issue that many people can viscerally relate to and want to see improved. This movement must be led by both transit riders' organizations and transit workers' unions, whose membership often bears the brunt of austerity measures and the ensuing anger of riders at transit's costs and unreliability. Labour and fare strikes are great weapons to collectively exert power and demand rapid improvements.[47] Transportation is also linked to many other issues including housing, food, and access to healthcare, education, and social services: unless you can reliably get to a medical appointment or grocery store, improvements in those sectors can't be fully accessed. That opens up potential for partnerships between transit organizing and other struggles including tenants' unions, minimum wage campaigns, and anti-carceral activism—which allows for analysis of the interlinked impacts of austerity, racism, and the climate crisis. Unions representing workers in other sectors can fight to include improved transit access for their members, which can in turn improve service for everyone. Through a focus on the class dimensions of transit, victories can come from unexpected places. As transit activists are demonstrating around the world, the demand for free transit is an especially powerful one that unites struggles for climate action, police abolition, and disability rights.[48]

Public transportation represents an immediately build-able set of technologies that we can use to make and remake communities, combatting capitalism, colonialism, and racist state violence. Transit doesn't require years more testing, thousands of engineers, and tens of billions of dollars more in investments to perfect; we know that buses, trains, and street-cars work, as they have for over a century. The issue is about much more than physical bus chassis and routes. It concerns the ability for the working class to exert power over how cities and towns are built and for whom. The only thing that stands in the way of success is further capitulation to capitalist power that seeks to further remake the world in its own image. But first, we must come to terms with the existing state of transit and the promises of the "three revolutions" that seek to deliver its deathblow.

Part One

Depot >>> Depot >>> Depot >>> Depot >>> Depot >>> Depot
>>> Depot >>> Depot >>> Depot >>> Depot >>> Depot >>> De
pot >>> Depot >>> Depot >>> Depot >>> Depot >>> Depot
>>> Depot >>> Depot >>> Depot >>> Depot >>> Depot >>> De
pot >>> Depot >>> Depot >>> Depot >>> Depot >>> Depot
>>> Depot >>> Depot >>> **Depot** >>> Depot >>> Depot >>> De
pot >>> Depot >>> Depot >>> Depot >>> Depot >>> Depot
>>> Depot >>> Depot >>> Depot >>> Depot >>> Depot >>> De
pot >>> Depot >>> Depot >>> Depot >>> Depot >>> Depot
>>> Depot >>> Depot >>> Depot >>> Depot >>> Depot >>> De
pot >>> Depot >>> Depot >>> Depot >>> Depot >>> Depot
>>> Depot >>> Depot >>> Depot >>> Depot >>> Depot >>> De
pot >>> Depot >>> Depot >>> Depot >>> Depot >>> Depot
>>> Depot >>> Depot >>> Depot >>> Depot >>> Depot >>> De
pot >>> Depot >>> Depot >>> Depot >>> Depot >>> Depot
>>> Depot >>> Depot >>> Depot >>> Depot >>> Depot >>> De
pot >>> Depot >>> Depot >>> Depot >>> Depot >>> Depot
>>> Depot >>> Depot >>> Depot >>> Depot >>> Depot >>> De
pot >>> Depot >>> Depot >>> Depot >>> Depot >>> Depot
>>> Depot >>> Depot >>> Depot >>> Depot >>> Depot >>> De
pot >>> Depot >>> Depot >>> Depot >>> Depot >>> Depot
>>> Depot >>> Depot >>> Depot >>> Depot >>> Depot >>> De
pot >>> Depot >>> Depot >>> Depot >>> Depot >>> Depot
>>> Depot >>> Depot >>> Depot >>> Depot >>> Depot >>> De
pot >>> Depot >>> Depot >>> Depot >>> Depot >>> Depot
>>> Depot >>> Depot >>> Depot >>> Depot >>> Depot >>> De
pot >>> Depot >>> Depot >>> Depot >>> Depot >>> Depot
>>> Depot >>> Depot >>> Depot >>> Depot >>> Depot >>> De
pot >>> Depot >>> Depot >>> Depot >>> Depot >>> Depot

Chapter 1

Off the rails

A brief history of automotive domination

The combination of chronic underfunding, capitalist planning, and political bias toward the automobile has sabotaged transit at almost every step.

THE BATTLE FOR THE STREETS

It was the shot heard round the world—for transit experts, at least. "I think public transport is painful. It sucks," Tesla CEO Elon Musk opined at a 2017 convention. "Why do you want to get on something with a lot of other people, that doesn't leave where you want it to leave, doesn't start where you want it to start, doesn't end where you want it to end? And it doesn't go all the time. It's a pain in the ass. That's why everyone doesn't like it. And there's like a bunch of random strangers, one of who might be a serial killer, OK, great. And so that's why people like individualized transport, that goes where you want, when you want."[1]

Criticism of Musk's comments was swift and damning. Transit planner Jarrett Walker tweeted that the billionaire's "hatred of sharing space with strangers is a luxury (or pathology) that only the rich can afford," while Rich Sampson of the Community Transportation Association of America quipped:

"When you're white, wealthy & emotionally estranged, you view everyone else as an inconvenience at best and a threat at worst."[2] In response, Musk tweeted at Walker: "You're an idiot," clarifying a few hours later that he "meant to say 'sanctimonious idiot.'"[3]

The online fireworks weren't only entertaining—but also instructive in how automobile dominance is justified and defended by its proponents. Musk's anti-transit comments contained an age-old myth of a "love affair with the automobile" that has been weaponized for a century.

There is nothing inevitable about widespread automobility. Contrary to elite opinions, the daily deluge of car commercials, and the implications of every related political announcement—to fund a new road, expand a highway, or offer electric vehicle subsidies—there is no such thing as an inherent "love affair with the automobile" that needs to continue. What we think of as car culture, and increasingly as truck and SUV culture, is the product of a century-long onslaught of corporate lobbying, propaganda, and mythmaking, along with massive state subsidies that produced the infrastructure required for suburbanization and automobile dominance. It has largely worked. By and large, transit systems in North America are underused, dilapidated, and overpriced.

Some urbanist explanations of this ideological coup revolve around the alleged conspiracy of National City Lines between 1938 and 1950, in which General Motors, Firestone Tires, Standard Oil of California, and other companies that were invested in automotive dominance bought up and destroyed complex networks of electric streetcars in cities across the U.S. and Canada. There is some truth to the story, which found a popular retelling in *Who Framed Roger Rabbit*. In 1949, participating companies were convicted for violating the Sherman Antitrust Act via National City Lines' monopoly over diesel bus sales and products, which further entrenched automobiles as the basic form of transportation. Functional streetcar systems were replaced by buses, which eventually lost out to cars. But while the so-called GM streetcar conspiracy is a particularly memorable example of how automotive and oil interests collaborate to pursue profit, the story of how car dominance came to be is considerably longer and more complex. As argued by Australian writer Jeff Sparrow about the so-called conspiracy: "In many ways that missed the bigger point: simply, streetcars, trains and other transport systems required state support to be viable, and that support increasingly went to automobiles."[4] Let's review some of that history's highlights (and lowlights).

The first Model T was sold in 1908, and the first U.S. federal road program was inaugurated in 1916.[5] Peter Norton, author of *Fighting Traffic: The Dawn of the Motor Age in the American City*, told me that by the 1920s cars were viewed by much of the public as extremely dangerous, understood as forcing pedestrians off streets, crowding curbs, delaying streetcars, taking up excess space by sitting idle, and failing to serve a large portion of the people in a dense city. Judges, juries, and newspaper editorial pages blamed the car every time one killed a pedestrian on the street.

Dan Albert, author of *Are We There Yet?: The American Automobile Past, Present, and Driverless*, observed: "The upper classes used automotive violence to drive the working classes and urban poor from the streets—relatively wide open spaces in dense urban neighborhoods. Vigilantes responded with attacks on the millionaire motorists who raced through working class neighborhoods."[6]

The automobile was seen as a clear threat to the peace and safety of urban residents. As a result, municipal engineers took a series of steps to limit private car use. Those included banning curb parking, designing intersections and signal timing in a way that deliberately delayed traffic, and encouraging pedestrians to cross the street anywhere they liked. In their early era, North American cities were explicitly designed for the pedestrian and the streetcar.

"That status quo just terrified people who wanted to sell

cars," Norton says. "People were actually not buying very many cars in cities." The automotive industry then realized that "the obvious solution lies only in a radical redefinition of our conception of what a city street is for."

A concerted propaganda campaign by the automotive industry ensued. When a pedestrian was killed, the industry worked to ensure the victim was subject to public blame. Norton says that huge efforts were poured into a "campaign of organized ridicule against people who walk in streets," including collaborating with local police departments to physically pick up jaywalkers and carry them to the curb in order to embarrass them into never repeating the "crime." When cars collided, auto interests called for wider roads to improve safety rather than slowing down traffic.

In 1932, the National Highway Users Conference was officially inaugurated by General Motors, the American Automobile Association, and other interests.[7] Every safety issue that arose was solved in a way that didn't slow or restrict cars.

"It was a really substantially successful effort to create a car-dependent city," Norton says. "And the car-dependent city became self-perpetuating: to survive in the car-dependent city, you have to get a car. And once you have a car, now your interests do align to some degree with the proponents of the car-dependent city because they're the people who say, 'If you're stuck in traffic, we'll get you another lane.'"

Private companies that were contracted by cities to provide streetcar service, sometimes along with electricity and road paving, began to fail en masse.[8] Throughout the twentieth century, many major transit systems were taken over by municipalities. The Public Utility Holding Company Act of 1935 divided the previously close relationship between the transit industry and electric utilities, and the rise of suburbs, highways, and automobile dominance further undermined the financial viability of private transit operators. Yet even after being taken over, many transit systems were losing out to auto-mobility in state support.

Franklin D. Roosevelt's New Deal of 1933, premised on mass consumption of cheap energy, played a major part in this process. Matthew Huber, author of *Lifeblood: Oil, Freedom, and the Forces of Capital*, told me that prior to World War II, American workers didn't have high enough wages or the public infrastructure to consume in a way that created sufficient demand for capitalism to expand. The Wagner Act of 1935 dramatically altered those conditions by guaranteeing the rights of labourers to organize into unions and collectively bargain without fear of being fired. Higher wages for white workers combined with a massive mobilization of public resources to create the capacity for widespread private car ownership and highly segregated single-family suburban living. The GI Bill of 1944 further entrenched this trajectory by offering very low-interest mortgages for new suburban homes to returning white soldiers while systematically denying them to Black soldiers through bureaucratic restrictions, violent intimidation, and redlining; a huge majority of Federal Housing Administration (FHA) loans dispersed over the following decades were for suburban homes.[9]

The automotive industry tirelessly advocated for grade-separated, divided, controlled-access highways through cities. The Federal Aid Highway Act of 1956 was largely financed by a gas tax. This process satisfied industry, as it understood that highways would be able to expand much faster via a gas tax than toll roads.[10] The $128.9 billion interstate highway system, covering 90 percent of highway costs, was planned out by the auto industry and highway engineers—not urban planners or local communities.[11] These freeways were antithetical to bus service, which relied on frequent opportunities to stop.[12]

The mass buildout decimated communities of colour, destroying local neighbourhood economies, displacing residents, cutting off access to other parts of the city, and compounding racist oppression that had been institutionalized by redlining and blockbusting.[13] Violence and intimidation was also used by white residents, especially against Black families.

As historians Becky Nicolaides and Andrew Wiese wrote about the development of the suburbs:

> African American, Asian American, and Latino families battled for access to the suburbs, challenging not only the presumed whiteness of suburbia but the ideology of white supremacy implicit in postwar suburban ideology. In response, white suburbanites in concert with other crucial players—including government—created a web of discrimination that secured links between race, social advantage, and metropolitan space.[14]

This racist and ecologically devastating process became self-reinforcing. Transit usage dropped drastically after the war, leading to more cuts.[15] White suburbanites became convinced of their inherent right to drive gas guzzlers to and from their homes in increasingly sprawled cities, while simultaneously opposing higher taxes. This culminated in the rise of so-called taxpayer revolts like California's 1978 Proposition 13, which stunted the ability of municipalities to gather property taxes and has been described as "the antitax measure that ignited the Reagan Revolution and the conservative era."[16] Huge public resources had been used to produce geographies of privatism; such a revolt was an almost inevitable endpoint. As Huber explains: "Privatized geographies lead to privatized forms of politics, which are not good."

Throughout this time, automobile companies lied and evaded regulations. Famous examples include the following:

> General Motors hiring private detectives to slander Ralph Nader's reputation after the publishing of his ground-breaking 1965 investigation *Unsafe at Any Speed*
> Ford's refusal to fix a known problem with its Pintos that caused the fuel tank to catch fire in crashes

> Toyota's cover-up of a defect that jammed the accelerator with fatal consequences
> the Ford Explorer–Firestone Tire rollover scandal due to shredding tires
> Volkswagen's massive diesel emissions scandal[17]

Car companies have gamed fuel economy standards for years, with a 42 percent gap between test and actual performance.[18] American automobile manufacturers spent almost $50 million in 2017 lobbying the federal government to lower fuel economy standards.[19] "At each step of this industry's evolution, they have lied and they have lied in a way specifically that causes harm to human beings," Matthew Lewis, a climate and energy policy consultant in Berkeley, told me.

University of Iowa law professor Gregory Shill has made the case that the U.S. is "car-dependent by law" at every level of government: "traffic laws, land use, criminal law, torts, insurance, environmental, vehicle safety regulations, and even tax law provide incentives to cooperate with the dominant transport mode and punishment for those who defect."[20] These structures, Shill argued, not only displace costs onto non-drivers but institutionalize a "state of dependency and inequality."

A similar argument by Brown University anthropologist Catherine Lutz identified five "automobility-induced pathways to inequality," concluding:

With the aid of unremitting state support over the course of a century, car and oil corporations emerged at the center of a regime of accumulation that directs massive amounts of daily spending by all car owners and users, directly and via the tax system, to a small number of people and groups at the very top of the U.S. economic system.[21]

Public transit was a victim of this legal and ideological coup. The only transit services that were able to retain ridership through the upheaval were the grade-separated rail lines in large cities like New York and Chicago. "Only when transit didn't need to share the road with the car, and frequent service continued, was it able to survive," Jonathan English wrote.[22]

The massive Urban Mass Transportation Act of 1964 committed $375 million over three years of federal capital aid for transit, mostly rapid transit systems.[23] But the new rail systems failed to coordinate service with buses, leading to low ridership in many places. The same error was echoed in the commuter rail and light rail eras of the 1980s onwards.[24]

THE NEOLIBERAL COUP

Starting in the late 1970s, neoliberalism ushered in a new phase of privatization, gutting of spending on public services, and fragmentation of transit service. Under U.K. prime minister Margaret Thatcher, buses were deregulated and privatized in 1985, along with a series of state-owned enterprises related to rail infrastructure. Between 1995 and 2013, bus fares outside London shot up by 35 percent above inflation, while many routes were cut.[25]

Most transit services in North America have remained relatively public in terms of ownership and operation. But that's changing fast—particularly through the public-private partnership (P3) model of development. There are many different kinds of P3s, ranging from basic service and management contracts, to design-build arrangements (in which the private companies construct the asset), to design-build-finance-operate-maintain, to build-own-operate (in which the private sector maintains ownership on behalf of a government without full privatization).

The appeal of P3s for neoliberal governments is that short-term risks and costs can be transferred to the private sector, keeping debt off the books despite the likelihood of costing more in the long run. Toby Sanger, executive director of Canadians for Tax Fairness, explains: "This really hides the cost. There's no actual accounting rules for the public sector that specify how you need to report P3s. Those future costs are largely kept off the books. It's impossible to find out what these are unless governments open their books or the auditor general looks at them."

In Toronto, all of Metrolinx's proposed light rail transit (LRT) lines are being constructed with P3 arrangements. In 2015, a consortium of private partners under the name of Crosslinx Transit Solutions agreed to design, build, finance, and maintain the Eglinton Crosstown LRT line. In July 2018, Crosslinx Transit Solutions filed a notice of motion alleging that the provincially appointed Metrolinx and the Ontario Infrastructure and Lands Corporation had delayed their work, requesting more time and compensation to finish the project. The two sides eventually reached a settlement, but Metrolinx wouldn't disclose how much more money it was giving the consortium in order to meet the deadline.[26]

Shelagh Pizey-Allen of TTCriders told the *Globe and Mail*: "It sort of shatters that rhetoric around P3s keeping cost down and downloading the cost onto the private sector."[27] A December 2018 report by the Ontario auditor general revealed the payout was $237 million, euphemistically criticizing the alternative financing and procurement (AFP) process: "In an AFP project, a private-sector consortium is paid a premium to bear the risks of project delays and cost overruns. However, under the Eglinton Crosstown LRT AFP contract, the responsibility for these risks was not fully transferred to the AFP consortium."[28]

Meanwhile, Ottawa's Confederation Line—a 7.7-mile light rail line that uses a P3 deal—has faced constant delays, criticisms of lack of transparency, and concerns about operations in winter.[29] Since opening in September 2019, the transit line has been plagued with operational issues, requiring a fleet of twenty replacement buses to remain on standby in case of delays and breakdowns.[30] Few media reports have bothered to note that a private consortium designed, built, and maintains the line.

The DC Circulator—a downtown bus service in Washington, DC—is operated by RATP Group, Paris's publicly owned transit operator, in partnership with Washington's transit agency.[31] Detroit's infamous streetcar line was known as the M-1, until the founder of mortgage lending company Quicken Loans bought the naming rights for five million dollars and changed the name to the QLine. The 3.3-mile QLine, described by *CityLab* as "hardly mass transit" and "a boon for local developers" due to its lack of coordination with the rest of the city's transit system, was funded by a gaggle of local capitalists in partnership with the state and federal governments.[32]

Stephanie Farmer, a sociology professor at Roosevelt University, told me that the city put together the Chicago Infrastructure Trust to explicitly work on P3 projects, streamlining private finance into public works projects. Hence Elon Musk's absurd proposed Hyperloop project to the airport that would fire autonomous sixteen-person pods through dedicated tunnels, though Chicago already has a dedicated rapid transit service to the airport called the Blue Line.[33] (The Chicago Hyperloop was effectively killed off with the election of new mayor Lori Lightfoot in May 2019—but a similar project remains on the table for Cleveland.[34])

Due to the expected rate of return for private investors, P3 projects tend to cost more than if they were publicly built.[35] Privatization has also been criticized for its negative impacts on system coordination and the city's ability to build up its own capacity for future infrastructure projects. The "value for money" found via P3s is often found through undermined labour practices that threaten workers' well-being.[36]

The construction of Montreal's Réseau express métropolitain (REM), owned by pension fund Caisse de dépôt et placement du Québec (CDPQ), has been criticized for its potential to pull riders from existing public transit systems and undermine the potential for coordination with or expansion of other systems. It also lacks financial transparency—particularly around fares.[37]

In many instances, such as the London Underground refurbishment in the early 2000s, private partners in P3s have walked away and shut down their project subsidiary with bankruptcy if escalating costs threaten its profitability, which in turn leaves the public forced to cover costs.

Transit riders and the general public can also be deprived of opportunities to give input, because of the quasi-private nature of many P3 arrangements. Representatives of Toronto's TTCriders said that the governance structure of Metrolinx—an unelected board appointed by the province with decisions made behind closed doors—exhibits characteristics of "creeping privatization" despite technically being a public body.

Privatization can also manifest at much smaller levels, such as Calgary's failed contracting out of the design for an electronic fare payment system. It was eventually cancelled and a lawsuit was filed over the project in 2015; the city still doesn't have an electronic fare payment system.[38]

This ever-increasing commodification and fragmentation has bred considerable distrust of transit agencies, which, in turn, undermines their ability to secure new funding through tax referendums. That matters a great deal, as considerable transit funding has been downloaded onto states, provinces, and municipalities, requiring highly visible and often regressive methods including sales taxes and property taxes.[39]

Marta Viciedo, of Miami's Urban Impact Lab, told me that a half-penny sales tax was passed in 2002 specifically for public transportation. It was intended to double rail service on Miami's Metrorail, but only three miles of the proposed twenty miles was ever built, while bus routes were cut.

Viciedo says that there's a bitter fight underway in South Dade because part of county leadership wants a modernized bus rapid transit (BRT) line, while residents emphatically desire the Metrorail extension that they've paid the half-penny tax for, for sixteen years—a situation that became increasingly hostile in 2018.[40] "A lot of that money has been misspent," she told me. "It is unlikely that a referendum for additional dollars will pass, simply because of the broken promises and the immense lack of trust that we have right now." Construction on the BRT corridor is expected to start in mid-2020; the county transportation board voted against light rail in 2018 but pledged to covert it into light rail if the BRT met certain ridership requirements.[41] In response to that proposal, Miami-Dade County Commissioner Dennis Moss said: "We always find a reason why we can't do something."

Other cities have simply voted down proposals at the outset. In 2015, 62 percent of Metro Vancouver residents voted against a 0.5 percent sales tax to fund plans for public transit expansion.[42] The question of increased transit funding should never have gone to referendum, David Moscrop, a political theorist and postdoctoral fellow at the University of Ottawa, told me. The decision represented a "very cynical abuse of participatory democracy" by then-premier Christy Clark. Moscrop says there were plenty of other issues at play in the TransLink referendum. The "yes" side was uncoordinated and poorly framed, relying on billionaire Jim Pattison to be its spokesperson instead of someone like a single parent who depends on public transit. Meanwhile, the opposing side—led by the right-wing Canadian Taxpayers Federation—successfully made the vote about TransLink's alleged inefficiency and bloatedness.

In Nashville, the Koch brothers financed the astroturf group Americans for Prosperity, which helped defeat a $5.4 billion transit referendum in 2018.[43] Americans for Prosperity had been involved in anti-transit campaigns across the country since 2015, including in Arkansas and Utah.

SERVICE AND DEVELOPMENT

The combination of chronic underfunding, capitalist planning, and political bias toward the automobile has sabotaged transit at almost every step. Budget constraints restrict a transit agency's coverage (how much of a city or region is adequately serviced), affordability (what fare hikes are required to make up for lack of public funding), and frequency (how often a bus or train arrives, and if they can be accessed at non-peak times). Almost all transit agencies now suffer from serious unreliability. An assessment of 2018 bus data found that weekday on-time performance—defined as arriving at a bus stop between one minute early and four minutes late—ranged enormously between eighteen U.S. cities, from 44 percent in Baltimore to 75 percent in Portland.[44] As described by New York's TransitCenter, which compiled the numbers, "If these were grades in school, even the highest performing agency, [Portland's] TriMet, only receives a 'C.'" An analysis of forty bus routes servicing the Toronto suburb of Scarborough found a total of 11,000 delays of greater than ten minutes in 2018, averaging 15.25 minutes each.[45]

Because of austerity, transit services run buses or trains less often, making a late or missing bus even more calamitous for riders—especially for shift workers who ride transit outside of peak hours. Inadequate budgets also force arbitrary decisions about whether to prioritize increasing ridership—which usually means building new routes for the rich—or attempting to improve service for poor and low-density areas.

In many cities, the only public transit modes and routes that receive sustained investment are rail lines built to primarily serve affluent commuters, including to airports and stadiums. These projects receive popular support from chambers of commerce and the business press, linking transit to global competitiveness. Meanwhile, investments in buses often languish, leaving low-income residents without a dependable means of getting around. That's particularly the case for uncoordinated bus and rail services operated by separate agencies without single-fare models. In Toronto, for example, this means that while riders of the TTC can transfer between subways, streetcars, and buses, they have to pay a considerable premium to take Metrolinx's commuter trains.[46]

University of Pennsylvania sociology professor Daniel Aldana Cohen emphasizes that the bus is the service that most poor people ride, and that the new urbanist "smart growth" agenda often ignores its critical role. "People just kind of hate buses. And the public sector hasn't done much to make buses more comfortable at all. There's nobody defending buses, on the one hand, and on the other hand bus routes are probably under the most sustained and direct attack from the coming collective private rideshare."

Atlanta is a prime example of this deeply racist funding approach, which has been described as "highways for the largely white suburbs and a chronically underfunded public transit system for people of color and low-income people."[47] In 1968, Martin Luther King Jr. said about Atlanta: "The system has virtually no consideration for connecting the poor people with their jobs. There is only one possible explanation for this situation, and that is the racist blindness of city planners."[48]

The same dynamic has played out in Chicago. Professor Farmer told me that transit investments have consistently been made to benefit wealthy neighbourhoods and sectors including tech and finance, while depriving low-income communities in South Chicago of funds for improved rail service. "What you see amongst the 1 percent and wealthy in Chicago is that they're mobilizing the city's resources to build transit projects that benefit them," she says.

The introduction of new rail or bus rapid transit infrastructure in a community can trigger rapid gentrification and displacement of low-income residents from the area. Transit-oriented development—planning for density and walkability around transit—is often initiated by governments in the interest of attracting real estate development. "Upzoning," or changing zoning for increased density and mixed uses, also creates its own consequences if it is not done in a way that protects low-income residents.[49]

The very language of "densification" can be code for privatized real estate development that results in pushing low-wage jobs and residences to the outer suburbs. This creates an ironic inversion: the people who most need affordable transit are displaced in the process of its construction.[50]

Harsha Walia, an organizer with No One Is Illegal and author of *Undoing Border Imperialism*, told me that the argument of densification has been powerfully weaponized in Burnaby, a community to the east of Vancouver with a high percentage of Chinese, South Asian, and Filipino residents. Walia says that transit routes and SkyTrain routes in particular have had displacing effects, with higher-end condos pushing out existing residents. With gentrification comes increased policing, which leads to harassment and incarceration of Black and Indigenous people—especially those who are unhoused, criminalized for using substances or selling sex work, or living with untreated mental health issues.[51]

It's a similar situation in Pittsburgh. "Our city is being gentrified and a lot of people are being displaced," Crystal Jennings, housing and transit co-ordinator for Pittsburghers for Public Transit, told me. "It's hard to try to find housing near a good transit stop or service. A lot of people are getting pushed out to the suburbs."

P.E. Moskowitz, author of *How to Kill a City: Gentrification, Inequality and the Fight for the Neighborhood*, explained to me that public transit is now almost exclusively built as an income generator and tool of gentrification that in turn displaces the very people who rely on it the most. In fact, it's partly *because* of unequal and often segregating transit service that areas with quality transit gentrify and generate enormous profits. "With a more equitably distributed and more extensive public transit network, you would take the pressure off a lot of neighbourhoods that are currently experiencing gentrification," Moskowitz says.

The construction of Toronto's Eglinton Cross LRT has been lambasted by Black business owners in Little Jamaica for obstructing customer access and threatening property tax hikes that will likely displace their multi-decade presence for condos.[52] Businesses complaining about construction, especially of transit projects, is a tale as old as time, but the racialized impacts of such processes shouldn't be ignored.

Rather than trying to fundamentally challenge these inequalities, many transit agencies and planners are forced to tinker around the edges while they try to maintain their existing funding by demonstrating ridership growth. Bus network redesigns, which have been described as the "hottest trend in transit," can illustrate the pitfalls of obsessing over ridership growth over other metrics.[53] Maryland's Republican governor cancelled a proposed light rail line in Baltimore after election in 2015, but agreed to fund a bus system redesign as what was described as a "consolation prize."[54] Costing $135 million, the overhaul included a "high-frequency grid, dedicated bus lanes, and transit signal priority corridors that would dramatically improve service." These were all critical steps to improving transit service, but the process hasn't resulted in a major uptick in ridership.

Some may argue that it's not necessarily supposed to; rather, the redesign was to clear out inefficiencies and make sure transit vehicles are running on the most sensible routes, allowing for easy integration of more routes in the future. Yet there are still plenty of no-show buses and lack of frequent

"Like austerity anywhere else, the responsibility to finance cascades downward. It fell increasingly on cities, which means cities need robust tax bases. The way you create a robust tax base is you cluster people with high salaries in your city. And increasingly, the companies that pay the highest salaries are the gentrifying companies: your Amazons, your tech companies. The way you get the money to build the transit system you dream of is by inviting things that destabilize the rest of your social environment."

—ALEX BIRNEL, MOVE Texas

service. The one thing reported as the most lacking component of the Baltimore revamp? Money. As explained by *CityLab*:

> Underfunding is a problem for transit agencies around the country, but it especially stings for Baltimore—a city where 30 percent of the population doesn't have access to a car, affordable housing tends to be far from job centers, and where public schools rely on the [Maryland Transit Administration] to transport 27,000 students to school every day.[55]

That isn't to suggest that improvements like bus network designs are inherently harmful: some can be done with great consideration and consultation.[56] But they can often be used to make it seem like transit can be improved without challenging the crisis of funding cuts and neoliberal car-centric planning. The same goes for solutions like dedicated bus lanes and all-door boarding: excellent in theory, but easily undermined by lack of money. Such policy tensions are a microcosm of the crisis facing transit. This financial situation has led many people to ignore or be complicit in oppressive systems, and it has widened the door to allow venture-capital-backed capitalists to poach transit ridership. Issues of gentrification, air pollution, rising fares, policing, and neglect of many riders—including seniors, people with disabilities, and women, trans, and gender non-conforming people—are not inherent to public transit. They are the result of transit operating within a specific political context, the dominant objective of which is the restoration and maintenance of ruling-class power—with severely racist and classist repercussions.

These material conditions can change. But they are the ones that we face at this present moment, and that advocates of the "three revolutions" are successfully appealing to with their next-generation automotive technologies.

Chapter 2

Manufacturing automobility

The anti-transit underpinnings of the "three revolutions"

The "three revolutions" in automobility must be viewed as deeply political projects that depend on sustained austerity, weak regulations, and complicit politicians.

THE HEAVEN SCENARIO

Public transportation has already been undermined by decades of austerity and political infatuation with the private automobile. Even if nothing were to change technologically in how cars operate, most transit systems would still be in seriously bad shape. In the U.S., 17.3 million new vehicles were sold in 2018, close to the highest number in history.[1] The share of households without a vehicle in the U.S. dropped from 21 percent to 9 percent between 1969 and 2009, with low-income households increasingly owning vehicles.[2] Conditions are, predictably, getting worse with Trump's presidency. His administration cut federal transit funding from 28 percent of transportation grants to 8.5 percent, while increasing funding to highways, roads, and bridges from 34.8 percent between 2014 and 2016 to 70.4 percent.[3]

Existing political institutions are doing more than enough to marginalize transit as it is. But the "three revolutions" in automobility—electrification, sharing or pooling, and autonomous vehicles—threaten to deliver a fatal blow. This isn't because of any sort of innate technological superiority over buses and trains. Rather, these so-called revolutions are capturing political and public attention by further commodifying transportation, reiterating the myth that public transit is an outdated approach. In this chapter I'll discuss what these alleged revolutions are, their claims and failings, and why public transit remains the best option to anchor collective struggle. Let's start with some basic definitions.

First, and already well under way, is the *electrification of vehicles*—the replacement of vehicles running on gasoline- or diesel-powered internal combustion engines with electric motors that use battery power generated by charging stations and regenerative braking. Electric motors are far more efficient than their fossil-fuel-propelled counterparts, converting between 60 and 73 percent of energy to actually power the vehicle down the road, compared to only 12 to 30 percent for gasoline vehicles (much of the energy is wasted as heat).[4] That means that even in regions of the continent where electricity is mostly generated by burning coal, a switch to electric vehicles has a potential for significant emission reduction; when more electricity is generated by low-carbon sources, it is even cleaner.[5] Switching to an electric motor can greatly decrease the emission of local air pollution like nitrogen dioxide, along with noise pollution and other harmful impacts.[6]

Personal electric vehicles are already gaining political traction around the world, and many governments are offering generous subsidies to drivers as an incentive to make the leap. The top-selling electric vehicles in the U.S. are manufactured by Tesla, Chevrolet, and Nissan.[7] Note, however, that such vehicles don't offer benefits for a wide range of automobile-caused problems such as congestion, pedestrian and cyclist safety, or affordability. They are also highly resource-intensive, requiring large quantities of materials to build batteries, and necessitate continued investment in expensive infrastructure like roads and highways. Electrification is by no means limited to private automobiles: buses and trains are prime targets. They have much higher per-rider efficiency, and it's possible to rapidly replace a transit system's fleet. Outside of China, though, electrification of transit is happening very slowly; most of the focus is on personal electric vehicles.

The second revolution is the *sharing or pooling of vehicles*, which has far less to do with the physical vehicles themselves than with the platforms they're organized by. Rather than only one or two people being in a car, the objective with pooling is to increase the number of riders at any given time and reduce unnecessary transportation. Currently, sharing can look like using a ride-hailing service like Uber or Lyft, or the more transit-like services of UberPool and Lyft Line. Genuine car-sharing services like Zipcar and Car2Go are promising but, due to their limited scope, don't tend to be prioritized by the venture capitalists who bankroll mobility services. For example, Zipcar, now owned by Avis, boasts a fleet of 10,000 vehicles worldwide and a market capitalization of $1 billion. By comparison, Uber, with an estimated 3.9 million drivers around the world, went public at an $82 billion valuation.[8]

Transportation experts agree that sharing or pooling is the only way to maximize the potential benefits of next-generation automobiles: failing to do so will mean as many or more personal vehicles on the road, a nightmare scenario of induced demand that leads to far more congestion, pollution, and urban sprawl.[9] The "heaven" scenario—an expression popularized by Zipcar co-founder Robin Chase—would get more people into empty seats: it would see fewer cars on the road, less square footage dedicated to parking, and more ability to spontaneously take a trip. Some critics argue, though, that sharing isn't remotely guaranteed, given the sizable behavioural shift it will require from riders.

The third revolution is the *automation or self-driving of vehicles*. Vehicle autonomy is often imagined as a singular "on/off" switch in which a complex computer takes over all driving processes. But it's more helpful to understand autonomy as a spectrum, ranging from minimal intervention in cruise control and acceleration, to partial navigation of open highways, to the full-blown ability of a vehicle to self-navigate busy pothole-strewn streets without any driver control.

The Society of Automotive Engineers International has devised a standard of six levels, ranging from Level 0 (no automation), to Level 2 (partial automation, like Tesla's contro-versial Autopilot system), to Level 5 (full automation, in which the steering wheel and pedals are completely removed).[10] Small advances in autonomous technologies can make sig-nificant differences in safety, with lane centring and brake support. But full automation—Level 5, capable of driving in all conditions—requires a much more complex set of tech-nologies, including radar, high-resolution lidar (radar, except pulses of lasers instead of microwaves), multiple ultrasonic sensors, high-definition mapping, cameras, and immensely powerful computers to process the data.[11]

Ride-hailing companies like Uber and Lyft are banking on Level 5 autonomy for their future profitability, as such tech-nology would eliminate the need for costly human labour. And many of the world's largest companies—including Apple, Huawei, and Microsoft, along with the usual automotive com-panies—are working on autonomous vehicle technologies.[12]

These next-generation technologies are expected to emerge in tandem, helping to improve public transportation as a by-product by providing connections between work-places, transit stations, and homes. But as I will argue, that hope is loaded with politically naive assumptions that ignore the history of automobility and that may end up trigger-ing a death spiral for transit systems if they are not directly challenged—and unless vastly improved alternatives are quickly built up before it's too late.

There is great financial incentive for these next-generation projects to succeed. Total revenue of autonomous vehicles is projected to hit $2.8 trillion by 2030, of which Google's Waymo will represent 60 percent.[13] Autonomous ride-hailing services may account for nearly $4 trillion in global economic activity by 2050, with another $3 trillion coming from driverless delivery and business logistics.[14] Larry Burns, a University of Michigan engineering professor and former vice-president of research and development at General Motors, said in 2015: "This is an arms race. You're going to see a new age for the automobile." Burns suggested that annual profits for the "first mover" could be $30 billion.[15]

Uber went public in 2019 with a valuation of $82 billion, while Lyft priced its initial public offering at $24 billion.[16] These ride-hailing services have come to dominate markets by imposing ongoing pressures on drivers through repeated rate cuts, a refusal to pay benefits, and an insistence that they are exempt from regulations such as minimum wage and overtime. Jarrett Walker told me, "A lot of PR dollars are being spent trying to pretend it's about something else: that it's about Uber and Lyft being more efficient or more innovative. No, it's about racing to the very bottom on driver compensation and still not being able to make money."

Ride-hailing companies are indeed struggling to turn a profit. In 2018, Uber lost $1.8 billion despite $50 billion in sales and $11.3 billion in net revenue.[17] Lyft logged $8 billion in bookings that same year, collecting $2.2 billion in revenue—but still lost $911 million.[18] But investors don't see that as a problem. Uber's executive team has often appealed to the growth of Amazon, which didn't turn a profit for almost two decades, as an example of how it plans to eventually succeed.[19]

Uber and Lyft survive—and attract ever more venture capital—due to their success at dodging or resisting rules that apply to other transportation modes, including taxis and limos. The companies have poured enormous resources into opposing proposed limits on the number of cars on city roads, mandatory data sharing with regulators, the provision of wheelchair-accessible vehicles (WAVs), and requirements for basic background checks or insurance for drivers. In 2016, Uber spent over $1.4 million on federal lobbyists, and millions more are spent at municipal, state, and provincial levels.[20]

In the first half of 2018 alone, Uber spent $876,000 lobbying the New York City Council, mostly over the proposed cap on ride-hailing vehicles and minimum wage for drivers.[21] Another $73,000 was spent by Lyft.[22] Transportation expert Hubert Horan has argued that Uber successfully exploited gullible business and tech industry journalists into propagating a "heroic innovator" myth, "apparently oblivious to the fact that they were amplifying claims crafted by Koch-funded groups designed to undermine market competition, the concept of urban transport as a public good, and the legitimacy of any form of regulatory authority."[23]

Many of the next-generation automobile companies have a well-established revolving door with senior government officials. In 2017, Valerie Jarrett—a long-time adviser to former president Barack Obama—joined Lyft's board of directors.[24] A few years earlier, Uber had hired Obama's 2008 campaign manager, David Plouffe, for a senior vice-president position. In 2017, Plouffe was fined $90,000 by the Chicago Board of Ethics for illegally lobbying mayor Rahm Emanuel, having failed to register as an Uber lobbyist.[25]

In 2016, Google, Uber, Lyft, Ford, and Volvo combined forces to create the Self-Driving Coalition for Safer Streets lobby group. The group is headed by David Strickland, the former administrator of the National Highway Traffic Safety Administration under Obama. As reported by *Verge*: "NHTSA is currently working on a set of rules and policies, pitting

Strickland against his former agency in the race to clear the road for fully self-driving cars."[26]

Many municipalities that have attempted to introduce meaningful restrictions have been beaten back by such interests. Uber and Lyft ceased operations in Austin due to safety concerns but wormed their way back into the city after appealing to the state's legislature.[27] A report by the National Employment Law Project and the Partnership for Working Families concluded that Uber and Lyft have successfully lobbied forty-one states to strip municipalities of their ability to establish regulations, a process that the report summarized as "barge in, buy, bully, and bamboozle."

The report concluded: "In many cases, using these strategies and tactics, Uber has secured a high level of access in multiple state and city legislative processes, enabling it to draft its own bills, heavily influence the vetting, and even effectively staff elected officials on the issue."[28] Consumer rights group SumOfUs compiled a list of the seven steps that Uber uses to successfully gain access to a city, including attempts to "convert riders into a political base" by recruiting the support of celebrities including Kate Upton and Ashton Kutcher.[29]

According to Horan, Uber riders only pay 41 percent of costs—the rest is subsidized by private capital. Horan argued

"[Ride-hailing companies] have an interest in trying to undermine regulations and squeeze out those profits where they can. You can definitely try to keep playing catch-up and cutting them off when they're trying to game you. But frankly, your chances of success are not that high. Even if it is technically possible, practically you're probably going to end up getting gamed."

—MICHAL ROZWORSKI, co-author, *The People's Republic of Walmart* that "unlike most startups, Uber did not enter the industry in pursuit of a significant market share, but was explicitly working to drive incumbents out of business and achieve global industry dominance."[30]

These companies also rely on tax loopholes for massive gains. Uber's main corporate structure is based in the Netherlands; it operates through a network of Bermuda-registered subsidiaries and shell companies that exploit byzantine rules concerning royalty payments and offshore havens. Only 1.45 percent of Uber's net revenue is subject to U.S. taxes.[31] A *New York Times* investigation suggested that Uber was improperly downloading the burden of sales tax payments to New York Uber drivers, rather than to passengers—which could represent over $200 million in compensation owed to drivers.[32]

Uber and Lyft are vehemently opposed to sharing data about their operations. So governments are often deprived of urgently needed information on driver statistics and ridership patterns, which in turn undermines their ability to plan for changes like increased congestion or depressed transit usage. Researchers have been forced to devise a range of methods to track the impact of ride-hailing services. Northeastern University built a software script that analyzed vehicle location data to help model drop-offs by ride-hailing services, while Boston's transit agency conducted a rider intercept survey to assess impacts.[33] Katie Wells, an urban geographer and postdoctoral fellow at Georgetown University's Kalmanovitz Initiative for Labor and the Working Poor, says that "we have no idea how many drivers there are" on the roads, as Uber doesn't share any of its information with public regulators. Such data is even inaccessible via Freedom of Information Act requests. As University of California researchers put it: "Limited data in the public sector perpetuates less-informed decision making, which in turn results in transportation systems that do not meet the public's needs."[34]

The testing of autonomous vehicles has indicated that many companies will skirt rules and pressure local governments into allowing their presence on roads and highways without clear safety regulations. In 2017, thirty-three states had either passed or initiated legislation or an executive order to allow autonomous vehicles on public roads.[35] That was followed in 2018 by fifteen states enacting another eighteen autonomous vehicle-related bills.[36] In February 2018, California became the first state to allow fully autonomous vehicles to operate on public roads with a safety driver, who is responsible for overseeing the operations of the vehicle and intervening if necessary.[37] Arizona followed suit only a few days later.[38]

The Self-Driving Coalition for Safer Streets has successfully lobbied the federal government to keep collision data secret and worked against local governments being able to craft their own autonomous vehicle legislation to protect residents.[39] Significant lobbying efforts were made by various autonomous vehicle groups in the lead-up to the U.S. Senate vote on the AV START Act in early 2018, which several senators held up due to serious concerns about safety. The bill would have allowed companies to test and market autonomous vehicles to consumers before federal safety regulations were implemented and would block more stringent state regulations.[40] It failed to pass in late 2018, but Congress continues to meet about advancing legislation.[41]

Indiana state legislator Ed Soliday introduced a bill to regulate the autonomous vehicle industry, which passed both the House and Senate but eventually died due to lobbying efforts by the Self-Driving Coalition for Safer Streets and General Motors' Auto Alliance.[42] Soliday said at the time:

> You can ask legislators all over the country. [Automotive lobbyists] come in and they want one of two things—and they will do anything to get it. They either want unlimited, unfettered, total access to every street and road in your state with no accountability

whatsoever and no federal safety standards, and if they can't get that, then they want to kill any legislation. They are powerful lobbyists—they will tell any story, they will make any exaggeration.[43]

It's not entirely impossible to regulate these companies. They can be corralled to a degree, as was demonstrated when the New York Taxi Workers Alliance pressured New York City Council to vote for a twelve-month cap on Uber and Lyft vehicles (with the exception of those accessible to people in wheelchairs) and establish a $17.22/hour minimum wage for drivers.[44] Transport for London, the transport regulator for the British capital, suspended Uber's licence in November 2019 after finding out 14,000 trips had been taken with drivers who faked their identity on its app, although the company is allowed to continue operating during the lengthy court battles to come.[45] And battles are unfolding—including California's sweeping AB-5 legislation—over the employment status of ride-hailing drivers that may significantly impact the industry.[46]

THE THREAT TO PUBLIC TRANSIT

Ride-hailing and autonomous vehicle companies have long positioned themselves as friends to transit, looking to share cities and towns rather than dominate them. It's a public relations gambit.[47] Many major firms have already indicated they wish to replace public transportation as we know it by creating citywide mobility-as-a-service (MaaS) networks, including scooters, e-bikes, autonomous vehicles, flying cars, and van-pooling.[48] In 2018, new Uber CEO Dara Khosrowshahi said, "I want to run the bus systems for a city. I want you to be able to take an Uber and get into the subway ... get out and have an Uber waiting for you."[49]

This clear threat to public transit was confirmed in Uber's filing to the Securities and Exchange Commission in April 2019 for its initial public offering, stating: "We believe we can continue to grow the number of trips taken with our Ridesharing products and replace personal vehicle ownership and usage and public transportation one use case at a time."[50] Specifically, Uber described "all public transportation miles in all countries globally" as part of its total addressable market.[51]

Uber and Lyft are having serious impacts on public transit. Transportation policy expert Bruce Schaller calculated that ride-hailing services transported 2.6 billion passengers in 2017, a 37 percent increase from 2016.[52] Ride-hailing services have added 5.7 billion miles of driving *per year* in the nine largest markets: the metropolitan areas of Boston, Chicago, Los Angeles, Miami, New York, Philadelphia, San Francisco, Seattle, and Washington, DC. These services are not only replacing existing automobile travel but expanding it. Between 2015 and 2019, the average U.S. household increased the amount it spends on for-hire services, including Uber and Lyft, from twenty dollars to seventy dollars, while spending on transit decreased by 15 percent.[53]

A widely circulated study from the UC Davis Institute of Transportation Studies indicated an average net loss of 6 percent had occurred in transit usage in seven major American cities due to Uber and Lyft.[54] A survey in 2018 by the Metropolitan Area Planning Council of Boston found that 42 percent of ride-hailing users would have used public transportation, while another 12 percent would have walked or cycled.[55] "Despite what the companies say, ultimately they see transit riders as potential customers," Kafui Attoh of the City University of New York, and author of *Rights in Transit: Public Transportation and the Right to the City in California's East Bay*, told me.

Ride-hailing companies have actively worked to replace transit systems in smaller municipalities. Altamonte Springs in Florida contracted Uber for a one-year pilot to do the job previously done by public transportation, subsidizing 20 percent of Uber fares in the city and 25 percent of Uber fares connected with rail service.[56] The director of transportation policy for Lyft has said that it's "very interested" in expanding the Altamonte model across the country as an opportunity to take hold in suburban areas.[57]

By early 2018, Uber had stuck thirty-five partnerships with public transit agencies around the world.[58] In March of that year, the city of Arlington, Texas, announced that vanpooling service Via was completely replacing its bus system.[59] A number of concerns emerged early on in Altamonte Springs: the lack of options for people with disabilities or who don't have smartphones and credit cards, and the requirement that Altamonte sign a far-reaching nondisclosure agreement about the deal.[60] But many other small cities in the area opted for a similar deal. Over 100,000 residents in the northern Orlando area were brought into an Uber-operated "public transit" arrangement by 2016.[61] Altamonte's efforts to maintain transit usage with a further 25 percent discount on Uber fares if the rider is travelling to or from a train station failed to take hold: the city manager said that "the monstrous majority" of rides weren't of that nature.[62]

The same has happened in Innisfil, Ontario, where the municipality is subsidizing Uber for any trip over three to five dollars (the rate varies based on destination) in order to complete routes that bus lines would otherwise have served.[63] In early 2018, it was reported that the subsidized Uber program in Innisfil cost "just" $165,535 over the first eight months, with 3,400 residents taking 26,700 trips. That works out to a per-trip subsidy of $6.20, extremely high compared to the subsidies that transit agencies receive in other municipalities—and, crucially, it relies on precarious, non-unionized labour.[64] In 2019, it was reported that the so-called Innisfil Transit was raising its flat fare by one dollar per trip and implementing a thirty-ride-per-month cap for users. A regular user of the Uber service told *CityLab*: "I would never get on a bus in Toronto and hear the driver say, 'Sorry, but you've hit your cap.' Uber was supposed to be our bus."[65]

The "three revolutions" in automobility must be viewed as deeply political projects that depend on sustained austerity, weak regulations, and complicit politicians. As Hana Creger, environmental equity co-ordinator at the Greenlining Institute, put it to me: "Uber and Lyft became popular because as a rider it's a great service. It's cheap, it's convenient, it's fulfilling a transportation gap that transit was not providing in many cases. There's been a massive deterioration of our public transit system because of underfunding. That in itself allowed ride-share services to fill that gap and take advantage of that. I think part of the solution is increasing funding for the construction, operation, and maintenance of mass transit in order to make it a more competitive, cheaper, and more efficient option."

Quality public transportation represents a direct threat to attempts by these companies to remake communities: transit agencies offering free, frequent, and accessible service that reaches all parts of a city or region at any time of day—and maybe even offers a functional app for trip planning—would significantly undermine the growth potential for ride-hailing services and autonomous vehicles. As argued by Jeff Sparrow: "Car culture will only be defeated by destroying its foundations. Once it is cheaper and more convenient to catch the train, the car will no longer represent freedom but will instead signify expense, waste and frustration."[66] As a result, the continued stagnation and eventual demise of public transit is very much in these companies' interests. To that end, they are actively breaking up the remaining network of transit by poaching riders from the most profitable lines.

It's a process that Daniel Aldana Cohen described to me as companies slipping into cracks in service in order to "pry those cracks open." By the time transit agencies and regulators sum up the willpower to respond, it may well be too late. The entrance of ride-hailing companies into communities represents a quiet but fierce competition over space, labour power, and decision-making: one that Peter Norton describes as a "low-grade war, as it always has been."

The "three revolutions" aren't about technology superiority. The most effective and viable transportation modes already exist: the bus, train, bike, and wheelchair. It's a question of political priorities—and whether the next century of transportation is guided by a neoliberal privatism or aims for a more collective and livable society.

"We're making alternatives less possible by pursuing these high-tech futures," Norton says. "And we saw this all historically. When we made it more possible to get to work by driving your own car, we inevitably made it less possible to get to work by any other means. We are making that mistake again right now."

Part Two

arture >>> Departure >>> Departure >>> Departure
re >>> Departure >>> Departure >>> Departure >>> Depart
arture >>> Departure >>> Departure >>> Departure
re >>> Departure >>> Departure >>> Departure >>> Depart
arture >>> Departure >>> Departure >>> Departure
re >>> Departure >>> Departure >>> Departure >>> Depart
arture >>> Departure >>> Departure >>> Departure
re >>> Departure >>> **Departure** >>> Departure >>> Depart
arture >>> Departure >>> Departure >>> Departure
re >>> Departure >>> Departure >>> Departure >>> Depart
arture >>> Departure >>> Departure >>> Departure
re >>> Departure >>> Departure >>> Departure >>> Depart
arture >>> Departure >>> Departure >>> Departure
re >>> Departure >>> Departure >>> Departure >>> Depart
arture >>> Departure >>> Departure >>> Departure
re >>> Departure >>> Departure Ture >>> Departure >>> Depart
arture >>> Departure >>> Departure >>> Departure
re >>> Departure >>> Departure >>> Departure >>> Depart
arture >>> Departure >>> Departure >>> Departure
re >>> Departure >>> Departure >>> Departure >>> Depart
arture >>> Departure >>> Departure >>> Departure
re >>> Departure >>> Departure >>> Departure >>> Depart
arture >>> Departure >>> Departure >>> Departure
re >>> Departure >>> Departure >>> Departure >>> Depart
arture >>> Departure >>> Departure >>> Departure
re >>> Departure >>> Departure >>> Departure >>> Depart
arture >>> Departure >>> Departure >>> Departure
re >>> Departure >>> Departure >>> Departure >>> Depart
arture >>> Departure >>> Departure >>> Departure
re >>> Departure >>> Departure >>> Departure >>> Depart
arture >>> Departure >>> Departure >>> Departure
re >>> Departure >>> Departure >>> Departure >>> Depart
arture >>> Departure >>> Departure >>> Departure

Chapter 3

Running on empty

Climate and environment

It simply isn't possible to slow climate chaos and environmental issues without a radical recommitment to public transportation.

A FABRICATED VISION

Fossil-fuel-powered transportation is killing the planet and our communities. That's no exaggeration. Burning coal to create the steel used to make the chassis of a vehicle. Extracting the crude oil that's refined into gasoline and diesel and combusting that fuel to emit toxic air pollution and greenhouse gases. The ecological devastation of highways and concrete jungles. Petroleum-propelled vehicles are exacting catastrophic harms in seemingly endless ways.[1] Climate chaos is only beginning.

Proponents of the "three revolutions" are convinced that a new generation of vehicles can help fix this situation. Electric vehicles, they say, will radically reduce greenhouse gas emissions and air pollution, and sharing the vehicles will mean fewer cars are required to transport more people. Autonomous technologies are promised to nearly eliminate the need for parking spaces, opening up large portions of cities and towns for densified redevelopment that further cuts down on the need for motor vehicle travel. Uber CEO Travis Kalanick once gloated about an Uber-oriented city as "a cleaner city, where fewer cars on the road will mean less carbon pollution—especially since more and more Uber vehicles are low-emission hybrid vehicles."[2]

All things considered, it sounds like a promising vision. The problem is that it's almost completely fabricated. Given the incredible lobbying powers of private industry and its ability to rebuff or delay regulatory impacts, the chances of best-case conditions emerging are extremely slim. Though public transit has also routinely dropped the ball on the environment, it remains the best opportunity to make rapid progress if political power is democratized and leveraged.

THREE REVOLUTIONS: ENVIRONMENTAL IMPACTS

A Cleaner Car

Compared to internal combustion engines, electric motors do offer greater energy efficiency and emit less toxic air pollution.[3] So it's easy to see why proponents of the "three revolutions" in automobility view environmental benefits as a justification for rolling out a new generation of personal vehicles. While manufacturing an electric vehicle emits about 15 percent more greenhouse gas emissions than a gasoline-powered equivalent, the driving of the vehicle is staggeringly more efficient. The U.S. average greenhouse gas emissions for an electric vehicle are equivalent to those of an 80-miles-per-gallon gasoline vehicle, ranging from 38 miles per gallon in the coal-heavy Midwest up to an incredible 191 miles per gallon in Upstate New York.[4] To put that in perspective, the average U.S. vehicle on the road in 2016 reached only 24.7 miles per gallon.[5]

Many governments that offer subsidies for electric vehicles make explicit reference to climate change and air pollution as a motivator. In 2018, California governor Jerry Brown announced a whopping sixteen bills to accelerate the rollout of electric vehicles, as they "will help get more clean cars on the road and reduce harmful emissions."[6]

The sharing of electric vehicles via ride-hailing apps has also been marketed as accelerating low-carbon transportation. Lyft's founders have written on the company's blog that cost savings from its future electric and autonomous vehicles "will dramatically accelerate the rollout of electric vehicles, displacing millions of gasoline-powered cars and helping the U.S. and world reach their climate goals."[7] Studies have suggested that if all three "revolutions" happen simultaneously and within predicted timelines, they have the potential to cut greenhouse gas emissions compared to the business as usual scenario by an incredible 80 percent.[8]

But electric vehicles, ride-hailing services, and autonomous technologies all come with significant impacts of their own. Both the lessons of history and contemporary research indicate that, if these developments are not severely limited, they may rapidly worsen climate and environmental conditions.

Raw Materials

Let's start with the most widely critiqued environmental impact of electric vehicles: their immense use of raw materials, which requires a massive escalation of mining around the world.[9] The global market for lithium-ion batteries—the main type used in electric vehicles—is projected to skyrocket from 15.9 gigawatt hours in 2015 to 93.1 gigawatt hours by 2024.[10] That will result in an unprecedented spike in demand for materials. Some 63 kilograms of lithium carbonate—more than 10,000 cell phones would use—is required for a 70 kilowatt hour (kWh) battery to power a single Tesla Model S.[11]

Many high-tech devices in our society require such materials. But personal electric vehicles will explode demand to a much greater level. Replacing all two billion cars worldwide with electric vehicles would require a 70 percent increase in the production of neodymium and dysprosium, a doubling of copper output, and over a tripling in cobalt mining.[12] Mining giant Glencore has estimated that about three times the copper is required for an electric car than for a regular vehicle.[13]

Hypothetically, mining can be done responsibly and ethically. As in every sector, processes could be dramatically improved with strong union density, environmental regulations, and public accountability. But there's very little precedent for that in the places where the most mining takes place and where its impacts are unfolding. Peter Norton, author of *Fighting Traffic*, told me that an explosion of personal electric vehicles and autonomous ride-hailing services could quickly accelerate resource depletion, abusive labour exploitation at mines, and toxic waste. As he puts it, "Electric vehicles and autonomous driving don't necessitate these things, but they do entail the risk, and the profitability means that there will be a strong pressure to go in this direction."

Over half of the cobalt mined in the world comes from the Democratic Republic of the Congo, where mining practices have resulted in devastating pollution, illnesses, displacement, and use of child labour.[14] Graphite mining in China has also caused rampant pollution of air, water, and soil.[15] The extraction of rare earth minerals necessitates large quantities of toxic chemicals and waste products, while copper can result in heavy metal contamination and major tailings dam breaches.[16] Thea Riofrancos, author of *Resource Radicals: From Petro-Nationalism to Post-Extractivism in Ecuador*, told me that mining in the so-called lithium triangle of Chile, Argentina, and Bolivia has major effects on the hydrology of the water-scarce salt flats, compromising an already vulnerable water system that over a dozen Indigenous communities rely on. Bolivia's Indigenous president Evo Morales has attributed the Western-backed coup that forced his resignation in late 2019 to the country's nationalization of lithium resources, which private corporations desired control over. "I'm convinced that it's a lithium coup d'etat," he told the *Intercept*'s Glenn Greenwald.[17]

By 2030, the world may have created 11 million metric tons in lithium-ion batteries that need to be recycled.[18] Recycling rates of lithium batteries currently range between 2 and 5 percent, depending on the country.[19] Analysts predict that a recycling industry will emerge in tandem with the increased demand for materials, but many questions remain about how much can and will be recovered.[20] Recycling plants are expensive to build and operate, require specialized equipment to mitigate toxic pollution, and cannot recover all the material. Further, wide swings in materials costs may undermine the economic case for large-scale recycling.[21]

Energy Use and Particulate Matter

Private cars as a whole are a wildly inefficient way of using energy, even if that electricity is generated by low-carbon power plants. The average weight of a passenger vehicle in the U.S. dropped from 4,060 pounds in 1975 to 3,220 pounds in 1987, only to rebound to 4,070 pounds in 2014 due to a significant increase in pickup truck and SUV sales.[22] Although a great majority of trips are taken in the city—perhaps 30 or so miles per day—some electric vehicles are being built with over 250 miles of range.[23] Manufacturing for longer ranges, and bigger batteries, decrease the energy efficiency that electric vehicles boast.[24] The battery alone makes up about 20 or 30 percent of an electric vehicle's curb weight, ranging from 650 pounds for a Nissan Leaf to 1,200 pounds for a Tesla Model S. That mass requires more electricity to run. David Roberts of *Vox* observed: "Personal vehicles are probably the most challenging to electrify cost-effectively" and "dragging one or two passengers around over long distances in a 2-ton vehicle takes a lot of energy."[25]

Electric motors also fail to reduce the amount of fine particulate matter emitted from tires and road surface wear, a problem that has links to cardiopulmonary toxicity and a wide range of respiratory issues.[26] New research indicates that automobile tire particles also contribute an enormous amount of microplastics, which wash into nearby water sources.[27]

Autonomous vehicles are expected to weigh even more and use even greater amounts of energy than standard electric vehicles. An autonomous vehicle's on-board computer currently accounts for 45 percent of its weight and consumes 80 percent of the power; there's a risk that energy efficiencies from electrification could be "diminished or vanish completely" if factors like computer demand and weight aren't meaningfully addressed.[28] Prototypes for autonomous vehicles consume the equivalent of having 50 to 100 laptops continuously running in the trunk, "giving engineers a fuel economy headache."[29]

It might not be immediately clear why such energy consumption matters, given that electricity is often much cheaper than fossil fuels and comes with less supply volatility and damage to the climate and environment. Electric vehicles do indeed use energy more efficiently than their internal combustion engine counterparts, but they require a huge amount of electricity for operation and manufacturing; an estimated 50 percent of an electric vehicle's lifetime emissions comes from producing the battery itself.[30] That, along with the power to operate the vehicle day to day, has to come from somewhere.[31] In many parts of the U.S., electricity generation still requires the burning of coal or natural gas—which can have significant climate and environmental impacts, even if consuming electricity is proportionately less harmful than burning gasoline or diesel.[32]

At current rates, it will take many more decades to transition away from fossil fuels, especially natural gas. Jeremy Michalek, director of the Vehicle Electrification Group at Carnegie Mellon University, observed: "Some plants, like nuclear, hydro, wind and solar are generally fully utilised and will not change their generation output if you buy an EV [electric vehicle]. What changes, at least in the short run, is primarily that coal and natural gas plants will increase generation in response to this new load."[33] Renewables are being deployed at an alarmingly slow rate, exacerbating this concern.[34] The International Energy Agency has warned that a stagnation in the world's annual growth in renewables is "deeply worrying."[35] As Daniel Aldana Cohen of the University of Pennsylvania put it to me: "The less energy people are consuming for heating and cooling and transit, the less new clean energy you need to build."

Timing and Uptake

New electric vehicles—whether for personal or shared use—will take a very long time to proliferate: time that we don't have, given the imminent threat of climate change. A vast majority of North Americans travelling by automobile continue to do so in vehicles that don't include *any* of the three revolutions and likely won't for a long time yet. Only 2 percent of the 17.3 million new vehicles sold in the U.S. in 2018 were electric.[36]

Many people who purchase electric vehicles aren't replacing gas-guzzling SUVs and pickup trucks, but highly fuel-efficient hybrids and other smaller vehicles, lessening the relative improvement in emissions.[37] And the rapid rise in popularity of SUVs and pickup trucks, at 68 percent of sales in 2018, is greatly undermining fuel efficiency gains. The class of "light trucks" receives a larger pollution allowance under fuel economy regulations, incentivizing manufacturers to produce larger vehicles that they can sell for more money.[38] In late 2019, General Motors announced a new generation of fossil-fuel-powered SUVs "whose profits will help fund development of electric vehicles that the automaker promises for the future."[39] In other words, auto manufacturers plan to keep rolling out climate-change-causing vehicles for many years yet.

There's also a curious tendency by car owners to stick with driving even when a public transportation mode would be far cheaper and more predictable in service.[40] This matters a great deal because new vehicles are lasting longer than ever. The turnover of household vehicles has slowed since 2009; an average vehicle in 2017 lasted 10.5 years.[41] "The thing that we forget is that cars are capital assets," explained Costa Samaras, the director of the Center for Engineering and Resilience for Climate Adaptation at Carnegie Mellon University, in a 2018 interview. "This idea that people are going to give up a capital asset because a newer product is maybe saving some operational cost is not in line with what we've typically seen."[42] Another report echoed this concern. It calculated that the average American vehicle remains in use for 16.6 years, and that if every U.S. vehicle sold were electric starting today it would take until 2040 for 90 percent of the vehicle fleet on the road to be electric.[43]

That's very contrary to current vehicle buying trends. It also assumes that ride-hailing and autonomous vehicle companies actually embrace electric vehicles, which, as evidence suggests thus far, is an awfully big assumption. Fewer than 0.2 percent of vehicles driven for Uber and Lyft are electric.[44] Uber announced that it would start paying drivers with a small per-trip incentive of between $1 and $1.50 to switch to using electric vehicles, hoping to increase rides taken in electric vehicles from four million in 2017 to five million over twelve months in both Canada and the U.S.[45]

But Uber provided a total of four billion rides in 2017, meaning electric vehicles are only a tiny percentage of the total (and will likely be for a long while yet).[46] As Peter Slowik, researcher in the International Council on Clean Transportation's passenger vehicle program, put it: "Even their more bullish announcements about future electrification activities still amount to less than 5% of their operations by 2025."[47] Almost all operating costs of ride-hailing are downloaded onto their drivers, who often live in precarious, near-poverty conditions. It's difficult to imagine how a one-dollar-per-ride bonus—or even grants to encourage drivers to make the change—would help foster the financial stability to purchase a new electric vehicle. Slowik noted that time spent charging an electric vehicle is lost revenue for a ride-hailing driver, with faster and convenient charging infrastructure requiring large upfront costs.

Lyft has committed to one billion trips in autonomous electric vehicles by 2025, but that commitment may make up less than 5 percent of the company's rides by then.[48] The company has introduced an electric vehicle option to its app that allows riders to request a low-carbon ride, rewarding drivers who opt to use such vehicles.[49] Lyft also announced that it would be going "carbon-neutral" by purchasing carbon credits to plant trees, build wind farms, and capture greenhouse gases from landfills.[50] However, the purchasing of emissions offsets doesn't fundamentally address the reality that cars spew significant quantities of greenhouse gases and air pollution into the atmosphere; it only displaces the solutions elsewhere.[51]

A serious problem with ride-hailing is the amount of "deadhead" miles between trips without any passengers, which accounts for roughly half of the 600 million miles that these services have added to New York City's roads since 2013. The offsets that Lyft purchases don't include those miles—and the company has opposed the introduction of a zero-emissions vehicle mandate in California that would require all ride-hailing vehicles to be electric by 2028.[52]

Going Autonomous

So far, Ford, Waymo, and Uber have used hybrid vehicles for most of their autonomous vehicle testing.[53] The Waymo fleet that's racking up million of miles in testing is made up of hybrid Chrysler Pacifica minivans; in May 2018, the company ordered another 62,000 of the models.[54] While hybrids have a higher fuel efficiency than regular vehicles, such testing still requires a significant amount of gasoline.

Waymo doesn't disclose how often they charge their hybrid vans, leading some to speculate that batteries are being used to power the energy-intensive computer systems while gasoline is being used to actually drive the vehicles 25,000 miles per day. This could represent massive greenhouse gas emissions and air pollution.[55] Waymo announced in early 2018 that it would also purchase 20,000 all-electric Jaguar SUVs—but new hybrid purchases would continue to outweigh all-electrics by a ratio of roughly three to one.[56]

It was reported in late 2017 that "Ford expects its vehicles will be on the road for roughly 20 hours a day, and [Ford's president of global markets Jim] Farley said using battery-electric vehicles doesn't make business sense because they would need to recharge multiple times a day, cutting into profits."[57] Farley explained that hybrids also help provide the immense electricity required to run the autonomous sensors and computers.[58]

In response, California Air Resources Board chair Mary Nichols tweeted: "Earth to Ford: what part of sustainability do you not understand? Driverless hybrid vehicles running 24/7 delivering pizza and passengers means more tons of pollution/GHGs in cities!"[59]

Bringing It All Together

Pulling off the "three revolutions" in tandem could mean an 80 percent decrease in emissions. But if vehicles are only automated and electrified—but not shared—and electricity isn't completely decarbonized by 2050, we will face a scenario that, euphemistically, "may produce more CO_2 emissions in 2050 than is consistent with targets to limit global temperature rise to 2°C (or less) compared to preindustrial levels."[60]

Only automating vehicles while failing to ensure electrification and sharing would increase vehicle travel by 15 to 20 percent, with an alleged "increased efficiency of AVs" meaning that energy consumption and greenhouse gas emissions would remain around the business as usual levels that will likely result in global collapse.[61] It's a spectacular gamble. Failure could mean a massive overshoot of the 2°C threshold, greatly jeopardizing the survival of humanity—especially in the Global South and in low-income communities in the Global North.

A truly enormous behavioural shift would be required to achieve widespread pooling. Americans are not in the habit of sharing private automobiles. From 1980 to 2013, carpooling decreased by 19.7 percent of workers to a mere 9.4 percent.[62]

Decades worth of high-occupancy vehicle (HOV) lanes and car-sharing programs haven't proven to be successful.[63] Tesla's growth strategy is oriented around the continued sale of personal vehicles to consumers, with increased autonomous technologies baked in.[64] Waymo and Fiat Chrysler announced in 2018 that they were working on a licensing agreement to sell autonomous vehicles directly to consumers.[65]

Options like Lyft Line and UberPool are arguably incentivizing a return to genuine carpooling; Lyft has pledged that 50 percent of all rides by 2022 will be shared. But even if Lyft does achieve that goal, it will still produce 2.2 ride-hailing miles for every personal vehicle auto mile taken off the road, as some of every shared trip involves just one passenger between pickups.[66] These shared rides are widely despised by drivers, who are effectively forced to accept the most labour-intensive rides to keep their acceptance rate up. Uber's Express Pool and Lyft's Shared Saver are new services that require riders to walk to a designated pickup spot to reduce driver detours. One review of Uber's version observed that it "takes a few minutes for the app to determine the pickup and drop-off locations, and then it takes a few more minutes for a car to arrive," concluding that readers should take a bus instead.[67] The constraints facing genuine ridesharing are huge, and largely unresolved outside of wishful thinking and fundraising hype.

Even an absolutely best-case scenario of rapid and widespread electrification, sharing, and autonomous technologies will necessitate the maintenance and expansion of the ecologically devastating infrastructure of roads, highways, and suburbs. Highways have destroyed hundreds of thousands of acres of wetlands that serve as complex ecosystems for a tremendous variety of species, as well as natural flood mitigation—until they are wiped out by roads to facilitate more and faster passenger vehicles.[68] Road systems result in high runoff of toxic pollutants including grease, road salt, and pesticides into streams and rivers.[69] Making driving easier will likely result in induced demand that makes people more comfortable with living farther away from their work, in turn requiring more of this ecologically devastating infrastructure.

"The extensive land dependency will not change," says Stefan Kipfer, an associate professor at York University who focuses on urban politics. "The energy use remains very high compared to public transit, irrespective of what the source of energy is. The profit orientation of the for-profit platforms, of course, means that there's an incentive on these people's part to push that means of transportation for its own sake."

PUBLIC TRANSIT: CHALLENGES AND OPPORTUNITIES

Pollution

Much of the public transit in North America is currently noisy, dirty, and very bad on fuel economy—with disproportionate impacts in working-class communities. Constant stopping, starting, and idling by diesel buses to pick up riders creates plumes of nasty air pollution and undercuts fuel efficiency. This effect is worsened by pothole-strewn roads that slow vehicles and require more acceleration.[70] Resulting fumes can cause and worsen respiratory issues, including asthma.

Diesel buses have an average fuel efficiency of only four or five miles per gallon.[71] That matters a great deal from a climate perspective, given that city buses can be driven between 40,000 and 60,000 miles a year.[72] Relative improvements have been made with the proliferation of natural-gas-powered buses (28.5 percent of the U.S. fleet in 2018) and hybrid electric buses (21 percent).[73] But the production of natural gas is plagued by methane leakages, a serious concern given that, over a 100-year period, methane has a global warming potential 25 times greater than carbon dioxide.[74] Passenger rail also has issues with spewing pollutants. Fine particulate matter in the Toronto subway system, for example, is around ten times higher than the levels found outside.[75]

Madeline Janis, executive director of Jobs to Move America, emphasized to me that the environmental impacts of transit are most pronounced in low-income communities of colour, as public transit vehicles are often maintained in such areas. West Harlem Environmental Action (WE ACT), for instance, has long fought the presence of polluting bus depots near the community's homes and schools.[76] Moreover, frequent exposure to peak noise levels at subway, bus, and streetcar stations can cause hearing loss, particularly for passing cyclists.[77] Decades of austerity have resulted in people with the least access to reliable service coping with the worst environmental consequences of dirty transit. These are extremely serious issues.

Yet even in its current underfunded state, transit remains *far* less polluting on a per-passenger basis than personal automobiles. A lot of it comes down to sheer weight. An average automobile weighs around 4,000 pounds without passengers. A standard two-axle forty-foot transit bus weighs in at between 20,000 and 33,000 pounds.[78] With only eleven passengers, a transit bus gets better mileage and emits slightly less in greenhouse gases than a passenger car with one rider (which is how most cars are driven).[79] It requires considerably less energy to propel one passenger a single mile on a semi-full bus or train than in an automobile.

There are a wide range of factors for this. Trains are more efficient because of the very low "rolling resistance" of steel wheels on steel rails, compared to rubber tires on pavement. There are also efficiencies from reduced aerodynamic drag in closely coupled vehicles (the same case that autonomous vehicle proponents make for "platooning" on highways, and why freight rail is more efficient than trucks).[80] But all transit, including buses, can fit far more people in a vehicle than a private automobile with five seats. This passenger capacity—combined with the efficiencies found in fixed-routed transportation, due to not having to drive to pick up every individual rider from different locations—makes public modes far less energy-intensive than private counterparts.

Critics of public transit will point out, often accurately, that buses and trains frequently run with only a handful of passengers aboard at any time. But that ignores the tremendous ridership potential uniquely available to those modes. Transit's historically low fuel efficiency can be rectified in many ways: driving in dedicated lanes with priority at intersections, faster loading systems like all-door boarding, and encouraging densification of communities through building and preserving public housing.[81] These are not particularly radical changes. When combined with free fares and comfortable rides, expanded transit service can trigger a virtuous cycle of less vehicle ownership and congestion as people feel more confident in their ability to rely on transit. The better the service, the more people who ride buses and trains. That in turn lessens the amount of energy required on a per-person basis. Increasing ridership on existing transit is far better climate policy than getting everyone into their own electric vehicle.

Existing air pollution problems can be mitigated by transit agencies with just a bit of commitment, a process far easier than trying to regulate and retrofit all personal automobiles on the road. After all, a transit agency has only a few thousand vehicles and can deal with them and related systems in a relatively rapid fashion. A study of Toronto's dirty subway system recommended improved ventilation, filtration, and rail dust cleaning: all fairly straightforward solutions, although the TTC has repeatedly refused to implement such changes, which the union is fighting. (In late 2019, a retired TTC worker filed a private prosecution against the transit agency for alleged adverse health effects resulting from air pollution in the subway system.)[82]

Following a study into Toronto-area commuter GO trains, Metrolinx installed new filters that removed 80 percent of black carbon and 25 percent of ultrafine particles. Upcoming electrification, long fought for, will eliminate them altogether.[83] Centralized control over a transportation system makes it possible for change to happen far more rapidly than if it is privately owned.

Electrifying public transportation will massively cut emissions, air, and noise pollution. It takes an estimated 100 personal electric vehicles to provide the same "environmental relief" as can be gained by a single sixty-foot electric bus.[84] Every 1,000 electric buses on the road displace 500 barrels of diesel, while 1,000 battery-electric vehicles only remove 15 barrels of oil demand.[85] Unlike personal vehicles, which tend to be used for only an hour or two per day, buses run up to eighteen hours per day. Electric motors have extremely high torque that can be administered at low speeds, making them a perfect fit for buses that have to constantly start and stop, and through regenerative braking, the kinetic energy from frequent braking can be captured to recharge batteries rather than lost as heat.[86] An electric bus running in peak conditions can be at least five times as efficient as an old diesel bus.[87]

Of course, electric transit would require resource-intensive materials and inputs to manufacture the required batteries and components. But quantities would be hugely reduced on a per-person basis compared to widespread ownership or use of personal electric vehicles.[88] Given the sheer number of passengers they can carry and the hours per day spent on roads, electric buses prove to be a far superior use of resources than personal vehicles, even if those cars are occasionally shared.

While electric buses are currently more expensive to buy than diesel buses, transit agencies would end up paying much

> "It's not a solution to climate change to create a billion Teslas. Each of those cars has an enormous carbon footprint for everything that's extracted and all the energy-intensive processes to create it. The more we can just make one bus instead of twenty cars, the better."
>
> —THEA RIOFRANCOS, author of *Resource Radicals*

less to operate them than current models. It's about 2.5 times cheaper to power a bus with electricity than with diesel, and maintenance costs would be considerably lower as well.[89] There are several ways to charge a bus, including a plug-in overnight at the bus depot or an overhead charger at main bus stops. Charging en route requires a massive amount of electricity at once, which may cause sudden spikes in load demand and requires an integrated approach between transit operators and the grid; rapid charging can also cause faster battery deterioration. There are ways around such harmful effects, such as committing to an off-peak overnight charge when electricity demand and costs are at the lowest, or a hybrid trolleybus-like approach using overhead wires for a few miles between longer stretches that are wire-free.

Transit agencies across North America are experimenting with different ways of charging buses and integrating them into their networks. It's not enough to simply purchase electric buses: a great deal of collaboration is required with electrical utilities to prepare the infrastructure before rollout.[90] There's plenty of talk about the potential for personal electric vehicles to serve as "batteries on wheels" that fill up in off-peak times and sell electricity back to the grid during peak times if they're not in use. But there's no reason that public transit agencies couldn't do that as well—and potentially better. Buses have more battery capacity, are often parked for long periods of time, and run on predictable schedules.[91]

Unfortunately, there have been challenges in deployment of electric buses in some places. Both Los Angeles and Albuquerque experienced performance, battery range, and mechanical issues in buses from the Chinese manufacturer BYD.[92] There are also ongoing issues with battery range in electric buses, particularly in cold weather; immense heating requirements can suck up almost half of the battery power, reducing the number of hours a bus can spend driving its routes.[93] However, they continue to spread: New York City's MTA introduced its first 60-foot electric bus for service on the new 14th Street Busway in late 2019, with plans to buy 500 electric buses by 2024 for all five boroughs.[94]

Moataz Mohamed, a civil engineering professor at McMaster University, told me that every brand of bus has its own unique plug-in technology. That means that transit agencies trying out a certain type of bus, like a New Flyer or BYD, become effectively married to that technology. They would have to install a new set of charging stations if they changed brand. Transit agencies are notoriously risk-averse, so they'll tend to stick with the technology they know—even if it's a dirty diesel bus. Mohamed says having operational data for electric buses would help agencies decide if the mode is right for them, especially given questions around wintertime battery life and breakdown histories. But private bus manufacturers usually require nondisclosure agreements with municipalities, keeping that data unavailable to the public.

While electric buses cost considerably less to operate over their lifetimes, few transit agencies are in a financial position to invest in replacing a significant portion of their fleet with what many consider a still-unproven technology. Mohamed told me that his team interviewed a dozen transit managers in Canada about electric buses. "They said repeatedly, 'I don't want to see my picture on the front page of the newspaper saying I wasted taxpayers' money.' The risk-averse mindset is controlling a lot in the industry." Austerity by another name.[95]

Battery-related concerns about resource usage and range can also be meaningfully addressed by providing transit agencies more funding to experiment, and investing in public transportation modes that don't require batteries in the first place. Trolleybuses, streetcars, light rail, and subways run on electricity delivered through overhead power lines or third rails. Trolleybuses are arguably the best option for cities at the present moment. The mode has a century-long track record of proven success in places including Beijing, Milan, and Vancouver, and, without the need to carry a heavy engine or battery, higher energy efficiency.[96] Range issues are also solved with these vehicles. They're far less reliant on battery power; some alternate between requiring charge from overhead lines and driving without connection, which requires a smaller battery than standalone buses.[97]

Essentially, the more coordinated and well-funded a transit system is, the fewer batteries it will likely require. Instead, the system will rely more on fixed-track options like trolleybuses, streetcars, trains, and subways—with buses filling the gaps. Each of these options greatly decreases the amount of space that needs to be dedicated to roads and highways, which are accompanied by wetland destruction, road salting, and toxic runoff.

Well within Reach

Low-carbon solutions that dramatically reduce greenhouse gases, air pollution, and other ecological impacts are well within reach. All they need is increased and sustained public funding, political support, and a desire by all for a greener city and world. And they can have near-immediate, desperately needed effects in communities poisoned with air and noise pollution. There's no need to wait: the transition can happen immediately.

Cohen told me that in the wake of protests in 2013 in response to worsening congestion and a nine-cent hike in bus fares, the mayor of São Paulo, Brazil, demarcated hundreds of kilometres of dedicated bus lanes just using paint (rather than constructing separated bus rapid transit lanes). Cohen says that within about six months, the new lanes resulted in commute time being cut by about 15 percent, with a corresponding reduction in diesel and greenhouses gases. That demonstrates the speed at which a city can massively improve bus service and environmental conditions, he says.

A similar example can be found in Everett, Massachusetts, which saw an incredible 20 to 30 percent decrease in commute times at peak hours after using red paint to install a "tactical transit lane."[98] "I don't think there's any form of land-use politics in the city that can be as dramatically reshaped as quickly as you get when you make dedicated bus lanes with paint," Cohen told me.

Such projects can help reduce political opposition and give a tangible example to riders and other commuters who may have doubts about the possibilities. With escalating enthusiasm from creatively deployed interventions, a transit agency can build constituencies of support for further advances, including electric buses and more well-planned options that reduce the need for resource-intensive batteries.

There are many recent instances of public transit offering a lifeline to impacted communities: following the 2013 floods in Calgary, the devastating 2016 wildfire in Fort McMurray, and the Houston Metro's evacuation of thousands of people with buses following hurricanes Harvey and Irma. "Public transit remains the number one travel option for mass transportation, and for those who don't own a car in times of natural disasters, that can mean their only chance of survival," the Canadian Urban Transit Association wrote.[99]

Getting people out of spatially inefficient vehicles and onto buses, trains, bikes, and sidewalks also allows cities and towns to take steps to mitigate harms from climate change impacts—including flooding, sea level rise, and extreme temperatures.[100]

Public transit as it exists has clear environmental issues. But such issues are proportionately far less significant—and easier to fix—than the impacts of maintaining and expanding the supremacy of private automobiles. We can very quickly electrify and expand public transportation in a coordinated and predictable manner. That's much better than naively hoping that dozens of Silicon Valley–backed companies competing for monopoly control of city streets will somehow save the day by convincing million of drivers to self-select for low-carbon vehicles. It simply isn't possible to slow climate chaos and environmental issues without a radical recommitment to public transportation as a communal force for good and a collective struggle for a decarbonized, ecological, and decommodified future.

"What's optimistic is people organizing in whatever form that takes," author and academic Kafui Attoh told me. "Elon Musk and Silicon Valley capitalists are organized to some degree. What that requires is organization from below and by those who will be immediately affected by ecological disaster."

Chapter 4

Race to the bottom

Inequality and poverty

Communities that genuinely desire to confront legacies of racism, poverty, and dispossession have to prioritize free, frequent, and comfortable public transportation alongside public housing.

THE COST OF ACCESS

Driving—as anyone who's ever owned a vehicle knows—is an incredibly expensive activity. The average cost in the U.S. to own and operate a new vehicle in 2019 was calculated at $9,280 per year.[1] That figures includes everything from fuel to maintenance and repairs, to insurance and licence fees, to depreciation of the vehicle's value. While upfront prices to purchase used cars are lower, less fuel efficiency and more maintenance issues can lead to higher ongoing costs over time. Americans owe banks a total of $1.1 trillion in car loans.[2]

Quite predictably, such costs lead to unequal and inaccessible transportation, exacerbating existing divisions along race and class lines.[3] Almost 20 percent of households in the U.S. without a vehicle are Black and 13.6 percent are Native American, compared to a national average of 9.1 percent.[4] Low-income households spend 16 percent of household income on transportation; high-income earners spend 8 percent.[5]

This lack of access to transportation impedes access to employment, food, healthcare, education, and social services. Many jobs require a licence and a vehicle, an expectation that excludes applicants who can't afford to drive or have had their licences revoked after being unable to pay fines for infractions as small as a burnt-out taillight.[6] Distance from a job can have a significant impact on hiring practices. Callback rates fall by 1.1 percent for every mile an applicant moves away from a job; commuting distance and neighbourhood poverty can account for a full two-thirds of the penalty in job callback rates in Washington, DC.[7] One study indicated that low-wage workers in San Diego with access to a car had thirty times as much access to jobs as workers who didn't.[8]

Most households in food deserts don't have access to a vehicle.[9] Lack of access to reliable transportation also compromises the ability for people in low-income communities to get to medical appointments on time; about one of every four low-income patients have missed or rescheduled appointments due to mobility constraints.[10] Gentrification of many cities has displaced low-income residents out of downtowns. Having relied on active and public transportation, they are now required to own personal vehicles for the first time in their lives—at greatly disproportionate cost.[11]

THREE REVOLUTIONS: THE EFFECTS ON POVERTY

Genuine Car-Sharing

One of the chief appeals of ride-hailing services like Uber or shared autonomous vehicles as promoted by Waymo is that individual riders don't have to own a car. They can simply use an app to summon one when desired. Proponents argue that eliminating the large capital cost of owning and operating a vehicle will make mobility more accessible, particularly for households that don't currently own their own car and aren't served well by transit or taxis.

The proliferation of privately owned electric vehicles doesn't fit particularly easily into this vision, given the typically high cost of a new car. But various groups concerned with transportation equity have proposed state-led solutions that expand subsidies for electric vehicles, with a focus on low-income residents. Jurisdictions in California are leading the way, offering up to $9,500 in funding to purchase an electric vehicle if a low-income resident trades in an older gasoline- or diesel-powered vehicle.[12] And utility companies in San Diego and Santa Rosa are working to improve access to charging stations in low-income neighbourhoods.[13]

The shared usage of electric vehicles is another commonly suggested remedy. Some cities, mostly in California, have introduced genuine car-sharing options using electric vehicles with a specific focus on low-income communities. BlueLA in Los Angeles charges a sliding scale between fifteen and twenty cents per minute, and features 100 cars and 200 charging points.[14] Sacramento is introducing a similar program called Envoy, featuring electric vehicles available for rent at 71 spots around the city, including in low-income areas.[15]

There are promising examples of ridesharing in the Central Valley of California, where many rural low-income farmworker communities suffer from air pollution and isolation from basic services. In Cantua Creek, a community-led ride-sharing program that recently acquired a seven-seat Tesla Model X allows residents to take trips at the rough cost of a bus trip.[16] In addition, they provide alternative ways to pay for the service, Spanish service, and the option to book over the phone. In the nearby community of Huron, a similar service described by its mayor as "indigenous Ubers" provide low-cost rides to residents in electric vehicles.[17] Similarly, Winnipeg's non-profit Ikwe Safe Rides, organized by Indigenous women, seeks to provide a rideshare service to mostly Indigenous women who, fearing sexual harassment, prefer to avoid taxis.[18] New York

City's legendary "dollar vans" also provide an informal ride-sharing network.[19]

Industry Response

Of course, this isn't the model of ridesharing that "three revolutions" boosters are talking about; in fact, the headline for the *New York Times* profile of Huron's ride-sharing service was "The Anti-Uber."[20] The modes that are redefining cities and towns and attracting by far the most political attention and venture capital are ride-hailing services like Uber and Lyft.

One assessment of 6.3 million Lyft rides in Los Angeles County seemed to confirm the political appeal of such services, finding that 99.8 percent of the county's population was served by Lyft—and that low-income residents used it the most.[21] Lead researcher Anne E. Brown wrote: "Users living in low-income neighborhoods ... may have low—or zero—personal car access and therefore use Lyft to provide rather than supplement auto-mobility."[22]

In mid-2018, Lyft announced $1.5 million over a year for free rides to low-income people and military veterans for situations like job interviews and medical appointments. This followed its Relief Rides program, initiated in the wake of Hurricane Irma and California's 2017 wildfire season to offer free rides to shelters, hospitals, and blood donation clinics.[23] Lyft has also partnered with the Washington, DC, anti-poverty organization Martha's Table for a six-month program to offer $2.50 shared rides so that 500 families can access grocery stores as a way to confront the crisis of food deserts. That program has been replicated in other cities, including Portland and Indianapolis.[24]

Autonomous vehicles are already being marketed as offering the same kinds of accessibility to low-income residents, improving transportation to places that would otherwise suffer continued neglect. Transportation policy expert Ashley Nunes has written of the importance of governments subsidizing access to autonomous vehicles for America's poor, calling it "more effective than improving mass transit." Nunes argued that low-income people are more likely to suffer from poor job prospects from mobility restrictions and to die in traffic crashes because they use older vehicles that don't have features like cruise control and pedestrian detection. "That's the real promise of driverless technology—lifting millions out of poverty without having them pay for it with their lives."[25]

Personal ownership of electric vehicles does cut some costs by a significant margin. It costs about 40 percent as much to charge an electric vehicle as to fill a car up with gasoline, and electric vehicles have fewer moving parts and therefore lower maintenance costs.[26] But the vehicle itself still costs a significant amount, even with a generous $7,500 U.S. federal tax credit: a Nissan Leaf, the cheapest popular option, is $22,500, while a Chevrolet Bolt costs $29,995 and a luxury Tesla Model S rings in at $72,000.[27]

That federal tax credit, introduced in 2008, is non-refundable, which means that a tax liability can be reduced to zero but no refund will be provided beyond that. In other words, an electric vehicle buyer would have to earn at least $52,000 per year to owe $7,500 in federal tax—and therefore get the full amount in a tax credit.[28] Just over 57,000 taxpayers (both individuals and corporations) claimed $375 million in electric vehicle tax credits in 2016; 78 percent of those were claimed by filers with an annual gross income of at least $100,000.[29] An estimated 70 percent of electric vehicle owners would have bought them without a subsidy, according to research published in 2019, which calculated owners' average income at $140,000 per year.[30]

The future of the federal tax credit is uncertain. The legislation was designed to be phased out once a manufacturer had produced 200,000 electric vehicles; the supposed idea was to kickstart the industry rather than permanently support it. Tesla and General Motors have already surpassed that level of sales, so the subsidy for their vehicles is being phased out.[31]

Appeals to ride-hailing as a remedy to lack of access to automobility for low-income communities is similarly flawed.[32] Using Uber on a regular basis would be about 80 percent more expensive than driving a personal vehicle, already an extremely expensive mode of transportation.[33] Even at base rates, ride-hailing is inaccessible as a regular means of transportation for low-income riders. That becomes even more of an issue with surge pricing, in which rates multiply many times the regular fare at certain times based on supply and demand. People with a household income over $200,000 per year are far more likely to use ride-hailing options than people making less income.[34]

Transportation expert Hubert Horan has explained: "Surge pricing reduces wait times for wealthier people returning home from restaurants and nightclubs by eliminating all service for lower income people working late night shifts that have no transit options."[35] Surge pricing results in a form of redlining of low-income communities of colour when drivers choose not to operate in such areas.[36] Low-income riders can certainly use these services from time to time, but they're by no means a reliable form of transportation. "A lot of our residents can't even afford it," says Crystal Jennings of Pittsburghers for Public Transit. "Sometimes Uber trips can skyrocket with surge charges during the course of the day. A lot of people can't pay for that."

Alex Birnel, advocacy manager at MOVE Texas, told me that he spends a significant amount of money on ride-hailing because he has cerebral palsy and can't drive. He says that public transit in his hometown of San Antonio is too unpredictable for many people to use it on a consistent basis. "When a city doesn't have these resources or this infrastructure, you fall back on incredibly budget-busting private options," he says. "So much of my monthly paycheque will go to Uber or Lyft. That's because transportation at a moment's notice is what's desired. I want to be able to on a whim decide to go somewhere and not have to plan my day with three- to four-hour windows because of public transit."

Part of the calculus has to do with basic costs of operation. Ride-hailing options, even when shared, are very inefficient compared to fixed-route transportation.[37] Rides are artificially subsidized by venture capitalists because they can't make enough money. But ride-hailing companies are also looking to make as much profit as possible.

Drivers, too, are seeking returns, and they get to decide on the hours they drive and where. Ride-hailing drivers may not always provide service to poorer communities, as those rides tend to be shorter and not taken during times of surge pricing.[38] Additionally, as noted by Hana Creger of the Greenlining Institute, "there are no specific procedures to prevent discriminatory practices such as drivers going offline to avoid requests in lower-income areas."[39]

Some research has indicated less prejudice by Uber and Lyft drivers compared to taxi drivers.[40] But other studies have suggested that ride-hailing passengers with African American–sounding names face significantly longer waiting times and more frequent cancellations.[41] Language barriers can also impede access, and ride-hailing services don't offer alternative payment or reservation methods for riders who have no credit card or smartphone.[42]

About 8 percent of Americans are unbanked, meaning they don't have access to credit cards or bank accounts, so they can't use ride-hailing services.[43] Only 67 percent of people who earn less than $30,000 a year own a smartphone, and 46 percent of people over the age of 65.[44] Combined, that means that tens of millions of people—mostly low-income and/or seniors—effectively can't use ride-hailing services at this point, and their access to transportation is worsening with the ongoing decline in transit. There is no indication that things will substantially change with the eventual shift toward autonomous vehicles. In fact, they could get even worse, depending on which scenarios governments allow.

Todd Litman of the Victoria Transport Policy Institute has said that there's a popular idea that we may arrive at a moment when autonomous rides cost so little that the rate will be paid for by advertising. But he thinks such estimates fail to look at what the actual cost profile might look like, including maintenance and cleaning, empty vehicle travel, insurance, and roadway costs. Others disagree. *Vox*'s David Roberts has warned of an impending nightmare scenario in which a race to the bottom will lead to a company offering free service, which would require much higher vehicle miles travelled (VMT). "Insofar as they get revenue from advertising, owners of shared vehicle fleets will want more people to go more places in cars. Their revenue will rise with VMT, so they will strive to maximize VMT."[45]

In such a scenario, well-off people would likely have the option of paying to avoid all of that tedium, like subscribers to Spotify's premium service to listen without ads. Conversely, low-wage workers attempting to get to a job or grocery store would be subjected to a specific route that was based on whichever company had paid the most for the right.[46]

Far from a predictable, affordable option for people, the mix of heavy advertising, data collection, and potentially unpredictable pricing would only reassert accessibility for the wealthy. Due to rampant gentrification, wealthy residents could continue to live in downtown areas closer to their work, reducing any commute time in an autonomous vehicle to a fraction of what displaced workers would have to face at a higher personal cost. Regardless of whether riders are charged with money or advertising—or both—autonomous vehicles will likely replicate existing systems of inequality and racism that deprive entire communities of the ability to secure, safe, and affordable transportation.

Barriers to Access

Since urban transit is chronically underfunded, that lack of money must be made up from other sources: mostly through constant fare increases. A 2017 analysis found that an average monthly transit pass in the U.S. costs $67, but can range up to $121 in New York and $122 in Los Angeles.[47] Single fares are often more expensive per ride, especially if a transit system is zoned (additional price for travel into different regions) or tickets are restricted to one-way travel on a network or don't include transfers. Low-income riders often can't afford to purchase a weekly or monthly pass, so they usually pay more in the form of single tickets. Larry Hanley, the late international president of the Amalgamated Transit Union (ATU), told me: "Putting higher fares in is a completely inadequate and unfair strategy. Most of what's going on in our society today is lowering taxes on the rich and raising taxes on the poor."

Anti-poor discrimination in transit systems can manifest in other ways as well, particularly around the type of service prioritized in particular areas. Low-income bus riders are often disregarded as "captive riders," suggesting they will continue to use transit regardless of how bad the service gets.[48] The biases of political elites and the desire of transit agencies to boost ridership and revenues funnels most funding to attract affluent "choice riders" onto new rail service. Affluent residents, as a result, tend to have by far the best access to transit. Low-income households in Toronto's inner suburbs, for example, have almost four times less access to transit service than do high-income neighbourhoods.[49]

This bias is also evident in where transit agencies choose to build infrastructure that improves overall rider comfort: heated bus shelters, shaded benches, public washrooms. A lack of such amenities in a neighbourhood represents a hidden barrier for residents to use transit. Other barriers include limited bus service on evenings and weekends, which disproportionately impacts low-wage shift workers, and snow accumulation on sidewalks that makes access to transportation even more difficult for people using strollers, walkers, canes, or wheelchairs.[50]

Transit Planning

Much of this dynamic has to do with who's calling the shots about how communities are planned. Metropolitan planning organizations (MPOs) play a major role in deciding how U.S. transportation funding is allocated, but their board members are disproportionately white; Hispanic and Black communities are underrepresented.[51] Creger told me that the voting structure of MPO boards can give a small suburban community the same voting power as a large urban area. A Brookings Institution report suggested that most of the substantive discussions in MPOs take place among specialists on technical committees, not elected officials.[52] Such organizational bias further disenfranchises low-income residents from having a real say over transportation decisions.

The same goes for the boards of transit agencies. A 2018 assessment of boards across North America found that most were overwhelmingly white: both Montreal's and Vancouver's had no Black, Indigenous, or people of colour (BIPOC) representatives on their boards. Of eight boards examined, only two included a rider representative: in Montreal and Washington, DC.[53] The income or class position of board members wasn't reported.

There are ways to democratize this process. Creger points to the increasing role of participatory budgeting in California, where public money must be dedicated from the start of a project in order to improve community involvement. She says that San Francisco's Metropolitan Transportation Commission recently allocated one million dollars to such processes, to be specifically implemented in low-income communities of colour. "The more money that is allocated toward these projects, the more we can ensure that this actually results in tangible benefits," she told me.

But as Steven Higashide has written in *Better Buses, Better Cities: How to Plan, Run, and Win the Fight for Effective Transit*, the "open house" approach to transit planning often structurally benefits wealthy residents and business owners, as they have more time and resources to organize. He stressed the need to proactively seek out the perspectives of transit riders and allies, abandoning lengthy development plans for much faster deployments of infrastructure like tactical bus lanes. A key part of this process, he has argued, is for planners to focus on maximizing access to destinations including grocery stores and healthcare facilities, not just jobs; most of the trips that people take, after all, are not for work.[54]

Development without Displacement

Transit development can cause displacement—but it doesn't have to. Seattle council member Kshama Sawant told me, "We should not draw false causal relationships between public transit expansion and that being detrimental to the lives of working people. It's exactly the opposite."

Many tools have been used to ensure that low-income residents gain better transit and active transportation in their neighbourhoods without fearing that they will lose their homes, most notably the genuinely public ownership of housing stock, including government-owned housing and co-ops. Struggles for public transit and housing are closely linked and must be fought together.

In April 2018, Sound Transit—the regional transit authority that operates the Seattle metro area's light rail and commuter rail services—announced that it was updating its policy for equitable transit-oriented development to apply an 80-80-80 rule ordered by the state legislature. It would offer 80 percent of "surplus property" following construction of new light rail lines to affordable housing developers, who would be required to make at least 80 percent of constructed units available to people earning 80 percent or less of the region's median income.[55]

Several organizations in Toronto, including the Toronto Community Benefits Network, have been working to ensure that a community benefit agreement (CBA) is secured with Metrolinx as new light rail lines are built in coming years. The Toronto and York Region Labour Council explained in a statement that such an agreement would help address social inequalities by including employment and training opportunities for members of low-income communities.[56]

Some cities are also moving to mass-rezone single-family zones to allow for higher-density housing. Vancouver's city council voted in 2018 to rezone 99 percent of single-family lots; a few months later, Minneapolis abolished single-family zoning entirely to allow for duplexes and triplexes.[57] California Senate Bill 50, proposed by San Francisco state senator Scott Wiener, would require cities to allow construction of apartment complexes near transit stops while protecting existing renters from displacement.[58]

Many groups across the country are struggling for genuine community ownership and control of land and housing. Samuel Stein, author of *Capital City: Gentrification and the Real Estate State*, has argued that relying on zoning for housing justice is a dead end, and that we have to fight for "public housing, particularly, but also rent control and community land trusts."[59] Community land trusts, which are typically non-profit, community-led organizations that own the land via donations or purchase the land and lease it to individuals, provide an alternative long-term solution that can help slow gentrification.[60] Universal rent control, limiting the ability of property owners to hike rents, is a particularly important tool in this struggle. Banning or seriously limiting the spread of companies like Airbnb, which further entrench the commodification of housing and drive up rental prices, would be another strong step.[61] In June 2019, tenant activists in New York won what Stein described as a "historic expansion of rent stabilization, rent control, and anti-eviction measures." While universal rent control was missing from the bill, it's an excellent example of what's possible when tenants organize.[62]

Public Ownership; Public Activism

While ride-hailing companies might host an occasional PR campaign for a few hundred people to access groceries for a month, publicly owned and operated transit agencies are in a position to dramatically reorient funding and operations to benefit everyone, including low-income communities. Residents can fight back and build a far more equitable system. And there are plenty of examples over the years of this exact struggle unfolding with resounding success.

In the mid-1990s, the Los Angeles Bus Riders Union famously sued the Metropolitan Transportation Authority under Title VI of the Civil Rights Act for "intentionally discriminating against racial and ethnic minority groups in the delivery of transportation services" by dedicating disproportionate funding to rail service that served predominantly affluent white riders while depriving the bus network—which mostly carried low-income people of colour—of needed investments to reduce costs and buy more buses.[63] A judge awarded a temporary injunction against the transit authority, and a deal was later struck that cut fares and required hundreds more buses to be purchased. However, the transportation authority failed to uphold many of its promises, an impasse that was met by escalating tactics including a militant "no seat, no fare" campaign.[64] That pivotal moment for transit organizing in North America inspired the formation of many bus riders' unions and advocacy groups.

In 2009, several Oakland organizations filed a similar civil rights complaint against Bay Area Rapid Transit for failing to conduct an equity analysis of the Oakland Airport Connector project. As a result, the project lost $70 million in federal funding, which was reallocated to regional rail and bus improvements.[65]

Jennings says that Pittsburghers for Public Transit recently won a series of victories. For example, they blocked proposed service cuts to a low-income community that would have required inconvenient transfers—and actually leveraged it into a new bus rapid transit route. She told me about riders that she worked with: "We open them up to the possibilities of if they fight for what they believe in, that their service can and will be resolved and stay current or get better. We basically use a lot of community engagement: teaching them and helping them get their voices heard, speaking out about the issues that they have in their communities."

Stephanie Farmer of Roosevelt University says that United Working Families—a Chicago-based independent political group made up of unions and community organizations—is agitating for transit investment for all of Chicago rather than allowing more ground to be ceded to private vehicles and grandiose plans. Creger says that there are good news stories emerging out of California, including the building of an all-electric bus rapid transit route in South Stockton, a low-income community of colour in Central Valley.[66] She adds that progressive cities including Portland, Seattle, and Oakland are creating race equity departments that are being integrated with departments of transportation to help address injustices—but that there are still many examples of low-income residents not being at the decision-making tables, so many needs and priorities are still being left behind.

Toronto's TTCriders has had success over the years, helping to pressure the city to introduce low-income fares, increase annual funding to reduce overcrowding, and implement two-hour transfers, which allow for more than one trip, reducing the amount spent on fares for a short or multi-stop outing.[67] When it launched in 2015 ahead of the Pan American Games, Toronto's Union Pearson Express to the airport cost $19 per trip for riders with a Presto payment card or $27.50 for riders without one. Following several years of organizing by the Our Union Pearson Coalition—made up of many groups including TTCriders and the Toronto Airport Council of Unions—Metrolinx cut those fares to $9 and $12, respectively (airport workers pay $3.50 for a one-way ticket). When the coalition formed, TTCriders argued: "Let's make this line for everyone, and not just the 1%."[68] That organizing worked.

Low-income passes are also being increasingly discussed across North America. In 2017, Calgary introduced a sliding scale pass, available for $5.05 per month for the lowest-income segment of the population. The city sold 70,000 passes in the first three months, 70 percent of which were the least expensive option.[69] Portland's TriMet transit agency brought in a low-income fare program in July 2018. Qualifying riders can buy single tickets for half the price and monthly passes for almost three-quarters less.[70] Amy Lubitow, a sociology professor at Portland State University who researches public transit ridership experiences, emphasized to me that the policy was "the result of lots and lots of community organizing," rather than something benevolently gifted by the agency.

Discounted fares for low-income people are a good start—but they can rely on inconvenient and humiliating means-testing processes that require the user to prove their worthiness to administrators. In early 2019, it was reported that only 30,000 low-income New Yorkers would be eligible for half-priced transit passes, excluding most of the 800,000 people living below the poverty line.[71] Low-income fares also maintain a relationship to public transit as a commodity, rather than a universal public service that everyone shares in and has access to regardless of income. That's where the free transit (or more exactly, "fare-free transit") movement, which is gaining rapid support around the world, comes in.

Almost one hundred cities and towns around the world have introduced fully free transit, over half of them in Europe.[72] Free transit has produced extremely positive ridership outcomes. Chapel Hill in North Carolina saw annual ridership increase from three million to seven million passengers after eliminating fares, while in Missoula, Montana, a "zero fare" initiative and high-speed routes led to a 70 percent increase in bus ridership. The regional transit authority in Tampa, Florida, eliminated fares and improved service on a downtown streetcar thanks to a $2.7 million state grant, resulting in a tripling of service in only six months.[73] In 2019, municipal governments in Victoria, British Columbia, and Kansas City, Missouri, voted to abolish fares on transit.[74] And a week after Kansas City's decision in early December, it was reported that Portland's TriMet board was studying the possibility as well.[75]

Free transit expert Wojciech Kębłowski has explained that governments pursue the policy for a wide range of reasons: reducing car usage and pollution, improving access for low-income residents, or redefining the relationship of riders to transit as a public service.[76] Eliminating fares for transit can result in significant ridership increases, requiring funding boosts to meet demand and increase service.[77] Polling of 2,000 transit riders in Dunkirk, France—which made buses free to use in 2018, found that 50 percent of riders were new users and an incredible 48 percent were taking the bus instead of driving.[78]

As will be discussed in chapters 7 and 9, abolishing fares eliminates the need for fare enforcement—an overwhelmingly racist and classist practice—and protects transit workers from assaults related to fare disputes. By funding free transit through general revenue, preferably from higher income and wealth taxes on the rich, communities can directly confront the climate crisis (and other issues discussed in this book) while improving transportation access for low-income communities. When combined with greatly improved service, this policy offers a far more rapid and politically popular transition away from automobility than carbon pricing and other user fees—and has the incidental benefit of making boarding a bus more efficient, as there's no fare to be paid or card to be swiped.

As transit wonks will often point out, free transit isn't enough. We need a radical improvement in service, most notably improving frequency so that buses and trains show up more often and for longer stretches throughout the day. Some critics oppose the policy because of its potential to strip away reliable funding from agencies when they need it most. But free transit advocates aren't suggesting abolishing fares and leaving it at that. They want to replace user fees with revenue from higher taxes on the rich, and significantly *increase* funding to anticipate higher ridership and improved service.

Here's an example, using my home city of Winnipeg. The transit agency receives almost $90 million a year in fare revenue.[79] Anticipating at least a 50 percent increase in ridership and a desire to greatly improve existing service, higher levels of government could completely abolish fares and increase frequency of buses for somewhere between $150 and $200 million a year—a paltry sum when compared to the urgency of the climate crisis. By comparison, the city's police department has an annual budget of over $300 million. Free transit is *incredibly* achievable, as the organizing in Kansas City, Missouri, and elsewhere should remind us.

Struggles can be fought and won against ride-hailing companies.[80] But they tend be defensive campaigns to prevent a transportation coup from spreading even further. While valuable, the win doesn't change the material realities for low-income riders desperately in need of free and reliable transportation. That's where community organizing for public transportation, especially free transit, comes in. Through bus riders' unions and similar organizations across North America,

"Complaining about the TTC is an everyday part of life in Toronto. People are really angry about the constant delays. What we do is we try to turn that anger into political action. If everyone who's angry about the TTC joined our organization and got active, we can make a lot of changes."

—SHELAGH PIZEY-ALLEN, TTCriders, Toronto

we can greatly improve service for the people who need it most. Regular people know what needs to change. When asked what could draw riders of New York's "dollar vans" back to the city's transit network, they identified cheaper fares, faster bus speeds, and better spacing of buses.[81]

Communities that genuinely desire to confront legacies of racism, poverty, and dispossession have to prioritize free, frequent, and comfortable public transportation alongside public housing, as well as the sustained expansion of a range of related policies to improve access: snow clearing, well-lit stops, public washrooms, easy-to-read timetables and routes designed for use by people with different abilities, shelters that protect from both heat and cold, and diverse ways to purchase tickets. The alternative is to knowingly deprive low-income communities of opportunities for employment, food, healthcare, and social services—leading to all kinds of preventable tragedies and suffering, and further entrenching automobile culture for the predominately affluent.

A real commitment to a massive buildout of public transportation—as well as safer streets for pedestrians and cyclists—that focuses on serving low-income residents, along with social housing and other anti-gentrification measures, will have tremendous impacts on the equality and well-being of communities. Every dollar spent on new roads, electric vehicle subsidies, and other privatized solutions is not only a distraction, it is oppositional to this goal. Knowing that, we must direct our organizing to the most equitable and just form of transportation available.

Chapter 5

Crowding out

Congestion and safety

Urban transportation is a question of geometry. We simply can't fit as many cars onto a city street as there are people.

PLANNING FOR HARM

You never see a driver in a car commercial stuck in gridlock. There's no footage of frantically circling a city block to hunt for a parking spot, or a driver with road rage lobbing slurs at a cyclist. In fact, few ads even take place in the city: exquisite aerial shots show vehicles hurtling through a secluded forest or navigating hairpin turns down a mountain valley (usually with a "closed course" or "professional driver" warning tucked at the bottom).[1] Universally hated day-to-day problems with automobility only make it to the screen as a means of demonstrating how *this* vehicle is the means to avoid such situations; the underlying message is freedom, tranquility, efficiency.

Of course, these are fanciful depictions of what we hope driving will be. Commuting by car tends to be alarmingly frustrating. Congestion leads to calamitous effects: mental duress, missed appointments, higher fuel consumption, road rage, and impeded emergency vehicles.[2] In 2018, traffic congestion cost the U.S. an estimated $87 billion in lost productivity.[3]

The chief policy response has been the constant expansion of roadways, which itself only incites more demand for driving and sprawl.[4] Urban road mileage grew by 77 percent between 1980 and 2014, while the U.S. population increased by only 41 percent; roads and highways receive far greater funding, with considerably less bureaucratic delay, than public transit.[5]

The average automobile is used for only an hour a day; it's parked for a stunning 96 percent of the time.[6] As each vehicle takes up about 100 cubic feet, that requires an enormous quantity of space.[7] In 2010, for example, some 14 percent of Los Angeles County's incorporated land was committed to parking.[8] This institutionalization of the car is deeply embedded in the U.S. federal tax system. The country spends about $7.3 billion per year to encourage people to drive to work through the federal income tax exclusion for commuter parking, which principally benefits higher-income earners.[9] Most cities also mandate that property developers install a certain number of off-street parking spots. About this policy of "mandatory parking minimums," TransitCenter wrote: "Few planning practices do so much harm to cities: Parking mandates induce more driving, increase housing costs, and put climate goals out of reach." Cities including San Diego, Minneapolis, and Sacramento are working to abolish parking mandates near transit stops.[10]

Driving isn't only frustrating and spatially inefficient—it's exceedingly dangerous. About 40,000 people in the U.S. died in motor vehicle collisions in 2018, while over 4.5 million people were injured badly enough to require medical attention.[11] Globally, an estimated 1.35 million people die each year in crashes.[12] Car deaths are worst in states with high speed limits (the state with the highest relative road fatality rate, Montana, has a rural interstate speed limit of 80 miles per hour), as well as in poor states where drivers are more likely to use older vehicles without crash protection.[13] Other key factors include alcohol, seat belt laws, and distracted driving. A full 10 percent of fatal crashes in the U.S. and 15 percent of crashes causing injuries resulted from distracted driving including cell phone use, eating, talking to other passengers, and adjusting the radio.[14] As National Safety Council president Deborah A.P. Hersman noted in 2018: "The price we are paying for mobility is 40,000 lives each year."[15]

It's not just drivers who are affected: 16 percent of Americans killed in motor vehicle crashes in 2016 were pedestrians.[16] While motorist deaths have declined slightly in percentage, the number of pedestrians killed by vehicles has increased by 35 percent over the last decade.[17] Pedestrians using wheelchairs are 36 percent more likely to die in a crash than pedestrians who are not in wheelchairs.[18]

These deaths are also highly racialized. Between 2005 and 2014, Native American pedestrians were almost five times more likely to be killed than white ones, while Black pedestrians were almost twice as likely to be killed.[19] Similarly, cyclists in communities of colour are more likely to be hit by a car due to lack of safe biking infrastructure.[20] That's despite polling that suggests low-income communities of colour rely the most on biking for transportation and recreation, and have a greater desire to bike in protected lanes than white people do.[21]

Much of the danger comes down to speed and size of vehicles. Gregory Shill of the University of Iowa has observed that speeding kills about as many people as drunk driving, yet there are no national campaigns to reduce speeding.[22] There's a direct correlation between the speed of a vehicle and the chance of a pedestrian surviving a collision; in Philadelphia, there are ten times more deaths on roads with average speeds of 45 miles per hour than on roads with speed limits of 25 miles per hour.[23]

The increased sale of larger vehicles further worsens the chance of a pedestrian or cyclist surviving a crash, as the person can be pushed under the higher vehicle body. Pedestrians are two to three times more likely to die when hit by an SUV or truck than by a passenger car.[24] In response to the unveiling of Tesla's controversial Cybertruck in November 2019, the head of Australia's crash test authority said its shape and materials would likely pose increased risk to pedestrians and cyclists.[25] A cycling website dubbed it "a rolling tank against cyclists & pedestrians."[26]

THREE REVOLUTIONS: DANGER AND DENSITY

Technological Upgrades

Many advocates of next-generation automobility are genuinely concerned about the realities of congestion, sprawl, and fatalities. The Shared Mobility Principles for Livable Cities, a manifesto of sorts created by a group of transportation NGOs and signed onto by Uber and Lyft, emphasizes the need to design compact cities, limit single-passenger and oversized vehicles, and promote mobility for pedestrians and cyclists.[27] No one transportation mode would dominate: users will plan out their trip on smartphones in a single app, switching between everything from scooters to ride-hailing services to public transit to get to their destination.

Most new vehicles, including electric vehicles, feature significant upgrades in safety software due to small advances in autonomous technologies. The proliferation of partial automation crash-avoidance features—including blind spot monitoring, lane departure warning, and forward collision warning—is expected to help prevent 133,000 injury-causing crashes and 10,100 fatal crashes in the U.S. every year.[28] The issue of electric vehicles being too quiet, endangering pedestrians and especially those with limited visibility, can be fixed by requiring a sound emitter. With that said, new features like a media player, climate control, and cell phone—available by using the seventeen-inch touchscreen display in a Tesla Model S, with expandable menus that require attention be taken off the road to use them—may compromise safety improvements with novel distractions.[29] A study by the American Automobile Association found that programming navigation can distract a driver for an average of forty seconds; a driver only needs to take their eyes off the road for two seconds to double the risk of a crash.[30]

The sharing component particularly excites next-generation automobility enthusiasts on this front. Rather than having to own a personal electric vehicle, users are soon projected to be able to summon a car with their phone that will be shared with other riders and, at least in the short term, driven by the contractor who owns the vehicle. This scenario is expected to result in many current car owners selling off their vehicles, in turn freeing up space that would otherwise be consumed by congested traffic and parking. Ride-hailing executives have embraced this rhetoric as a marketing opportunity. Uber CEO Dara Khosrowshahi said the company's entire plan is "aimed at eventually replacing car ownership itself. Cars are unused 95% of the time and take up enormous amounts of space, in parking etc—we want to give that space back to the city."[31] In 2016, Zipcar announced that it had surpassed the one million membership mark and had assisted in pulling over 400,000 vehicles off the road.[32]

Lyft has followed a similar trajectory in its marketing approach, emphasizing the dent its services have made in personal car ownership. In one promotion, it offered credits to users who gave up their vehicles for a month.[33] Being able to count on reliable transportation modes that don't require a single-occupancy vehicle adding to congestion, parking, and potential collisions seems an incontestable net positive.

The hype for fully autonomous vehicles goes a step further. In the future, according to this vision, all cars will interact with each other to ensure perfectly planned movements, eliminating most safety issues and congestion as we know it as each vehicle determines the most efficient means of getting to a destination. Downtown parking spots will be rendered irrelevant, as the autonomous vehicle can move riders at pretty much all times. In turn, this radical shift will allow for the densification of urban areas. Shared ride-hailing will no longer depend on the availability of drivers, so riders can be picked up within minutes at any time of the day. They can then spend their stress-free rides reading, working, or catching up on a Netflix show.

Because such a high percentage of crashes are caused at least in part by human error, the industry claims that fatalities and injuries will drop by at least 90 percent with the proliferation of their technology.[34] The National Highway Traffic Safety Administration has calculated that the "critical reason" for 94 percent of crashes can be attributed to human error. That doesn't mean it's the only cause; vehicle-related causes, including tire and brake failures, and slick roads also play significant roles. Rather, human error is the "last failure in the causal chain of events leading up to the crash." In General Motors' 2018 report on self-driving vehicles, it told readers to "imagine a world with no car crashes."[35] Almost every negative thing we associate with automobility, we're led to believe, will be erased by a highly intelligent robot.

A Zero-Sum Game

Yet fundamentally, the crisis of urban transportation boils down to a spatial argument. It's about the efficient use of a limited amount of square footage. Regardless of what's powering the individual automobile, the vehicle itself takes up an unavoidably large amount of space. Space in a city is a zero-sum game; every square foot that's prioritized to one form undermines the possibility of another. While demand-responsive services like Uber or Lyft don't rely on street parking in the same way that a personal vehicle does, they still require cars to drive in a meandering path instead of the straight line that a fixed-route bus drives—making them a highly inefficient mode of transportation.

Private motor vehicles can only transport between 600 to 1,600 people per hour.[36] On-street bus lanes can move between 4,000 and 8,000 people. A dedicated light rail or bus rapid transit lane can serve between 10,000 and 25,000 people per hour—or a full fifteen times what motor vehicles can in the best-case scenario. Peter Norton told me: "When we're talking about cars in cities, it's very often like trying to drive a nail with a wrench. It can be done. It just makes no sense to be done that way."

This spatial sensibility is already playing out in real time.[37] An estimated 59 percent of trips taken with a ride-hailing service add additional cars to Boston's roads (the remaining percentage would have either taken a taxi or a private vehicle).[38] Traffic congestion in San Francisco increased by 62 percent between 2010 and 2016, with Uber and Lyft bearing responsibility for over half that increase; travel time would have increased by only 22 percent without ride-hailing.[39]

Driving from one part of town to another for a pickup doesn't remove the presence of a vehicle: it only substitutes it. Ride-hailing vehicles are also notorious for blocking transit lanes during pickup and drop-off; ride-hailing vehicles made up two-thirds of the violations recorded in San Francisco in three months of 2017 for driving in transit lanes.[40] Over three-quarters of violations in that same period for obstructing a bike lane or traffic lane were against ride-hailing vehicles. Not only are companies like Uber and Lyft worsening gridlock by adding more cars to the street, they're slowing down and endangering more environmentally and socially beneficial modes of transportation in the process of loading or dropping off riders.[41]

The Promise of Protection

Partial autonomous technologies in newer cars do represent advances in vehicle safety—at least in theory. But recent testing suggests that test cars equipped with automatic emergency braking and pedestrian detection alerts strike dummy pedestrians 60 percent of the time during daylight, 89 percent of the time when it's a child-sized version.[42]

And such technologies don't yet apply to ride-hailing, as many drivers are using older vehicles. Traffic fatalities in the largest 100 cities in the U.S. have not declined since the arrival of Uber and Lyft; researchers in 2016 concluded this statistic "should provoke skepticism of broad claims regarding the city-wide effects of rideshare services in reducing traffic fatalities."[43] More recent studies indicate the launching of Uber or Lyft in a city actually increased traffic deaths by between 2 and 3 percent since 2011.[44]

While ride-hailing vehicles aren't inherently more dangerous, they do add more vehicles to the road and make it easier for people to be in a car, resulting in a range of negative effects, including fatalities.[45] One in every six vehicles being used by Uber and Lyft drivers in New York City and Seattle have outstanding recalls, including for issues like faulty airbags and potential engine failure; a safety advocate recommended that before using a ride-hailing vehicle, riders use the myCARFAX phone app to look up its licence plate for open safety recalls on an online database.[46]

There are a wide array of safety concerns with autonomous vehicles, including failures of hardware and software, increased risk-taking by passengers such as not wearing seatbelts, higher risks resulting from platooning (when autonomous vehicles travel closely behind each other to minimize drag), and the overall increase in travel by vehicles—which itself increases the chance of a crash.[47] Todd Litman of the Victoria Transport Policy Institute wrote that successfully operating an autonomous vehicle on public roads will require "orders of magnitude more complex software than aircraft" with extremely high stakes in case of failure.[48]

That's further complicated by weather conditions such as heavy rain or snow that may get in the way of essential radar and lidar sensors. "Even a half-second delay in processing could result in death," Litman told me. "There's good reason to be a little bit skeptical." Think of how many times your computer or smartphone may have glitched or crashed; now imagine that technology is controlling the vehicle that you're travelling in at high speed behind a semitrailer. There's also concern among autonomous vehicle watchers that cars might be hacked and hijacked.[49]

A massive challenge facing the industry is the mixing of human drivers with computer control in the mid levels of automation. Humans have proven to be very inadequate when they are required to monitor the driving but not control it at all times. Elaine Herzberg, a forty-nine-year-old unhoused woman, was killed by a "self-driving" Uber in Arizona when its backup safety driver was distracted, watching a TV show on her phone.[50] Several drivers of Tesla cars have died in crashes while relying on the vehicle's Autopilot system.[51] Tesla CEO Elon Musk has blamed several incidents on driver complacency, rather than the technology.[52] Yet Musk's claims of the unprecedented safety benefits of Autopilot are unverified outside of Tesla itself; government regulators lack sufficient data to confirm them.[53]

Up to 11 billion miles of autonomous vehicle testing will be required before completely reliable statistics are produced about average fatality rates compared to human-driven vehicles, a process that would take some 500 years of testing—and require 100 autonomous vehicles driving 24/7 at 25 miles per hour.[54] To help put that figure in perspective, Waymo, by far the most advanced company on this front, reached only 10 million miles on public roads by October 2018 with its 600 autonomous vehicles.[55] As a result, alternative methods of testing have been recommended such as accelerated testing, virtual testing, and simulations and mathematical modelling. Even then, Rand Corporation experts have concluded: "It may not be possible to establish the safety of autonomous vehicles prior to making them available for public use."[56]

A poll of 1,000 U.S. residents in May 2018 concluded that 73 percent of drivers wouldn't feel comfortable riding in an autonomous vehicle. That was up from 63 percent in late 2017; the spike was likely caused in part by a series of high-profile fatal accidents involving Uber and Tesla autonomous vehicles.[57] Fifty-four percent of the American public prefer that autonomous vehicle testing not be conducted in their munic-ipality.[58] Autonomous vehicle testing by Waymo has also been interfered with by local residents in Arizona. The vehicles have been the recipients of dozens of attacks, including slashed tires, rock throwing, and other vehicles trying to run them off the road.[59] In late 2019, the *Washington Post* profiled Karen Brenchley, a veteran computer scientist living in Silicon Valley who is extremely concerned about autonomous vehicle testing: "The problem isn't that she doesn't understand the technology. It's that she does, and she knows how flawed nascent technol-ogy can be."[60]

Autonomous vehicle proponents have already indicated that successful deployment of the technology will require persuading pedestrians not to jaywalk and to "behave less erratically."[61] In fact, it will likely necessitate a complete over-haul of cities and towns, making them even more hostile to pedestrian and cyclist traffic.[62] Gill Pratt, head of the Toyota Research Institute, has said "the trouble with self-driving cars is people"—a suggestion consistent with the century-long his-tory of automobility in North America.[63]

Andrew Ng, an autonomous vehicle investor, also received significant criticism for his response to the "pogo stick prob-lem," in which self-driving cars are expected to be able to sense and stop for a pedestrian on a pogo stick in the middle of a highway.[64] "Rather than building AI to solve the pogo stick problem, we should partner with the government to ask people to be lawful and considerate," Ng said in 2018. "Safety isn't just about the quality of the AI technology." Renowned roboticist Rodney Brooks wrote a scathing blog post in response to Ng's comments, suggesting they "completely upended the whole rationale for self-driving cars" and the idea of government forcing change would turn pedestrians into "the potential literal roadkill in the self-satisfaction your actual customers will experience knowing that they have gotten just the latest gee whiz technology all for themselves."[65] In 2016, Mercedes-Benz's manager of driverless car safety told *Car and Driver* that in the situation of a crash between an autonomous vehicle and pedestrian, the car would be programmed to save the driver over the pedestrian every time.[66]

There are growing ethical concerns about the programming of autonomous vehicles when it comes to decision-making about who lives or dies in a potential crash. Such dilemmas have included extreme hypotheticals such as "whether to run over a group of schoolchildren or plunge off a cliff, killing [the car's] own occupants."[67] Others have suggested that racial inequity is hardwired into autonomous vehicles, as they are less likely to detect dark-skinned pedestrians.[68]

Preliminary reports from the National Transportation Safety Board indicate that the self-driving Uber vehicle that killed Herzberg detected her a full six seconds and called for an emergency brake 1.3 seconds before contact. Uber had programmed the vehicle not to stop in that situation because frequent braking could make for an "uncomfortable and jerky" ride for passengers, which may undermine ridership and profits.[69] Arizona prosecutors announced in early 2019 that they wouldn't pursue criminal charges against Uber for the killing of Herzberg, which Angie Schmitt of *Streetsblog* argued "signals that tech companies won't be punished for taking egregious risks with their untested technology even when the worst happens."[70] The safety board's report released in late 2019 found the vehicle failed to classify Herzberg as a human because "the system design did not include consideration for jaywalking pedestrians."[71]

Ashley Nunes of Massachusetts Institute of Technology has suggested that these are signs of things to come, that autonomous vehicle promises are "on life support," and that

> even if robotaxis had an unrealistically high utilization rate and even if their investors lowered their profit expectations, the cost of providing safety oversight would need to be substantially reduced (to below existing minimum-wage levels) in order for robotaxi

fares to be cost competitive with owning an older vehicle.[72]

"It's the worst-case scenario," Greg Lindsay, senior fellow of NewCities, told me. "Autonomous vehicles are going to literally run roughshod over people and there's not going to be any real oversight over it."

Worsening Sprawl

To recoup the technology's significant costs, autonomous vehicles will likely have to be on the road almost 24/7.[73] Another fear for industry watchers is "zombie vehicles," or personal autonomous cars that continue driving around instead of finding a parking spot in order to avoid parking costs. While such an approach would feasibly reduce the amount of geographic space required for parking, it could massively increase emissions and gridlock. Without a punitive tax like congestion pricing to deter the practice, autonomous vehicles are very likely to cruise at low speeds rather than park. In a best-case modelling of San Francisco, only 2,000 autonomous vehicles would slow traffic to less than two miles per hour.[74]

Daniel Aldana Cohen warns that autonomous vehicles could help draw even more residents into ever-sprawling suburbs, rather than finding ways to live in more dense environments and making those areas equitable. He says that we should be "very, very worried" about cities repeating their histories of suburbanization and segregation in new iterations of "eco-apartheid." This kind of future could be highly lucrative for autonomous vehicle companies using data collection—every minute spent in a car is sellable information—as well as to developers seeking the next round of areas to gentrify.

Other questions remain about who would pay for road maintenance and construction in the future, particularly if sprawl continues unchecked. Autonomous vehicles will depend on high-tech roads that integrate sensors and 5G broadband—but advocates rarely address how such upgrades would be paid for.[75] If realized, autonomous electric vehicles would rely on this existing infrastructure while eliminating the gas and diesel tax, a main source of roads funding.[76]

Funding for roads is already in a difficult spot, as the U.S. gas tax has stagnated since 1993, decreasing its purchasing power by 40 percent.[77] Since 2008, $140 billion has been transferred to the Highway Trust Fund from general revenues to make up for the shortfall from the gas tax, with $70 billion transferred in 2016 alone.[78] An average household in the U.S. spends $597 per year in general tax revenue to fund road construction and repair, as well as more in subsidies.[79] Almost 90 percent of local roads—meaning non-highway infrastructure—were paid for by the public, and only 11 percent specifically by motorists.[80] "In major cities, capacity remains the major issue," Yonah Freemark of the *Transport Politic* told me. "We'd have to build new highways if we wanted to rely on autonomous vehicles for all our transportation needs."

Urban sprawl and road dominance also make climate-change-exacerbated extreme weather events more difficult to cope with. Rising temperatures will put stress on infrastructure like roads—many of which are already in poor shape. Since concrete is a highly impermeable surface, heavy rainfall isn't absorbed by soil and instead overloads stormwater drainage systems and basements. In recent decades, wetlands and marshes, which offer natural water storage and filtration

> "It's scandalous that drivers are getting away with socializing the cost of their pollution. But it's even more scandalous that autonomous vehicle companies are basically skipping that entire line in their assumptions. These are smart people. I think they're perfectly aware that cars don't pay the cost of their infrastructure."
> —MATTHEW LEWIS, climate and energy policy consultant, Berkeley

services, have been filled in for agriculture and paved over to build roads and suburbs. This worsens the effects of heavy precipitation.[81]

Next-generation automobiles fail to mitigate this growing crisis of public subsidies and resulting ecological destruction. The promise of mostly shared vehicles that prioritize integration with publicly owned modes of transportation ignores decades of history demonstrating the singular focus by automotive interests on securing market share and profits. The risks that cities and towns are being forced to absorb as result of these experiments could lead to greater congestion and traffic fatalities, and encourage sprawl, exacerbating flooding.[82] Given a long history of racist discrimination and segregation, it's very likely that these impacts will disproportionately harm low-income communities of colour.

PUBLIC TRANSIT: CHALLENGES AND OPPORTUNITIES

Dedicated Space

There's a popular meme that compares transportation modes by the amount of space that they require to move sixty people. The cars stretch into the distance, taking up all lanes of traffic. The bikes line up only slightly beyond the group of people huddled together for the photo. And, quite sensibly, the same number of riders fit into less space than the bus takes up. Variations of the meme will add extra frames of electric vehicles, or Uber rides, or autonomous cars. Of course, they take up the same amount of space as regular cars.

As Jarrett Walker often points out, urban transportation is a question of geometry. We simply can't fit as many cars onto a city street as there are people. Building new roads to ease congestion only leads to induced demand—and more congestion. The solution is to use space more efficiently and in a way that prioritizes people over vehicles. For while congestion is frustrating to everyone, it's often people who can't afford to live in or near the downtown that are punished the most by poor planning that encourages dangerous and inefficient modes of transportation. Luckily, these problems can be very simple and affordable to fix.

Toronto's year-long King Street streetcar pilot project—which ran from November 2017 to December 2018—is a glowing example of what is possible. At the outset, drivers represented only 16 percent of users on the downtown corridor but were allocated 64 percent of the space. Meanwhile, pedestrians (half of the users) got only 25 percent of the space, while transit was about evenly matched at one-third of users and space.[83] The presence of private cars has historically impeded speed and reliability of the busy streetcar route; as a result, the pilot project prohibited private vehicles from using intersections that crossed the streetcar route in the downtown core, giving full priority to streetcars. On-street parking was also banned in the pilot area.

As you might expect, the results were extremely positive. Streetcar travel time improved by five minutes in each direction. The slowest travel time during the pilot was in the same range as the average travel time before it.[84] Average ridership went up by 17 percent. Driving time on adjacent streets was impacted by a mere minute. Newly opened up public space along the curb lanes hosted dozens of amenities including cafes, public art, and seating areas.

In April 2019, Toronto city council voted to make the pilot project permanent.[85] Costing only $1.5 million to implement and another $1.5 million to make permanent, this project is a textbook example of how small changes that give transit modes priority can massively improve reliability and ridership.

Dedicated bus lanes succeed based on the same merits, removing the less spatially efficient private vehicles from their path and ensuring dependable transit. New York City's 14th Street Transit & Truck Priority Pilot Project, introduced in October 2019, reserved a lengthy stretch of the major Manhattan street for buses, trucks, and emergency vehicles between the hours of 6 a.m. and 10 p.m. A report written by renowned transportation engineer Sam Schwartz found that the dedicated lane resulted in a 36 percent improvement in average weekday travel times for buses and a 24 percent increase in bus ridership.[86] Automobile travel times on most adjacent streets increased by a single minute.

This isn't to suggest that pilot projects are embraced by all constituents: many are vehemently opposed, especially by business interests who fear loss of affluent customer access by car. Several businesses on Toronto's King Street erected ice sculptures of a middle finger facing the streetcar line, with one owner alleging that his delivery business had declined by 75 percent since the pilot project began.[87]

Promotion of transit and active transportation—rather than doubling down on automobility with a new generation of technologies—guarantees safer streets as well. In 2018, 251 people were killed by transit crashes in the U.S.[88] That represents a mere 0.7 percent of people killed in transportation-related incidents.[89] A 2017 study of a decade's worth of police reports along major traffic corridors in Montreal found that private automobiles were responsible for 95 percent of pedestrian and cyclist injuries, and that a 50 percent shift from people driving to using the bus would reduce transportation-related injury rates by 35 percent.[90]

There are many reasons for the inherent safety of public transportation, ranging from the expertise of transit drivers, to frequently maintained vehicles, to physically separated tracks or lanes. Reliable service can also reduce the chances of drunk driving by providing options other than a personal vehicle; as a 2014 *CityLab* article asked: "What If the Best Way to End Drunk Driving Is to End Driving?"[91] The more infrastructure built for transit—whether it be dedicated bus and streetcar lanes, or light rail lines—the safer it becomes, as such modes aren't required to interact with automobiles. The same goes for wider sidewalks and protected cycle tracks, which allow people to get places without fear of potentially fatal interactions with cars.

Not that transit is invincible or flawless. Several Amtrak

trains have derailed in recent years, resulting in several deaths and hundreds injured.[92] A brutal crash in early 2019 by an Ottawa transit double-decker bus into a station overhang resulted in three deaths and twenty-three injuries.[93] The American Public Transit Association has identified a wide range of safety improvements that can further protect riders and other street users, including more driver training, new transit vehicles, grade separation, and new station design.[94] Increased labour power and a requirement for transit agencies and city councils to take transit operators' demands seriously would also improve safety for everyone.

Transit crashes do happen, but at a far lower rate than for automobiles. Litman wrote in his 2018 report about safety that "disproportionate media coverage can also stimulate transit fear. Because transit accidents and assaults are infrequent, they tend to receive significant media coverage."[95] A 2018 investigation found that 1,235 people have died on subway and rail tracks in Canada since 2007, a "vast majority" of them ruled as suicides.[96] But there's a simple fix to help reduce such fatalities: platform edge barriers. These sliding doors that open only once a train has stopped have reduced deaths on transit by more than half in places where they have been deployed, like Hong Kong. Toronto's transit agency has estimated that it would cost between $1 billion to $1.5 billion to install platform barriers on all seventy-five subway stations, a seemingly small price to pay for reducing deaths.[97]

Public transportation is subject to extreme weather impacts. Hurricane Sandy in 2012 flooded the New York subway system, causing billions of dollars in damage that is taking years to repair. Other cities can follow the example provided by New York City, which has spent the last several years attempting to floodproof the thousands of street-level openings to the subway with flexible stairwell covers, portable vent covers, and waterproof gates.[98] While continually sprawling cities undermine attempts at such planning, more centralized communities and transportation systems allow for more coordinated infrastructure—flood walls, elevated tracks or roadways, dikes—to ensure mobility during and after extreme weather events.

Billy Fields, a political science professor at Texas State University and an expert in adaptation urbanism, told me that massive flooding experienced in Copenhagen in 2011 and 2014 encouraged the Danish capital to rethink its design of streets and open spaces. In one area, the city tore up asphalt for parking and redesigned it to better regulate the flow of stormwater into drainage systems. Such "green-blue" infrastructure includes flowerbeds and play areas with graduated levels that store water in a flooding event.[99]

But when large cities like New York City do think about building transit, it's often in illogical and climate-change-denying ways. In 2016, Mayor Bill de Blasio proposed building a $2.5 billion streetcar route from Queens to Brooklyn that would pass through a major floodplain. An investigation by the *Village Voice* argued that the plan "isn't just a clichéd amenity for developers and a waste of the administration's political capital; it also threatens to undermine the city's efforts to plan for the devastating and imminent effects of climate change."[100]

Designing for People

Transit and active transportation aren't one-stop shops for communities. It's going to require a much broader set of changes to accomplish improved safety and climate mitigation in a way that is genuinely just and protects low-income communities from gentrification and policing. Retrofitting suburbs and commuter towns for a less car-dominated future is an underappreciated step in this process. Currently, many transit agencies don't even try to provide adequate service to the suburbs; the logic is that the automobile reigns supreme today, so it always will. But these qualities are not inherent to the geographies of suburbia or rural communities; such places can boast high-quality and dependable transit.

The decision to render low-density communities as

unserviceable is chiefly a political one, and it ignores the reality that many residents require or prefer non-automotive transportation. In other countries around the world, an explicit decision was made in the 1960s to expand transit systems to new suburbs.[101] In a similar vein, many newer communities, built around the private car, are defined by cul-de-sacs and curving roads that, compared to the grid-like planning in older cities, make it difficult to access transit as a pedestrian.

It will cost a lot to play catch-up and foster the conditions for a cultural shift toward transit, but it can be done. Paul Mees—an Australian transit expert—argued that the appeal by urbanists to density as a prerequisite for quality transit was a fundamentally anti-transit argument. As he put it in his 2010 book *Transport for Suburbia*: "The notion that urban form, rather than transport policy, determines transport outcomes is convenient for [highway planning agencies]. It can also suit those responsible for providing public transport, because it pins the blame for poor services on suburban residents rather than public transport providers."[102]

Imagining that a minimum density threshold is required to support sufficient transit usage effectively writes off a vast portion of residents in communities across the continent. It doesn't mean density and urban form don't matter—only that they're not the end of the story. Just over half of U.S. residents, 55 percent, live in a suburban county, compared to only 31 percent in an urban county and 14 percent in a rural.[103] In Canada, an estimated 67 percent of the country's metropolitan population live in "automobile suburbs," while only 14 percent are in "active cores."[104] Demographics in the suburbs have been shifting dramatically in recent years, with steady increases in rates of poverty and new immigrants.[105] Commuter towns, or "exurbs," are rapidly growing in population.[106]

Plenty of reasonable cultural, environmental, and financial critiques can be made of suburbia. This pattern of urban development is unsustainable on many fronts, and should be seriously curtailed.[107] But given the persistence of urban sprawl and the fact that poverty is now suburbanizing, it appears critical for governments to make a serious effort to provide public transit for people living there.

Mees was by no means an advocate for suburban sprawl. But for him, the fundamental challenge wasn't urban form—which he said was used as an excuse for not addressing service quality—but urban structure, requiring transit service that used buses to shuttle people to more efficient rail service.[108] He called this "the network effect," when "public transport imitates the flexibility of the car by knitting different routes and modes into a single, multi-modal network."[109] While transit agencies obsessed with ridership numbers might worry about the fiscal feasibility of such a coverage-oriented approach, Mees and others have argued that it's the key to providing enough consistent ridership for high-efficiency rail lines to also succeed.

An example of this is happening in the suburban city of Brampton, Ontario, which has made serious progress in rehabilitating the car-heavy landscape for transit options by establishing a grid-like system and two-hour transfers.[110] In 2010, the city introduced an express bus service called Züm. It includes large heated bus shelters and traffic signal priority that allows buses to jump the queue at intersections. Ridership has tripled since 2006.[111] Residents who previously drove are retiring their cars for commutes and relying instead on frequent and dependable public transit.

Meanwhile, Calgary—often thought of as hopelessly sprawled—now has the second-highest light rail ridership on the continent, spanning to many parts of the farthest communities (although recent budget cuts to bus service now compromise that system).[112] Of course, it's going to take a lot more work to turn the suburbs into sustainable human-scale communities, particularly through government commitments to fund significant public housing.[113] These are objectives to be sustained over the next several decades.

But there is plenty of potential for interim measures—and mandated automobility, which disproportionately discriminates against low-income communities, isn't inevitable. To again quote Mees: "Transport policy can be changed more quickly and cheaply, and with less disruption, than city density, so it might even be possible to make the necessary changes in time to save the planet."[114]

It's something that we should take seriously. The ultimate objective is to densify existing residential areas with public housing and nearby healthcare, education, and social services to reduce the distance people have to travel to get what they need. That will rely on the power of activists fighting for public housing, universal rent control, anti-eviction measures, and community land trusts. But politicians searching for more excuses to cut public funding to transit shouldn't be allowed to weaponize an existing lack of density as a reason not to build transit now.

Next-generation automobiles—personal electrics, ride-hailing services, autonomous technologies—will almost certainly reproduce the spatial inefficiencies and wastefulness that enabled sprawl and tens of thousands of traffic fatalities per year in the first place. The profit margins of the venture-capital-backed companies depend on such wastefulness. Resisting the widespread proliferation of such modes and fighting for better access to transit will put us in a far better position to build denser communities rooted in public housing, climate mitigation, and community services.

Chapter 6

Locked down

Reimagining access for
marginalized people

*We need to reclaim power over buses, trains, and sidewalks to
create communities that genuinely serve everyone, not just
young, able-bodied cis men.*

INTERSECTING IDENTITIES

In the urbanist discourse of walkability and transit-oriented
development, the reality is often neglected that many residents experience transportation in profoundly different ways
than anticipated by city planners and politicians. That's especially the case for people with disabilities—which include
physical (or ambulatory), visual, hearing, and intellectual disabilities—seniors, and people who are subjected to increased
surveillance and harassment in public spaces due to gender
and sexual identity.

These identities of age, disability, and gender and sexual
identity frequently intersect. About 10.5 percent of Americans
between the ages of 18 and 64 have a disability of some kind,
as do more than 35 percent of people age 65 and older.[1] Black,
Native American, and Hispanic people are considerably more

likely than white people to have a disability.[2] People with disabilities are far more likely to be unemployed, earn lower wages, and live in poverty than those without a disability. They are also far more likely to be assaulted.[3]

As well, almost half of trans people have reported being verbally harassed in the previous year because of their gender identity; another 9 percent have been physically assaulted.[4] Almost two-thirds of trans and non-binary people who have disabilities have been sexually assaulted in their lifetime.[5] Traumas and oppressions can take on less visible forms as well, such as being misgendered and denied access to washroom facilities based on perceived gender presentation.

Everyone desires transportation that guarantees safety and comfort, especially if they have previously survived traumatic attacks or situations. That includes basic and predictable levels of dignity and respect expressed by transportation workers and fellow riders to people of all ages, abilities, and gender and sexual identities. Next-generation automobility claims to meet these needs.

THREE REVOLUTIONS: THE PROMISE OF ACCESS

A Ride-Hailing Niche

Uber's website boasts that the company has "transformed mobility for many people with disabilities, and [is] committed to continuing to develop solutions that support everyone's ability to easily move around their communities." Such solutions include the ability to request a ride using a smartphone's accessibility features, a contractual obligation to allow service dogs on rides, and the ability to request accessible UberWAV service in several cities.[6]

In 2016, Uber launched Uber Central, a means for businesses and non-profits to book and pay for rides on behalf of clients. It marketed the service as a means for seniors without a smartphone to use Uber to get to medical appointments and grocery trips.[7] Uber Health, introduced in early 2018, followed a similar model; it allows healthcare providers to order rides for patients who have limited access to transportation.[8]

At the end of that year, Uber launched a partnership with MV Transportation, which specializes in transportation for seniors and people with disabilities. At the time, Uber CEO Dara Khosrowshahi wrote: "Thanks to our work with MV Transportation and other providers, Uber riders in wheelchairs can now get picked up by a WAV in 15 minutes or less on average for trips in New York City, Boston, Philadelphia, Washington DC, Chicago, and Toronto."[9]

A 2018 research collaboration between Lyft and the University of Southern California Center for Body Computing awarded free Lyft rides to 150 people in the greater Los Angeles area who were over the age of sixty and living with chronic conditions.[10] It found, over the course of three months, that the amount of activity the seniors participated in increased by 35 percent, with a 74 percent increase in social visits and a 68 percent increase in ease of access to medical appointments.

A specialized ride-hailing app, GoGoGrandparent, has emerged to cater to seniors who don't own smartphones by offering a hotline to call to book an Uber ride.[11] Other apps specifically for female drivers and riders have launched across North America, attempts to increase the sense of safety that people feel when relying on strangers for transportation.[12] Meanwhile, major ride-hailing companies have taken steps to provide information to reduce the risk of danger. Uber, for example, advises riders to sit in the back seat of the vehicle, which "gives you and your driver some personal space," and to share your trip details such as driver's name and licence plate with loved ones via the app's "share trip status" option.[13]

Autonomous vehicles are heralded as improving accessibility still more. In 2016, Steve Mahan, a legally blind man, rode around Austin in an autonomous Waymo vehicle. He told the *Washington Post*: "This is a hope of independence. These cars will change the life prospects of people such as myself. I want very much to become a member of the driving public again."[14]

The head of the American Network of Community Options and Resources (ANCOR), which represents more than 1,600 private service providers to people with disabilities, penned a 2018 op-ed explaining the organization's committed support to the AV START Act—the federal legislation that would regulate autonomous vehicles. That support was explicitly based on the potential the technology has to improve access for people with disabilities, including those with intellectual and developmental disabilities, to employment opportunities.[15]

Such technologies could allow people with disabilities to set their own schedules without having to rely on other people. Waymo is reportedly working on a technology that would emit an audible signal when it arrives for a pickup if the rider is blind, while hearing-impaired riders will be able to see the route on a computer screen.[16] Seniors who can no longer drive, or prefer not to, will be able to determine where and when they travel unaccompanied.

There's a possibility of greater safety for passengers, as well. Some have speculated that autonomous vehicles could include "safe exit strategies" in the case of an uncomfortable or dangerous situation with other riders, such as being dropped off near one's destination instead of in front of one's home or using a safe word that would reroute the vehicle to the nearest police station.[17] Other suggestions include being able to route a trip through a populated area at night, and to stop for longer while a person with restricted mobility is exiting the vehicle to notify a contact at the destination for assistance.

The Harsh Reality

All of this sounds utopian compared to the heavy restrictions that people with marginalized access to transportation have to deal with today. But a long string of situations with Uber and Lyft, along with the whole history of private automobility, suggest that it's unlikely things will pan out in this way.

One indicator of this trend is the committed struggle by Uber and Lyft to continue to be legally categorized as technology companies that match drivers to riders, rather than as transportation companies. As a result of this categorization—which is why Uber is legally called Uber Technologies Inc.—the companies argue that they aren't subject to the Americans with Disabilities Act (ADA), which prohibits discrimination against people with disabilities in employment, transportation, and federal agencies. In 2015, Uber faced ADA-related lawsuits in California, Texas, and Arizona alleging discrimination against wheelchair users and blind riders. The company's response appealed to its inability to control what its independent contractors do.[18]

Lawsuits have been filed against Uber and Lyft in New York and California for failing to provide enough wheelchair-accessible vehicles.[19] A report by the New York Lawyers for the Public Interest found that Uber and Lyft consistently located non-accessible vehicles on request but met requests for a wheelchair-accessible vehicle only 30 percent of the time.[20] Wait times were also greatly different: four minutes for a non-accessible vehicle compared to seventeen minutes for a wheelchair-accessible vehicle.

In 2018, Uber, Lyft, and Via collectively sued New York's Taxi and Limousine Commission over its new rule that by 2023 every company has to dispatch 25 percent of trips in wheelchair-accessible vehicles.[21] The companies claimed that the percentage was arbitrary and that it could cost around one billion dollars to comply.[22] In a statement, Dustin Jones of United for Equal Access New York said: "This lawsuit proves once and for all that Uber, Lyft and other ridesharing companies just don't give a damn about providing equal access to New York's wheelchair users."[23]

Shortly before Lyft's initial public offering, the Disability Rights Advocates filed a lawsuit against the company in a California court, arguing that "Lyft's practice of excluding persons with mobility disabilities who need WAVs violates the Americans with Disabilities Act."[24] As a result of these consecutive incidents, Uber's partnership in late 2018 with MV

Transportation was regarded with serious skepticism. Joseph Rappaport of the Brooklyn Center for Independence of the Disabled said: "They've lobbied against proposals, they've sued, and they've spent millions of dollars to prevent a requirement that they provide accessible service.... The only reason that they're even doing this is because they face legal action."[25]

Ahmed El-Geneidy, professor of urban planning at McGill University, told me that many ride-hailing drivers aren't properly trained to deal with people with disabilities in a safe and respectful way, including safety precautions and etiquette.[26] Meanwhile, the seniors-focused app GoGoGrandparent has faced criticism over lack of additional compensation for drivers, lack of liability coverage, and expensive rates. One Uber driver suggested: "The whole thing screams of scam. On top of everything else, they seem to be targeting the people who are most vulnerable."[27]

There's also no guarantee that helpful private services will last. In December 2019, Ford announced it was ending GoRide Health, its non-emergency medical transportation service providing on-demand wheelchair service—leaving people dependent on such a service without an alternative.[28] This news came less than a year after Ford shut down its "micro-transit" service, Chariot.[29]

This precedent renders dubious the prospect of autonomous vehicles radically improving the mobility of people with disabilities. As Alex Birnel of MOVE Texas told me: "I just don't see a disproportionately poor demographic like the disabled, who are the number one in need of options, being the first to benefit from any new innovation." Alexander Stimpson, a senior researcher at Duke University, said that autonomous vehicle companies are aware that people with disabilities are a market, but it's not their priority: "The focus is how can we get these driving on the roads."[30] Similarly, University of Alberta design anthropologist Megan Strickfaden concluded that "the cars are being designed for drivers with normal competency levels, rather than a passenger perspective. The population they should be designing for is excluded."[31]

Further complications include the uncertainty whether a quadriplegic rider could enter and exit an autonomous vehicle without assistance, or that the vehicle wouldn't drop a wheelchair user off in front of a pile of snow in the winter.[32] Hana Creger of the Greenlining Institute told me: "Based on what we know about the lack of access that these shared mobility companies have for folks with limited mobility, that's a strong indication of how autonomous vehicle technology will roll out as well, especially if it's left to its own devices in the private sector."

There is ample evidence, both historical and contemporary, that people with disabilities and mobility restrictions simply aren't a priority for profit-hungry companies that routinely dodge regulatory requirements. Even if these companies came into compliance with existing accessibility laws, it remains unclear how the disproportionately poor demographic of people with disabilities would be able to regularly afford such services.

Plenty of lobbying and advocacy work is being done by disability organizations to change this reality. But it's an uphill battle. Outside of occasional PR-oriented pilot projects, ride-hailing companies don't seem willing to concede ground. Providing service to people with disabilities and seniors, who may require more driver training and time spent in pickup and drop-off, will likely continue to be low on these companies' to-do lists.

What about Safety?

Ride-hailing options also don't offer inherently safer rides for women (cis and trans), trans (of all genders), and gender non-conforming people (including non-binary, genderqueer, and Two-Spirit people). In early 2018, it was reported that at least 103 Uber drivers and another 18 Lyft drivers in the U.S. had been accused of sexually assaulting or abusing their passengers in the previous four years; at least 31 of the Uber drivers were convicted for crimes including forcible touching, false imprisonment, and rape.[33] At the end of 2019, Uber announced that it had received more than 3,000 reports of sexual assault in the U.S. the year prior.[34] Several states, including California, Colorado, Massachusetts, and Texas, have launched investigations into the ride-hailing services about alleged failure to properly screen drivers.[35] Two women who were assaulted by Uber drivers filed a class-action lawsuit in late 2017 that claimed "thousands of female passengers have endured unlawful conduct by their Uber drivers including rape, sexual assault, physical violence and gender-motivated harassment."[36] A 2019 lawsuit was filed by fourteen survivors of assault, including one blind woman, against Lyft for mishandling its "sexual predator crisis."[37]

In 2018, Uber was accused of attempting to force sexual assault survivors to settle cases through arbitration with confidentiality agreements, which would avoid a public trial.[38] Uber later announced that it was withdrawing the requirements of mandatory arbitration and confidentiality, and was installing a panic button in the app for riders to notify 911.[39] Yet a 2019 investigation by the *Washington Post* reported that Uber's so-called Special Investigations Unit, tasked with dealing with serious incidents, exists to protect the company from legal liability; investigators in the unit aren't allowed to direct complaints to the police or advise the customer to seek legal counsel.[40]

"We know that people are being assaulted and sexually harassed in those [ride-hailing] spaces as well," says Nicole Kalms, the director of the XYX Lab at Monash University in Melbourne, Australia. "I don't think they're necessarily safer. They don't have the same publicness and capacity to hold the ideology of right to public transport space and access in the same way."

An online survey conducted on behalf of the U.S. National Council for Home Safety and Security found that 23 percent of female respondents had reported an uncomfortable encounter to Uber; 8 percent stated they had involved the police over a driver's behaviour.[41] Women, trans, and gender non-conforming riders have developed techniques to avoid assault or harassment while using ride-hailing services. For example, they will share the GPS location of their phone with a few friends, and make sure that the driver matches the licence plate number and model of the vehicle listed in the app.[42]

A viral Twitter thread by writer Jill Gutowitz explained the constant need to lie about where exactly she's going in a ride-hailing vehicle when asked, protecting herself by telling drivers that she's going to a fictitious boyfriend's house. "Any time I Uber/Lyft home at night and it's a male driver, I risk being assaulted, or worse," she wrote. "Don't ever forget that women, especially WOC [women of colour] and queer women, have targets on our backs."[43]

Amelia Tait wrote in the *New Statesman* about being driven in an Uber all over London, completely off the predetermined route that Uber had instructed. In addition to costing her four times as much as it should have, the trip caused her to fear that she was going to be assaulted. "This wasn't the first time that it struck me how strange it is that Uber users entrust untrained strangers to drive us around simply because they operate via a sleek, shiny app," she reported.[44]

Writer and designer Robyn Kanner, a trans woman, wrote for *Mic* about the anxieties from being frequently misgendered by Uber drivers: "Here's what's going through my head: Are they stronger than me? If I call them out on gendering me properly, will they hurt me?"[45]

It's far too early to tell what safety technologies will be integrated into autonomous vehicles. Very little information has been made public about how safety would be guaranteed for riders. But the potential for women, trans, and gender non-conforming riders to be assaulted or harassed with no ability to easily escape on a trip seems of profound concern. That's especially the case for people with disabilities and seniors, who may be less able to respond to immediate threats in confined spaces.

The proposal of dropping a rider at a location near, but not at, someone's house appears rather short-sighted; a predatory rider could feasibly also get out of the vehicle and follow them. Unlike the relative anonymity that riding a bus or train can bring, a small pooled vehicle may make one's personal travel pattern overly visible to other riders.[46] Similarly, the idea of being able to redirect the vehicle to the nearest police station may be severely limited by the fact that it could take a long time to arrive, and that many people may have serious concerns about interacting with the police in any capacity. An ability to share one's location and vehicle information could potentially help respond to crises—but it's dubious that it would be particularly effective on a high-speed highway or deep in suburban sprawl.

Such concerns may motivate those who can afford it to buy their own autonomous vehicles or book the entire vehicle for themselves, which would undermine the anticipated environmental and congestion benefits of shared rides. Kalms told me that she fundamentally disagrees with the solution of female-only ride-hailing services or transit, like segregated train carriages in Japan and India, "pink taxis" in Mexico, or women-only ride-hailing services DriveHer and She Rides. Such options make women, trans, and gender non-conforming riders assume responsibility for their own safety, she says, and exclude many non-binary and trans people who don't want to declare a gender identity in public or may not pass as a cis woman.

People with marginalized access to transportation—whether due to disability, age, gender and sexual identity, or some combination of these factors—have the right to navigate a city in a safe and comfortable manner. While ride-hailing services and autonomous vehicles promise to revolutionize mobility for such riders, years of disturbing precedents from companies like Uber and Lyft along with the lack of priority by autonomous vehicle companies in challenging them indicate that the automobility of the future will simply be more of the same. People with disabilities will be largely ignored, seniors stranded or heavily reliant on others, and women, trans, and gender non-conforming riders subject to constant anxiety over harassment and assault.

Banking on autonomous vehicles as the solution to accessibility will leave many people waiting for years or decades more before they can use transportation in a safe and dependable way. That is extremely callous and unjust—especially since we have the opportunity to greatly improve systems of public transportation, fighting to guarantee access for all.

PUBLIC TRANSIT: CHALLENGES AND OPPORTUNITIES

Off the Map

It's partly because of the profound lack of transportation service for marginalized people that Uber and Lyft—and the prospect of autonomous vehicles—have acquired such momentum. Many communities have been routinely ignored, underserved, and insulted by transit agencies. Regardless of how improved safety and comfort really are, the idea remains that catching a private taxi with an app is less threatening than navigating a ride on a bus or train, for those who can afford it. In many instances, these criticisms aren't wrong.

Many transit stops are literally off the map for people with disabilities.[47] Of the 15 million people in the U.S. who have difficulty attaining transportation services, 40 percent have disabilities. Barriers include broken lifts and ramps, failing to stop for a rider with a disability, not providing adequate space, and lacking accessible alternatives to board if level-entry boarding isn't available. The top four barriers to transit listed in a survey of over 4,000 people with disabilities were inadequate transit service, drivers not calling out stops, inappropriate driver attitude, and lack of an accessible route to the stop or station.[48]

Here's how a 2019 report by Chicago's Metropolitan

Planning Council put it: "In many cases, bus stops and train stations can be impossible to reach, due to the lack of sidewalks and elevators. Paratransit options are limited and fractured with a multitude of funding sources, disconnected political jurisdictions, and providers with competing priorities."[49]

In New York City, only 92 of the subway system's 425 stations are accessible, and an average of 25 elevators a day are not working.[50] There's little information for riders when shutdowns happen, with no intercom announcements or reliable website updates.[51] The *New York Times* has described subway elevators as "often tiny, foul-smelling and hard to find, positioned at the far ends of stations, forcing long wheelchair rides along narrow platforms."[52]

Accessibility differs greatly by transit agency. All subway stations in Los Angeles, San Francisco, and Washington, DC, are wheelchair accessible, but only 68 percent of stations in Philadelphia and 67 percent of stations in Chicago.[53] In Toronto, 43 of 75 stations have elevators.[54] Steven Laperrière, vice-president of the Montreal-based disability rights group RAPLIQ (Regroupement des activistes pour l'inclusion au Québec), told me about the local situation: "One time out of two, if you want to take the regular street bus, well, you won't be able to. When it's summertime it's one thing. But when it's cold outside, or when you're expected at a medical appointment or job interview or just for your job, it's impossible to count on your being 100 percent sure that you'll be on time."

That obviously has direct impacts on the ability of people with disabilities to access employment, education, recreational opportunities, and engagement in public life. People with disabilities in Montreal have access to under half the jobs that non-disabled people have, due to inaccessible transit.[55] Accessibility is also impeded by factors including inadequate snow clearing, inaccessible public washrooms (if they exist at all), and lack of power wheelchair charging stations.[56]

New dockless electric scooters, rented by companies like Lime and Bird, aren't required to be returned to specific places.

Many are left strewn on sidewalks, which makes it very challenging for people with physical disabilities to navigate safely. In early 2019, a lawsuit was filed against several scooter companies operating in San Diego; the complaint read: "People with disabilities who wish to travel in the City using the City's walkways are being forced to either put their physical safety at risk or just stay home. This is not a choice that they should have to make."[57]

Most transit stations and buses don't include both visual and audible communication of schedule changes and stops, making it challenging for people with visual or hearing issues to use transit without a companion.[58]

Paratransit, which specifically services people with disabilities as a substitute for inadequate transit service, tends to be unreliable and restrictive.[59] Toronto's Wheel-Trans service has failed to strap riders in properly and frequently leaves riders waiting for up to an hour.[60] Polling of 1,500 paratransit users in the U.S. found that over half experienced scheduling problems and long wait times; one-third identified inefficient rides, inadequate service times, and inappropriate driver attitudes as additional problems.[61] El-Geneidy told me that an overreliance by a city on paratransit can have the added impact of segregating people with disabilities from the broader community.

Seniors, too, tend to have a tougher time accessing transit. Many bus stops fail to provide benches, let alone shelter,

"[With paratransit,] you're isolating the person with the disability. You're telling them 'you're on your own' and 'you're not part of the community.' Psychologically, it's not the best. The best and the cheapest is to use the good transit service that everybody else is using. It's the responsibility of the society to give them the freedom of transit."

—AHMED EL-GENEIDY, McGill University

making transit difficult and potentially dangerous for seniors to depend on. Marta Viciedo of Miami's Urban Impact Lab told me: "We're a very rainy place, particularly in the summer. It's very hot. So it's bizarre not to have any kind of protection, especially when most of our bus routes run at maybe thirty- to forty-five-minute intervals. You can conceivably be sitting in the sun for twenty or thirty minutes." The lack of easily accessible public washrooms can also limit seniors' ability to take trips.[62] And when older people can't walk to transit stops due to sprawl, parking, and other impediments, it can lead to debilitating isolation and depression.[63] Such issues aren't going away: most countries worldwide are experiencing an aging population.

Gender and Sexual Identity

Many women, trans, and gender non-conforming people also experience public transportation in significantly limited ways. Hollaback Vancouver, a local iteration of the global movement to challenge harassment in public spaces, reports that 58 percent of women surveyed said they don't feel comfortable on transit.[64] Kalms told me that recent mapping of safe and unsafe spaces in cities by young women, trans, and non-binary participants in Australia, Uganda, Peru, Spain, and India indicates that around 10 percent of all sexual harassment and assault occurs in public transportation spaces. She says that many women will have a traumatic experience in such a space and never return or use the system again.[65]

Kalms adds that transit agencies tend to implement measures that require women, trans, and gender non-conforming people to monitor their behaviour at all times, including not travelling alone and having to stand in certain well-lit areas in view of CCTV cameras and ride in certain train cars.

Such situations can become even more likely in congested transit or at stations with poor lighting, making it very difficult to get away if being harassed. "On the other end of it, it's very easy for perpetrators to be very anonymous on public transport spaces because they are so busy and very transitory," Kalms says.

Amy Lubitow, co-author of the 2016 journal article "Transmobilities," which featured interviews with twenty-five trans and gender non-conforming people, told me that interview subjects reported a sense of constant vigilance in public transit spaces, with a feeling that they couldn't easily get out of an uncomfortable situation.[66] She says that gender non-conforming riders she spoke with often restricted their movements to certain parts of the city and wouldn't take some trips during the evening.

These factors undermine the ability for a vast percentage of a city's population to get around efficiently and safely. But contrary to the messaging of ride-hailing and autonomous vehicle companies, the answer shouldn't be to further privatize transportation by getting everyone into ostensibly safer cars—that will only exacerbate environmental impacts, economic and racial inequality, and congestion. Rather, we should fight to pressure transit agencies to improve their service to people with disabilities, seniors, and women, trans, and gender non-conforming people, ensuring that everyone can be guaranteed public transportation where riders feel respected and included. As Angela Marie MacDougall, executive director of Vancouver's Battered Women's Support Services, put it:

> We don't believe that harassment is an unavoidable part of a woman's daily commute. We believe that women must be able to move about and occupy the public space without being placed in danger or threatened. It's a fundamental freedom. Safe public transit for women and girls is about recognizing our experiences and needs. We all have the right to feel safe in our cities. Let's make this a priority.[67]

Silicon Valley's investors would prefer us to throw our hands up at the dismal state of public transportation and opt instead for their ritzy but ultimately no better, unaccountable products. We need to reclaim power over buses, trains, and sidewalks to create communities that genuinely serve everyone, not just young, able-bodied cis men.

There are plenty of examples of this power being exercised. The legendary disability organization ADAPT, now known as American Disabled for Attendant Programs Today, formed in the late 1970s amid a fierce struggle to ensure that wheelchair lifts were added to buses in Denver. The group used a range of direct-action techniques to see their demands were met, including the famous "Gang of 19" rolling into traffic to block a bus and the destruction of sidewalks with sledgehammers to protest the government's failure to ensure accessibility.[68] ADAPT has repeatedly intervened with militant protests in the years since. Its members have been arrested countless times while calling for defence of Medicaid and the Disability Integration Act.[69]

Lawsuits are another tool to force transit agencies to pay sizable fines and improve accessibility. Boston only has fifty-three subway stations, but it is more than 90 percent wheelchair accessible due to a group of wheelchair users suing the transit authority in 2002 and gaining guarantees for the construction, maintenance, and monitoring of elevators.[70] Seattle is in the process of installing 22,500 curb ramps over the next eighteen years at an estimated total cost of $300 million in response to a class-action lawsuit filed by three people with disabilities.[71] A series of lawsuits have been filed against New York's Metropolitan Transit Authority for allegedly ignoring the ADA, including failure to install an elevator during renovations of a Bronx subway station.[72] Similar class-action lawsuits were filed in Montreal and San Francisco in 2017.[73]

In April 2018, a ritzy public discussion with the chairperson of the MTA held at the Museum of the City of New York was protested over lack of public transit accessibility, which led to the event being cancelled. An activist with The People's MTA, the group that shut down the event, explained that "the everyday frustrations experienced by riders, which are so much worse for people who use wheelchairs, exploded ... because people didn't want to allow the MTA to pull off a public relations stunt."[74] Advocacy by the Canadian Federation for the Blind in 2014 led BC Transit to implement an automated system to announce bus stops and require drivers to call them out if that technology isn't available.[75]

Chicago's Metropolitan Planning Council identified thirty-two recommendations to improve transit accessibility, including the integration of real-time accessibility information into trip planning tools, increasing audible cues at busy intersections, and building shelters with seating and restrooms.[76]

Struggles for accessibility are neither easy nor guaranteed to succeed. They are often multi-year fights, against obstinate bureaucrats and city councillors more concerned with keeping property taxes down than ensuring that residents with disabilities can genuinely access transportation. But these struggles can be won. Public agencies are often far more susceptible to legal and public pressure than venture-capital-backed private corporations are.

A 2019 paper presented at the national Transportation Research Board Meeting reported that women used Los Angeles's new Expo light rail line about half as much as men; 20 percent of women surveyed avoided it for fear of harassment.[77] Interviewees had suggestions to improve conditions: more lighting at stations, staff available to respond to situations, locating stops in busy areas where other people might be. These are not unreasonable or costly requests. They only require that a transit agency take them seriously—and they reinforce the importance of improving transit service to reduce overcrowding and lengthy waits. Importantly, they must also be implemented in a way that recognizes that feeling uncomfortable does not necessarily mean being unsafe; unconscious racist biases often contribute to discriminatory policing of Black and Indigenous people.

Similarly, Jana Korn identified three related solutions in a 2018 article for *Next City*: "investing in transport infrastructure, easing the process of filing a complaint, and raising public awareness." With more predictable and efficient transit, riders have less chance of being the victim of a crime, she wrote, while simpler reporting processes for survivors and witnesses, such as an anonymous texting or app service, can facilitate faster responses and prevention mechanisms. Hollaback Ottawa successfully pressured the city's transit agency into launching an anonymous online reporting system.[78] Kalms notes that there's a "huge case for not having such congested public transport in general because it has huge safety issues." That means allocating the funding to run more buses and trains.

Marketing campaigns proclaiming zero tolerance for harassment and assault can help, as can posters and commercials that encourage bystander intervention. Korn reports that an awareness campaign by Washington, DC's transit agency—fought for and won by Collective Action for Safe Spaces—doubled rates of reporting by people who had been harassed. Battered Women's Support Services in Vancouver created a brochure that lists ways that bystanders can intervene if someone is being harassed on transit, ranging from asking if the person is being bothered to offering to get off at the next stop with them, telling a transit worker, or dropping your bags to create a commotion.[79]

Lubitow and her "Transmobilities" co-authors recommended gender-sensitivity training for all transit employees, informing them of the threats of harassment and assault that trans and gender non-conforming people face. Interviewees in their study suggested installing signage to inform riders that everyone should be able to ride free of harassment regardless of gender presentation, and including gender identity as a protected class of riders. Lubitow told me that changes as simple as transit drivers not gendering people when they get on the bus by saying "sir" or "madam" can make a huge difference. Better lighting at stations and stops can also improve the sense of safety. However, the interviewees often specified that increasing police or security presence wouldn't help them feel safer, given the long history of police violence and incarceration of gender non-conforming people. One participant said: "My worst experiences ... have been TriMet police. I do not feel safe with any police officers, ever. I don't trust the police, just based on my personal history with them, but also being Black and trans and queer and disabled."

Governments also need to recognize the overwhelmingly gendered unpaid labour of childcare, grocery shopping, and running kids to and from school. Many women "trip-chain," making multiple and sometimes lengthy stops that can become very expensive if fares only allow for one-way travel.[80] A shift toward time-based transfers—or free fares—reduces the financial burden placed on riders in those situations. As urban planning professor Anna Kramer has argued, "good public transit is a feminist issue." In Toronto, 58 percent of transit riders are women, especially women of colour and recent immigrants.[81] Kramer wrote:

> What transit improvements would benefit women? Better service across the network: reliability, capacity, frequency, speed, coverage. Lower and more integrated fares. Safety and wayfinding. Better accessibility for those with strollers and large packages. Unsurprisingly, and happily, the same kinds of improvements that would benefit all kinds of riders, not just women, and help shift mode.[82]

There's a vast overrepresentation of able-bodied men in the transportation workforce; women make up only 15 percent of the industry in the U.S.[83] In Vancouver, 20 percent of TransLink's staff are women, while in Toronto a mere 15 percent of transit employees are women.[84] Transit boards are also disproportionately male.[85] But that can change under democratic and accountable processes that a publicly owned agency will respond to. Seniors, people with disabilities, and women, trans, and gender non-conforming people should be at the forefront of decision-making to improve transit service.

Transit agencies are underfunded and constantly subject to further austerity, making them less inclined to take on "extra" projects that don't produce immediate returns in the form of increases to ridership or funding. Private companies, though, are beholden only to their owners and shareholders and insist on ,downloading access issues onto their independent contractors. For public transit agencies and the communities they serve, we have the ability to force change. Decades of successful, though difficult, struggle have proven that such victories can improve conditions for people with disabilities, seniors, and women, trans, and gender non-conforming people. Faced with the prospect of a ride-hailing and autonomous vehicle sector that wishes to destroy what remains of public transit and further undermine access and safety, we must commit our collective power to making the drastic improvements to transit that are so desperately required.

Chapter 7

Data minecraft

Surveillance and policing

"Rider solidarity means we look out for each other and keep each other safe. Our vision is a ride without fares and a world with no police." (Unfare NYC)

THE DIGITAL AGE

A decade or two ago, it would have been unimaginable that so many of us would carry a small device in our pockets that can connect to the internet, take high-quality photos, and play videos and music. About 1.5 billion smartphones are now sold every year.[1] They're revolutionized every part of society—including transportation; services like Google Maps have enhanced our ability to find where we need to go via any mode of transportation.

Next-generation automotive companies have built on these technologies, not only with apps to summon rides but with integrated on-board computers. In a Tesla, you can now play video games or trigger fart sounds on command.[2] Transit agencies haven't managed to match these kinds of innovations. Compared to Elon Musk's schoolboy humour, most buses and trains remain relatively boring.

The sleekness and sheer aesthetics of such next-generation

automotive technologies can't be underestimated. But neither can the role these vehicles are already playing in greatly expanding the amount of data and surveillance available to corporations and policing bodies. A 2019 investigation by *Axios* reported that all vehicles built by Elon Musk's Tesla are generating an enormous amount of information including a driver's speed, charging locations, and video clips from the car's external cameras to capture footage of lane lines, street signs, and pedestrians.[3] The article noted: "It's not always clear who owns the data captured by vehicles and their networks, an issue that will only get fuzzier once shared, autonomous vehicles are here."

Police departments are predictably eyeing such vehicles as tools to aid their surveillance of communities, with legal experts suggesting that police may not require a warrant to collect data from them.[4] These technological marvels come with serious threats to our personal privacy.

THREE REVOLUTIONS: IMPACT ON PRIVACY

The New Oil

In early 2019, Kia unveiled its Real-time Emotion Adaptive Driving system, which will cater the lighting and music in an autonomous vehicle to the perceived mood of the rider, determined using "bio-signal recognition technology."[5] Meanwhile, Audi showed off its Immersive In-Car Entertainment, which turns the interior of a parked vehicle into a private movie theatre of sorts.[6] A recent feature in *Automobile* magazine boasted of a future of "energized glass coupled with augmented reality" that will display things like "information on history and culture" of an area and virtual reality depictions of various sites.[7] Such innovations are what consulting firm KPMG once described as the fostering of a "Sexy Dynamic Experience," with products constantly evolving and catering to the flexible desires of consumers and their environments.[8]

Car-generated data might become a $450 billion to $750

billion market by 2030.[9] Insurance companies are also rolling out tracking programs using an on-board diagnostic port or smartphone app to help calculate assessments for auto insurance.[10] These data-collecting ambitions also slot perfectly into, and are in many ways contingent upon, the development of so-called smart cities. Google's Sidewalk Toronto project is a prime example of this thinking. Proposed for a twelve-acre neighbourhood called Quayside on Toronto's eastern waterfront, the area is advertised as a high-tech hub combining autonomous vehicles, sensors and robotic delivery, and waste management systems.[11]

In 2016, Intel CEO Brian Krzanich stated that "data is the new oil," specifically pointing to the autonomous vehicle as a data collector. The average person, he said, "generates" a mere 650 megabytes of data a day using computers and smartphones; by 2020 the figure will increase by 1.5 gigabytes per day.[12] But an autonomous vehicle—with chips and hardware created through partnerships with Intel, of course—will collect data through cameras, radar, sonar, GPS, and lidar, generating an incredible 4,000 gigabytes of data per day. That includes technical data such as sensing pedestrian movement, "crowd-sourced" data such as how a vehicle gets from one place to another in the most efficient way, and personal data, which Krzanich described as follows:

> Data that tracks how many people are in the car, music preferences of each passenger, or even what stores or brands passengers prefer and, when you are near them, tees up sale items. Wearables and other sensors inside the car can also monitor behavior, focus, emotional and biometric status to increase safety and security. Whoever has the most personal data will be able to develop and deliver the best user experience.[13]

Private automobiles already collect enormous amounts of data about their drivers and passengers. As a *New York Times* feature explained, "cars have become rolling listening posts."[14] Newer vehicles can siphon information about everything from phone calls to music choices to diagnostic information about problems with a vehicle.[15] These are called connected cars, in contrast to older vehicles that are not connected to the internet. By 2020, one in five vehicles on the road worldwide, or 250 million vehicles, are expected to have some kind of internet connection.[16]

It's a situation that author Peter Norton is extremely concerned about—he goes so far as to call it a "nightmare scenario." The current trajectory, according to Norton, "exactly parallels" conversations in the petroleum industry of the early to mid twentieth century, in which people who were not dependent on cars were effectively forced into them in order to generate revenue. "You and me in an AV are the oil well," Norton says. "They are going to pump us for data. And they're going to sell it."

Autonomous vehicles will likely becomes a significant site of commerce, in which riders can buy all sorts of goods and services online while in transit.[17] Such opportunities will in turn encourage automotive companies to increase reliance on their technology and invasive surveillance; the more time a rider spends in a vehicle, the more personal data can be collected.

Police departments will also benefit from the transition. After all, the rise of police departments in North America occurred in conjunction with the proliferation of the mass automobile; warrants are not being required for cars despite the Fourth Amendment protections against unreasonable search and seizure.[18] There's little reason to believe that will change with the advent of a new generation of automobility; if anything, it will only strengthen police powers.

A History of Intrusion

In 2014, it was reported that in-vehicle communication systems Ford SYNC and General Motors' OnStar collected location data and call data, and shared them with business partners.[19]

Earlier that year, Ford's global vice-president of marketing and sales said during a panel discussion: "We know everyone who breaks the law, we know when you're doing it. We have GPS in your car, so we know what you're doing."[20] He later had to walk back those comments, saying, "We do not track our customers in their cars without their approval or consent."

That same year, Uber came under heavy fire for a series of infractions. Among them, the company's senior vice-president had recommended the doxing of critical journalists, collection of private location data, and unauthorized tracking of users. Uber retained possession of users' data even after the Uber app was deleted; a written request was required for complete deletion.[21]

The company was also busted for its use of the so-called God View, a software that allowed real-time tracking of passengers including celebrities, politicians, ex-partners, and journalists—and was sometimes unveiled as an entertainment of sorts at corporate parties.[22] In 2017, as a result of the scandal, the company agreed to comply with twenty years of third-party audits.[23]

In late 2017, Uber announced that it was finally winding down a series of invasive programs, including a feature of its app that allowed tracking of a user for up to five minutes *after* a trip.[24] Only a few months later, a letter written by the lawyer of Richard Jacobs—Uber's former manager for global intelligence, who had previously worked as a director of intelligence for the U.S. Department of Defense—was unveiled as part of a legal investigation.

The investigation alleged that the company had spied on rivals to acquire trade secrets and collect intelligence about public officials, regulators, and taxi groups.[25] Jacobs described the activities as "overly aggressive and invasive and inappropriate."[26] According to the letter sent by his attorney to the company, Uber hired ex-CIA field operatives to conduct such work and even bugged hotels.[27] An investigation into Uber's "Hell" spying program found that the company tracked Lyft drivers by creating fake driver accounts and finding out how many drivers were in a certain area before sending its own.[28] "Hell" was also used to track drivers who drove for both Uber and Lyft in an attempt to lure them to work only for Uber.

In November 2017, Uber disclosed that hackers had stolen data from 57 million driver and rider accounts—which the company had failed to inform affected persons about—and that it had paid a $100,000 ransom to the hackers to delete the data.[29] Formal investigations into the breach were launched in the U.S., Canada, U.K., and Australia. Only a few months later, allegations were made against Lyft that drivers were abusing customer data by collecting phone numbers and information about celebrities.[30]

In July 2018, an Uber and Lyft driver based in St. Louis was suspended after it was found that he had been secretly live-streaming passenger trips—sometimes including names, home addresses, and conversations—without consent.[31] He made about $3,500 by monetizing the livestreams on Twitch, where commenters would "rate" the attractiveness of passengers and make crude remarks. In early response to the revelations, Uber offered passengers a five-dollar credit and a pledge that they wouldn't be paired with the driver again, while also noting that under Missouri law the livestreaming was technically legal.[32]

A guideline banning the broadcasting of video collected of Uber passengers was introduced in September 2018, with a potential loss of account access as the punishment. Only a month later, an Uber driver in Phoenix uploaded a video of seven professional hockey players from the Ottawa Senators insulting the team and one of its assistant coaches. This was an industry-wide scandal and the players issued an apology.[33] Ontario's former privacy commissioner said that she was "appalled" by the video recording and described it as an example of "total unwarranted surveillance."[34]

Teresa Scassa, Canada Research Chair in information law at the University of Ottawa, told me that it's not possible to use ride-hailing services without "very significant amounts" of personal information being collected. Some have argued that Uber's addition of transit directions to its app was a PR stunt chiefly concerned with gathering trip data about how people get around cities.[35] Uber spent $50,000 on lobbying against the proposed California Consumer Privacy Act, which would "require companies to disclose the types of information they collect, like data used to target ads, and allow the public to opt out of having their information sold."[36] Other companies that lobbied against the act included Amazon, Microsoft, Facebook, and Google.

In the last six months of 2015, Uber received over five hundred data requests about riders and drivers from law enforcement agencies, and complied with 84 percent of them.[37] Uber's historically strained stance on police departments, most notably failing to disclose to police information about crimes and developing software to lock down computers in the case of police raids, has veered sharply toward collaboration. The company now has a "global law enforcement team" that works directly with police on sharing of data.[38] Retired NYPD detective Joseph Giacalone told Utah's *Deseret News* in 2019 that police usage of data from smartphone apps, including Uber and Lyft, has increased "infinitely" in the previous half-decade "with no abatement in sight."[39]

Scassa told me that the future of privacy and autonomous vehicles isn't clear at all. In the case of autonomous vehicles being used to perform quasi-transit functions, data collection could feasibly be limited to only payments and routes, "which is already a considerable amount of information." But she emphasizes that autonomous vehicles are explicitly meant to be much more than that: connected to the internet, with users checking their email, playing video games, and watching movies. "Of course, that will leave the kind of data trail that you don't normally get with taxis or public transit, which would be related to entertainment, shopping, consumer preference that might be collected as well," she says.

A district judge in New York ruled in early 2018 that software firm Vugo could advertise in the vehicles of Uber, Lyft, and other companies.[40] At the time, Vugo had contracts with some 3,500 drivers to display ads that can't be turned off and can only be "near" muted.[41] Such setups could be expanded for autonomous vehicles and potentially customized for each user based on previously collected data, the way customized Facebook posts are promoted based on interests and likes. This is a future that Adrienne LaFrance of the *Atlantic* also predicted, noting that companies may be prone to take advantage of the low probability that riders will read through the entire terms of service prior to usage. "In this near-future filled with self-driving cars, the price of convenience is surveillance," she warned.[42]

A start-up called Firefly is now mounting small billboards on the top of Uber and Lyft vehicles that have data-collecting sensors in them, collecting information about traffic, weather, and potentially noise. The company has already speculated about working with police departments on helping to identify where gunshots occur.[43]

Scassa says it's too early to tell what will happen when autonomous vehicles are integrated with smart cities. Assurances of privacy are still very much up in the air. In August 2018, an agreement for Google to develop the Sidewalk Toronto neighbourhood came under criticism for lack of transparency about data collection, especially the lack of assurances that Google wouldn't monetize the data.[44] Google's Waymo autonomous vehicles are considered frontrunners in the race for self-driving supremacy, and it's likely that such a tech playground would serve as an attractive proving ground for the cars.

The trajectory of connected vehicles and ride-hailing services has included the unaccountable mass collection of personal information by private companies that will monetize it for profit. Why would the future be any different, given that the same players are involved with the same lust for as much sellable data as possible?[45]

The Dangers of Data Sharing

Public transportation systems have serious Big Brother issues of their own. It's becoming difficult to ride on transit anonymously with the proliferation of reloadable tap cards, which can generate a data trail including travel time, boarding location, and transfers. Metrolinx—which operates Toronto's regional rail and motor coach services of GO Transit and the Union Pearson Express—has come under fire for sharing private Presto travel records with the police.[46] The data didn't include personal phone numbers and email addresses but did allow police to track a user's movements.[47]

Beauceron Security, a Canadian company specializing in cybersecurity, explained that "the ease with which card data is being disclosed should be concerning"; both Metrolinx and the police should be required to follow due process, even in an emergency having to "thoroughly explain why the normal process of acquiring data was subverted."[48] Scassa says Metrolinx's response to the public outcry was to claim that it's a public agency that is allowed to conduct data sharing between branches of government. She says the company came up with a new privacy policy and provided better notice, but that doesn't change the fundamental fact that they're sharing information without warrants.

This situation is even more concerning given the highly racialized nature of policing and incarceration. In the U.S. and Canada, a disproportionate percentage of Black, Indigenous, and Hispanic people are subjected to police violence and carceral punishment.

In recent years, transit agencies in both Canada and the U.S. have added video surveillance cameras to buses and trains. In the wake of the stabbing death of eighteen-year-old Nia Wilson at an Oakland transit station in 2018, board members of Bay Area Rapid Transit publicly discussed the possibility of introducing facial recognition technology to the existing 4,000 security cameras throughout the system.[49]

An investigation published in September 2018 revealed that data gathered by BART's automated licence plate reader, installed to scan thousands of plates per minute and alert the police of any related to criminal investigations, was being sent to U.S. Immigration and Customs Enforcement (ICE)—the agency that has become the subject of intense scrutiny for its detention of undocumented migrants.[50] While BART claims that ICE didn't access the data, the communication of it violated the transit agency's own Safe Transit policy, which clearly states that it won't "use any District funds or resources to assist in the enforcement of federal immigration law or to gather or disseminate information regarding release status of individuals or any other such personal information."[51] In response, Shahid Bhuttar of the Electronic Frontier Foundation said the technology "basically enables the government to create a time machine and uncover the historical locations of anyone, including for instance, undocumented workers and their families."[52]

Policing of fare evasion is constantly escalating in scope and severity, such as New York City hiring five hundred more police officers to patrol its dilapidated subway.[53] Toronto's TTC launched an ad campaign in mid-2019 threatening $425 fines for fare evasion, and added an additional fifteen fare inspectors and twenty-one transit enforcement officers.[54] This shift corresponded with implementation of all-door boarding on streetcars, with fares enforced through random checks rather than paying at the front of the car—but 18.5 percent of tickets given out by the TTC between 2008 and 2018 were to Black riders, despite Black people only making up 8.9 percent of the city's population.[55] The TTC's upswing in enforcement followed Metrolinx's addition of twelve fare inspectors to GO Transit lines only weeks earlier. In 2016, Toronto mayor John Tory said during a call-in show that he had suggested to the TTC the idea of publishing fare evaders' pictures in local newspapers, later claiming that he was joking.[56]

In Washington, DC, 91 percent of citations and summons for transit fare evasion are of Black people, and children as young as seven have been stopped.[57] A full 15 percent of citations and summons were issued at the Gallery Place station, a rapidly gentrifying part of the city.

In Brooklyn, 66 percent of people arrested for fare evasion are Black, and arrests are by far the most frequent at stations in high-poverty areas with a predominantly Black population.[58] Failure to produce a $2.75 fare can lead to jail time of up to a year, high court costs, and a criminal record that can affect the ability to find work, housing, and education.

Such surveillance and criminalization of riders predictably results in actual violence against people of colour, especially Black and Indigenous people, by transit police. On January 1, 2009, Oscar Grant—a twenty-two-year-old Black man—was shot and killed by BART police officer Johannes Mehserle while pinned face-down on a station platform. In May 2019 it was revealed that the police officer involved repeatedly lied to investigators, had instigated the conflict, called Grant a racial slur, and hit him in the face.[59]

In July 2013, nineteen-year-old Sammy Yatim, whose family had migrated from Syria only a few years earlier, was shot

"All of the surveillance technologies—as well as the implementation of transit police—very little of it is under the pretense of safety, the idea that they're on there to ensure people are safe from violent assaults. It's almost entirely around regulating public space with respect to people's ability to pay and looking for fare evaders. The issues are connected in terms of free access as well as criminalization."

—HARSHA WALIA, organizer with No One Is Illegal

nine times and killed on a TTC streetcar by Toronto police offi-cer James Forcillo.[60] In December 2014, twenty-three-year-old Gitxsan man Naverone Woods was shot and killed in a Surrey Safeway by a Metro Vancouver transit police officer.[61] In August 2018, a thirty-three-year-old Black man was tackled and choked by two transit officers in Montreal after reportedly using his girlfriend's transit pass to get through the turnstiles.[62] That fol-lowed a similar incident in February 2018, when two TTC fare inspectors tackled and handcuffed a young Black man; he and his mother are suing for "unlawful detention, assault, battery, negligence, discrimination, and racial profiling."[63]

Police violence and harassment can also have catastrophic effects on asylum seekers and undocumented migrants. Author and organizer Harsha Walia told me that Vancouver is unique in Canada for having a fully armed transit police force with the legal authority of law enforcement officers, including access to policing and immigration databases. In 2013, the transit police force reported 328 people to the Canada Border Services Agency, roughly 20 percent of whom were later deported from the country.[64] In December 2013, Lucia Vega Jiménez—a forty-two-year-old Mexican migrant and hotel worker—was detained by a transit police officer at the Main Street SkyTrain station due to an expired fare.[65] While in an airport holding cell at Vancouver International Airport staffed by private security guards, Jiménez hanged herself, and she died a few days later. Walia says the agreement between border services and the transit police was predicated on clear racial profiling; transit police only ask for immigration identification based on peo-ple's skin colour and accent.

In May 2017, Minnesota transit cop Andy Lamers was filmed questioning a man about his immigration status during a $1.75 fare check; a day later, ICE detained the man, who was an undocumented migrant from Mexico, and deported him within a week.[66] Lamers resigned from Metro Transit under public pressure but went on to work as a full-time police officer in New Hope. Months after the incident, Lamers received a $50,000 settlement from Metro Transit.[67]

In July 2019, Naomi Ramirez Rosales—a thirty-four-year-old undocumented trans woman—was arrested by police at a train station in Phoenix, Arizona, and later transferred to ICE custody. Rosales spent at least six months in detention, but migrant organizations said in late 2019 that she's being held in an all-male detention centre under threat of deportation to Mexico.[68] Stephanie Figgins of Trans Queer Pueblo said during a press conference: "Rosales's case is not unique: As a migrant community, we actually have fear of riding the light rail."[69]

Walia says about the practice of questioning transit riders: "It increasingly criminalizes people and makes it almost impossible for undocumented people to survive if they're not able to actually be mobile within the city."

Organized Resistance

These are horrific situations that exemplify the confluence of white supremacy, police violence, incarceration, and xenophobic anti-migrant policy. Many transit agencies have institutionalized policing and security regimes. But in publicly owned services, such racist and privacy-compromising incursions can be resisted and beaten back. This is the very point of the "right to the city," anchored in anti-racist and working-class struggles.

Following the death of Jiménez in Vancouver in 2013, local migrant rights organizers launched a campaign called Transportation Not Deportation to demand that the memorandum of understanding between the transit police and the Canada Border Services Agency be cancelled.[70] Some forty organizations and more than 1,500 people signed the petition to support the effort. In February 2015, the transit police announced that they were terminating the agreement, only days after meeting with members of Transportation Not Deportation.[71] Walia emphasized to me that the cancellation of the agreement wasn't enough. She advocates for the elimination of policing and surveillance that instills fear in communities of colour—as well as free fares, which would have prevented the arrest of Jiménez in the first place.

Crystal Jennings of Pittsburghers for Public Transit says their organization recently won a campaign to prevent the introduction of more armed officers onto buses. The proposal to issue citations and check riders who don't have a fare for criminal warrants was feared to lead to residents getting detained by ICE.[72] "We knew that was going to turn out pretty bad for a lot of our residents and immigrants here in the city," Jennings told me.

In September 2018, after revelations that BART police had been sharing licence plate data with ICE, the transit agency's board of directors approved a new policy that requires public notice and debate if any surveillance technology is considered in the future.[73] An attorney from the American Civil Liberties Union (ACLU) said that "this surveillance ordinance holds BART accountable to the community it serves and gives riders a seat at the table." The government relations co-ordinator of the Council on American-Islamic Relations said, "The passage of this ordinance will empower community members to have a say in the spaces they occupy—which will increase public safety in and of itself."[74]

Eight months later, San Francisco voted to ban the use of facial recognition technology by police and other government agencies, in a partial rebuke to the idea by BART's board to introduce it on the transit system. In July 2019, Oakland followed suit by banning facial recognition; Somerville, Massachusetts, banned it a month before.[75]

Transit agencies across Canada rely heavily on video surveillance technologies for investigating sexual harassment or assault. However, there are strict guidelines about how long that data can be stored. The TTC, for example, requires destruction of camera footage after seventy-two hours, while in Vancouver it can be reviewed for up to a week.[76] On the data-sharing front, Metrolinx in Toronto disclosed information in response to 37 percent of requests from law enforcement in 2018, down from 47 percent in 2017. The agency now publishes an annual report of such requests, which privacy expert Brenda McPhail told the *Toronto Star* is a positive step—although such reporting fails to state how many fulfilled requests lead to charges being laid. McPhail said having such information would "help determine whether law enforcement requests for Presto data are generally reasonable." [77]

These are far from ideal situations, and much more work needs to be done to corral the ability of transit agencies to collect and share personal data. But the rules around these issues are far clearer and more transparent than for their private counterparts—who have neither a responsibility nor the desire to disclose data collection and usage. In a similarly positive vein, cities across the country are considering the decriminalization of fare evasion, including in New York City, Portland, and Washington, DC. The latter voted in late 2018 to issue a $50 fine, instead of a $300 fine and potential jailtime. [78] In Oregon, transit riders pressured the local agency to allow people caught without a fare to perform community service, appeal the citation, or apply for a reduced-fare program. It would be considerably easier, of course, to simply abolish fares altogether.

In response to increased policing in New York City's subway and a string of viral videos in late 2019 documenting NYPD violence against transit riders (including police pointing loaded guns at a crowded subway and arresting a churro vendor for selling food in a station), several organizations including Swipe It Forward and Decolonize This Place organized mass protests and coordinated turnstile jumping to fight back. [79] Unfare NYC, an organization that provides alerts about fare enforcement on subways and buses, told *Patch*: "Rider solidarity means we look out for each other and keep each other safe. Our vision is a ride without fares and a world with no police." [80]

Fake ads made to look like official MTA marketing encouraged riders with unlimited monthly cards to swipe people into the subway system: "Maybe they don't have $2.75," one of the guerilla ads read. "Maybe they were laid off. Maybe there's an emergency and no time to refill. Maybe the ticket machines are broken. Don't snitch. Swipe."[81]

Nassim Moshiree of the ACLU of the District of Columbia told the *Washington Post*: "Activism like the Movement for Black Lives has had a positive impact on raising awareness that policing—and the explicit and implicit bias in policing—means that certain communities are impacted in unfair ways. Even when it comes to something like fare evasion."[82]

Concerns about public safety should be addressed by providing public housing, harm reduction, community services, and resources for mental health and substance use, not by reinforcing reactionary policies that do nothing to address root causes of criminalized behaviours. The racist and anti-poor policing of "disorder" must also be abandoned. Such efforts can unite struggles by transit and anti-police organizations that can collectively campaign for free transit and less policing. This is a politics of "excarceration," or funding services that help keep people out of contact with police and imprisonment.[83]

The response to the massive threat of surveillance and data collection by connected, ride-hailing, and autonomous vehicles isn't to pretend that public transit is doing a much better job on this front. Serious issues of policing and security endanger the lives of many low-income people, especially Black and Indigenous people. The promise with public transit, however, is that communities can effectively exert power over the institutions that govern them. The growing demand for free transit, motivating campaigns around the world, is the best example of this: abolishing fares and decommodifying transportation, although it's only one part of a broader struggle, is a powerful tool to limit the ability for police to stop and detain riders.

"Three revolutions" companies have lengthy histories of profound disregard for privacy standards and have faced only minor punishments for infractions like God View. Autonomous vehicles are by design intended to collect as much information as possible about their users, which will inevitably end up in the hands of police. While there are surely ways to limit the worst manifestations of that behaviour, the immense profit motive guiding some of the biggest companies in the world to perfect this technology should not be underestimated. Increased privatization of public transportation is making these fights increasingly difficult. Public transit agencies and the bodies that inform their policies are by far the best places for us to spend our time and resources protecting ourselves from increased surveillance.

The entrance of more ride-hailing and autonomous vehicles onto streets almost guarantees that any remaining semblance of privacy—beyond that which has already been compromised by our smartphones—will be commodified. The solution, once again, is a massive buildout of public transportation that keeps the control of transportation in the hands of the public.

Chapter 8

Old town road

Rural and intercity transit

Rural areas can attain autonomy for their residents without relying on the whims of ride-hailing companies that might hike fares or go bankrupt next week.

WHERE EVERYONE OWNS A CAR

So far, we have focused on public transportation in big urban centres. Cities are where the most people are concentrated, and they hold the greatest potential to rapidly get people out of personal automobiles and onto buses and trains—an imperative if we are to avoid the most catastrophic impacts of climate change.

But a large chunk of the population doesn't live in cities or close enough to city centres to access the kind of density that governments often insist on before they'll provide reliable transit. It's critical that we build a political project around public transportation that includes the unique needs of rural and small-town residents.

Rural areas—defined by the U.S. Census Bureau using criteria including population, housing density, and distance from urban centres—make up an incredible 97 percent of the country's land mass and 19.3 percent of its population.[1]

Of course, there's a wide range of what "rural" means within that framework: some counties are defined as completely (100 percent) rural, while others are mostly urban (less than 50 percent rural).[2] But generally, rural residents tend to be older, are more likely white, and have higher rates of disability than urban residents.[3] Rural communities of colour tend to be geographically concentrated; nine out of ten rural and small-town Black residents live in the U.S. South.[4] There has been a rise in Hispanic residents of rural and small-town areas.[5] In Canada, almost 39 percent of Indigenous people live in rural areas, with another 20 percent in "small population centres."[6]

Five specific demographics have been identified as facing transportation disadvantages in rural areas, similar to most places: older adults, people with disabilities, youth, low-income households, and women (especially mothers with young children and women fleeing from abusive situations).[7] Due to austerity measures, many services are consolidated in larger towns, forcing rural residents to drive long distances for healthcare, banking, post offices, pharmacies, and social programs.

Systematic neglect of intercity transit such as motor coaches and passenger rail has rendered many areas effectively unnavigable without a car or airplane ticket.[8] As a partial result of such policy failures, U.S. airlines flew over 778 million passengers on domestic flights in 2018, an all-time high.[9] Aviation emissions are expected to grow between 300 and 700 percent by 2050, making air travel the sole source of emissions that will continue to rise from developed countries.[10]

These realities have often been used by politicians to justify not investing in rural and intercity public transportation systems. After all, only 4.2 percent of rural households don't own a vehicle, and 31 percent own three or more.[11] These geographies—featuring wide roads, large parking lots, and multi-vehicle garages—are literally designed for the car. Political representatives can easily make the case that if everyone owns a car and has no trouble finding parking, why bother spending on subsidies for buses that are going to ride empty?

Chronic underinvestment in rural transportation can lead to a wide range of negative impacts, including debilitating isolation and loneliness. Young people without access to a car can feel trapped and lose out on opportunities; queer, trans, and gender non-conforming youth can especially need an option to leave their rural or small-town communities. Traffic fatality and injury rates are also high in rural areas. While only one-fifth of the U.S. population live in rural areas, almost half of fatal car crashes occur there.[12] These realities have made "three revolutions" thinking particularly appealing to many rural constituents. They offer the promise of lower emissions, improved access, and better service without requiring fundamental overhauls in taxation, funding, or planning.

THREE REVOLUTIONS: RURAL IMPACT

Savings and Convenience

Personal electric vehicles have obvious appeal to rural residents who can afford them. Electric vehicles are estimated to offer twice the cost-saving potential in rural counties and small towns as for urban dwellers, and considerably more emission reductions.[13] Rural residents currently spend a greater proportion of their income on gasoline than urban residents do, as they typically have to travel farther, more often, to meet basic needs.[14]

Many rural areas currently lack charging infrastructure, but that can change quickly with a bit of targeted investment from various levels of government. Access to a garage, which can be a rarity in urban centres, allows for the straightforward installation of home charging stations as well.[15] Several auto manufacturers are working on electrifying pickup trucks, which may prove useful in rural areas.[16] As the batteries of electric vehicles continue to grow in capacity and size, more fully electric vehicles will be able to make long trips without running out of power. Combining an electric vehicle with rooftop solar panels in rural areas offers up even more decarbonizing and cost-saving potential. A 2014 working paper from the National Bureau of Economic Research suggested that such a partnership may create "accidental environmentalists" because the sheer reduction in fuel costs will prove attractive.[17]

None of that changes things for people who can't drive or prefer not to due to age, disability, or income. Perhaps ride-hailing can help. Uber pitched the idea of rural service in early 2017; the company's policy director of New York stated: "We want to be everywhere in the state. The goal is to provide a car to people everywhere." Lyft announced in August 2017 that its service covered 94 percent of the country, anywhere in 40 states (including Alaska).[18] A month later, Uber boasted that it was serving 172 areas in California, 102 of which had populations under 30,000 people.[19]

Ride-hailing is often positioned as a means of solving the elusive suburban "last mile" problem: how a transit rider gets home from their stop or station. Failing to address that can lead potential transit riders to opt for their own vehicles. If an Uber or Lyft ride can take the place of that private car, all the better. The prospect of "100 percent coverage" of the country by a ride-hailing company would also be a huge marketing opportunity.[20]

Rural-focused ride-hailing services have also emerged, like start-up Liberty Mobility Now in Nebraska, Ohio, Texas, and Colorado.[21] Liberty Mobility Now's strategy was to recruit and train drivers from the local community and charge a fraction of what it cost for a taxi ride. However, the company was forced to shut down after less than a year due to an investor lawsuit.[22]

More successes have come from small community-owned operations, like the farmworkers' ride-sharing program in Cantua Creek, California, that was introduced in chapter 4. In the Canadian province of New Brunswick, three organizations partnered to provide a volunteer-run rural Tele-Drive service for seniors, people with disabilities, and low-income residents. The manager of Rural Rides Affordable Transportation said: "We have free health care, but if you can't get to the health care, it really is no good to seniors or people that have a low income."[23] Such community-based projects are by their nature small-scale and often depend on the time and resources of a few individuals. They can serve as stopgaps, but they don't constitute transportation policy.

This is where autonomous vehicles are supposed to step up. A March 2018 report by German consulting firm Roland Berger, with the lofty title of "Reconnecting the Rural: Autonomous Driving as a Solution for Non-urban Mobility," made this case clearly.[24] The report argued that autonomous vehicles will offer major cost reductions for rural areas, providing access to isolated communities that will in turn greatly increase quality of life—and further, offer a "strategic benefit" of serving as a testing ground for the technology, since there is less traffic and more predictable road systems.[25] It identified three constituencies who will benefit from such advances: youth not old enough to get their licences, people with disabilities, and seniors who can no longer drive. The report drew particular attention to the latter, given the rapidly increasing average age in many rural areas.

"Few central governments currently plan to invest in public transit in sparsely populated areas, and some are actively disinvesting from these areas," the authors wrote, calling explicit attention to austerity as an opportunity for privatized mobility.[26] Declining transit access leads to lower local spending and reduced business and government revenue. But the report claimed that autonomous vehicles would kickstart a positive feedback loop of more frequent travel, spending, and resources for both residents and tourists. However, in order for this to happen, the infrastructure of rural roads would need to be significantly improved: clear white lanes for navigation and top-notch telecommunication technologies to ensure lightning-fast transmission of data.[27]

Autonomous vehicles have also been heralded for their potential to help attract younger people back to rural areas and retain them.[28] Anyone will be able to summon a vehicle at any time of day or night and get where they need to go without worrying about safety, inebriation, or cost.

Reality Check

Yet personal electric vehicles face the same limitations for rural residents as they do in the city. They're costly, even with generous subsidies, so only well-off residents in these regions will be able to afford these cars and the associated charging infrastructure for some time to come. Improved safety technologies accompanying the vehicles may reduce the crash rate in some instances—but the risks of high speed, poor signage, and an aging population remain.

There are also unresolved questions about how funding for charging infrastructure would be allocated. Electrify America, the Volkswagen subsidiary that was required as a part of the settlement for the VW emissions scandal to fund highway charging infrastructure, has been accused by California politicians of investing far more of the settlement money into profitable areas like San Francisco and Beverly Hills than into low-income rural areas.[29] And as with any personal vehicle, the rise of electric cars means very little for people who can't drive or prefer not to.

A limiting factor for longer ride-hailing trips, especially to rural areas, is the cost of "deadheading." Ride-hailing drivers aren't paid when there is no passenger in the vehicle, and they absorb the gas costs. Rural rides can also be very short, even from one end of town to the other, making them rarely worth a driver's time and money. A 2017 forum on an Uber-focused subreddit about rural rides explained some of the disincentives for drivers: "Why as a driver would I ever accept a ride 20 minutes each way into the middle of nowhere?" one person asked. "The chances of a short ride or cancellation would be way too high for me to blow the better part of an hour + fuel costs on."[30] Another commenter noted: "The model breaks down in suburban and rural areas. It really requires significant density; otherwise people just own cars and drive everywhere."

Drivers aren't provided any additional incentive to service such areas, and Uber and Lyft haven't stepped up to change that in any meaningful way. Only 19 percent of Americans in rural areas use ride-hailing apps, compared to 45 percent in urban areas and 40 percent in suburban areas.[31] The one Uber driver in Haines, Alaska, which has a population of under 1,500 people, was repeatedly booted from the app as she wasn't logging enough rides. Also, some rural areas have not been thoroughly mapped by Google, which Uber depends on, so potential riders couldn't always mark their pickup location. Poor internet coverage also impeded pickups.[32]

Autonomous vehicles, if they come to fruition, will likely underserve rural communities for similar reasons. Companies will operate such technology where they can make the most trips for the highest returns. While some residents may be able to pay for access, those who arguably need it the most will once again be left behind. It strains credulity to think that massive corporations would voluntarily commit expensive assets to service people with the least ability to pay, rather than young white professionals in gentrifying parts of large cities.

Rural infrastructure will also require massive investments to prepare for the safe proliferation of autonomous vehicles, which require high-speed broadband capacity and sensors in pretty much everything around them: signs, telephone poles, curbs, bridges, bicycles. Complicating the situation further, self-driving cars are still unable to navigate snow, rain, or heavy weather.[33]

Such an overhaul doesn't just happen. Google's controversial Sidewalk Labs experiment on the Toronto waterfront is an attempt to build a geographically contained version of this future. But without immense regional and federal support, such a model would likely be hard to transplant to a town of a few thousand people. In an age of austerity and the anticipated reduction in gas taxes from electrification, it's unclear how such country-wide projects would be funded. Remote and rural communities have been deprived of meaningful public investment for decades; to imagine this trend would change with next-generation vehicles relies on truly magical thinking.[34]

Even if autonomous vehicles are introduced in rural areas with little delay, it remains likely that such advances will justify and enable even more driving. Like with ride-hailing, the owners of the service won't settle for providing only short mile-long trips when they can instead undermine the competition and then fill the void. Existing rural or transit routes could well be extinguished by subsidized ride-hailing and autonomous vehicles.

These are not problems that autonomous vehicle boosters acknowledge or address in any meaningful way. Rather, the consensus appears to be that self-driving cars will have entirely positive impacts on rural residents, especially for those in most need of transportation. That ignores the lacklustre experience of ride-hailing services in rural areas, and the profit imperatives of massive autonomous vehicle companies that will likely undermine the provision of adequate mobility for low-income seniors and people with disabilities. The response can't be to hope and pray that Silicon Valley decides to do the right thing. It's to recognize the benefits that rural transit already brings, and to commit to ensuring universal, free access.

PUBLIC TRANSIT: CHALLENGES AND OPPORTUNITIES

Spotty Coverage

Many rural communities do have some semblance of a transit system. In 2015, a total of 1,334 agencies across the U.S. provided service in such areas, while another 270 urban agencies extended their service into rural regions.[35] That gave 82 percent of counties in the U.S. rural transit service, up from 78 percent in 2011. Most are demand-response, meaning they are driven when summoned, more like a cab than a conventional bus.

But one-third of U.S. rural transit providers offer fixed-route service: a guaranteed trip from a certain place at a specific time of day. That provides access to transit to 70 percent of rural residents in the U.S., including seniors, people with disabilities, youth, low-income households, and women, trans, and gender non-conforming people.

But that still leaves a large chunk of the country without public transportation service. It's no surprise that many people drive enormous distances to get where they need to go. Almost one-third of rural residents commute a half-hour each way to work; 4 percent travel ninety minutes.[36]

Transit service that does exist in rural areas has been described by Aubrey Byron of the organization Strong Towns as "more of a spot treatment for the small number of individuals who are aware of the service, qualify for waived fees, and fall within the service area."[37] Service tends to be intermittent, available only a few times a week. Only 0.5 percent of rural residents use transit to get to work, and 27 percent (compared to 73 percent of urban residents) are able to get to a grocery store by transit.[38] Even when transit service is available, cultural norms can contribute to a perceived need to drive; 92 percent of trips taken by rural individuals over the age of 65 are by automobile.[39]

Here's how Scott Bogren of the Community Transportation Association of America described it in the late 1990s:

> The past two decades have seen many forms of public transportation virtually abandon rural areas. Small-town residents often travel hundreds of miles just to access the nearest airport; intercity bus service is a shell of its former self; taxi service is scant and expensive; and passenger rail service often streaks through the countryside in the middle of the night.[40]

Many rural transit services suffer from a lack of coordination and networking caused by jurisdictional limitations. At least one-quarter of the U.S. lacks public transit to travel to an adjacent county or state. As one report describes the process: "passengers have to ride to the boundary, disembark, and try to connect with another service."[41] The inconvenience of potentially being stranded or having to wait long periods for a transfer can further deter usage. A 2001 U.S. Department of Agriculture report described the situation as "primarily local in nature and, largely ... not connected to the nation's passenger service network."[42]

Conditions only become worse in periods of fiscal crisis. The loss of funding associated with the 2019 U.S. government shutdown led rural and small-town transit agencies to cut service hours and in some cases consider ending service permanently.[43] Already underwhelming service only gets worse under such pressures.

Intercity Service

Due to austerity and privatization, many regions have lost intercity bus service in recent years. Between 1970 and 2005, scheduled and regular route intercity bus ridership in the U.S. declined from 130 million passengers a year to only 40 million, with the number of communities served with daily intercity bus service plummeting from 23,000 in 1965 to 4,500 in 2005.[44]

Writing about his home state of Oregon in 2019, transit planner Jarrett Walker reminisced about the bus services that successfully linked small towns with Portland in the 1970s. "Almost all of those services are gone," he wrote. "Private intercity bus companies, including new players like Megabus, stick to linking big cities. All that remains is a minimal state-funded service called Point, one or two trips a day, mostly to feed Amtrak."[45]

Conditions are no better in Canada. After over seventy years of affordable service in rural areas, Canada's Saskatchewan Transportation Company was shut down in 2017 by the provincial government. The move was widely criticized for its disproportionate impacts on Indigenous women, people with disabilities, and seniors.[46]

Connie Deiter, an Indigenous woman living in Regina, filed a complaint with the provincial human rights commission alleging that the closure discriminated against her and other Indigenous women who can't afford to drive. "If you're poor, you don't have access to a vehicle," she said; "a lot of our people don't, the only option is to hitchhike and that's already happening."[47]

Mental health counsellor Marlene Bear said that she had witnessed considerably more hitchhiking since the closure of the STC, fearing that the situation in Saskatchewan may turn into a new Highway of Tears—a 450-mile stretch of highway in northern British Columbia where many Indigenous women have gone missing or been found murdered.[48]

A July 2018 survey of fifty-six staff members of domestic abuse shelters in Saskatchewan showed that women are finding it even more difficult to access help; 70 percent of workers reported that clients had hitchhiked to get to or from a shelter.[49] People with disabilities have also voiced serious concerns with the closure of the bus service, since private ride options do not guarantee wheelchair-accessible service.[50] In late 2017, a spokesperson for the Saskatchewan government told the CBC that "when we made the decision to wind up STC, we were confident that the private sector would recognize opportunities to provide services where demand warranted."[51] However, a research paper published by a University of Regina business administration student two years after the STC's closure indicated that the private sector had not stepped up to fill the gap, instead opting to focus on the busiest and more profitable corridor.[52]

In November 2018, private intercity bus operator Greyhound Canada pulled out of Western Canada (with the lone exception of a north-south route between Vancouver and Seattle), further exacerbating lack of access for marginalized communities. The company also cancelled its transit contract with Thompson, leaving the city of almost 14,000 people without public transit service.[53] In an interview with Global News, Grand Chief Arlen Dumas of the Assembly of Manitoba Chiefs said about Indigenous people travelling from northern Manitoba: "It is already well documented that our citizens have to ride the bus for hours, some longer than 14 hours, in order to see a doctor. How will they get access to adequate health care now?"[54] Only weeks earlier, a fifty-eight-year-old Indigenous man died on an intercity bus from northern Manitoba to an appointment in Winnipeg.[55] In October 2019, Amalgamated Transit Union Canada published a radio documentary paired with a petition calling for the "establishment of a national public intercity transit service as part of a Green New Deal for social, economic and environmental justice and tangible reconciliation with Indigenous peoples."[56]

Passenger rail—Amtrak in the U.S., VIA Rail in Canada—has also undergone decades of stagnation and decline. Arguably the greatest issue for both services is that they are forced to share tracks with freight transportation, which physically

"We call upon all governments to ensure that adequate plans and funding are put into place for safe and affordable transit and transportation services and infrastructure for Indigenous women, girls, and 2SLGBTQQIA people living in remote or rural communities. Transportation should be sufficient and readily available to Indigenous communities, and in towns and cities located in all of the provinces and territories in Canada."

—National Inquiry into Missing and Murdered
Indigenous Women and Girls (Canada),
Calls for Justice for All Governments:
Human Security, 4.8

pushes passenger rail to the side to wait, sometimes for hours. A 2015 background paper for the Government of Canada concluded that the need to share tracks "severely limits [VIA Rail's] capacity to deliver efficient and timely passenger rail service to the fullest potential, undermining VIA Rail's ability to fulfill its mandate."[57] About 97 percent of Amtrak's tracks are owned by other entities, making it subject to the other companies' schedules.[58] Unsurprisingly, this results in unpredictable scheduling outside of Amtrak's main Northeast Corridor.

As journalist Aaron Gordon has reported, catching an Amtrak train between Chicago and Cleveland has become near impossible, despite the fixes being simple: upgrading tracks, running more trains, giving passenger rail priority over freight. As a result of failure by government to prioritize passenger rail, Elon Musk's entirely theoretical Hyperloop proposal is being celebrated as an alternative between the cities, making these passenger rail improvements even less likely due to political distraction.[59]

High-speed rail, defined as rail transportation that runs at over 125 miles per hour, continues to be an elusive goal. China, Spain, and Japan are often looked to as inspiration for the mode, which can compete with short-haul air travel.[60] But governments are deterred by the costs; it would cost an estimated $150 billion over thirty years to upgrade Amtrak's Northeast Corridor for high-speed rail.[61]

California has considered a high-speed rail line between Los Angeles and San Francisco since the mid-1990s, and the plan was approved by Governor Arnold Schwarzenegger in 2008. But the project has faced continued delays, ballooning costs, and accusations of mismanagement; in early 2019, California governor Gavin Newsom effectively cancelled it, citing high costs, while keeping a 171-mile line from Merced to Bakersfield.[62] Only days later, Trump's Department of Transportation pulled almost $1 billion in funding for the line, adding that it was seeking to recoup the total of $2.5 billion for the "now-defunct project."[63]

Another plan by Brightline, owned by Richard Branson's Virgin, to build a high-speed project between Las Vegas and Southern California was delayed by two years after it didn't receive abatements for sales and property taxes.[64] Since 1970, some twenty-two studies have been conducted in Canada into the possibility of high-speed rail in Ontario and Quebec without anything coming to fruition.[65]

Plenty of Possibilities

As with transit service to suburban areas, there is nothing inherent about poor transportation options in rural counties and small towns. There are unique limitations to each area, of course: farmers and construction workers will continue to require pickup trucks to haul supplies (although much of that driving could likely be curtailed if production and distribution of equipment and supplies was centrally coordinated by public bodies). But publicly owned and operated transit can provide free, reliable, and accessible transportation to residents, regardless of population size and density. All that is required—you may be detecting a theme by now—is committed funding and planning from all levels of government.

Between 2007 and 2015, small-town and rural public transit ridership in the U.S. increased by 8.6 percent on a per capita basis.[66] There's a real desire for better transit in rural areas and small towns. A 2010 poll found that 79 percent of rural voters agreed with the statement: "The United States would benefit from an expanded and improved transportation system, such as rail and buses."[67] Funding such services would help create good long-term jobs in areas currently undermined by natural resource boom and busts and continued urbanization.

As with any jurisdiction, transit planning has to be done in close collaboration with the community. A 2017 profile by *American Prospect* of a van-based public transit system in Plainview, Nebraska—population 1,200—emphasized that municipal officials and related organizations surveyed residents to find out what improvements they needed, with public transit emerging as a priority.[68]

Good news stories are emerging, as new rural transit networks are regularly popping up. In Alberta, the County of Grande Prairie is providing bus service to and from nearby towns, while Red Deer established a regional transit service with Innisfail (population 8,000) and Penhold (population 3,200).[69] Montana increased its rural transit systems from nine in 2008 to close to forty in 2015 through partnering with federal and local governments.[70] North Central Montana Transit, founded in 2009, offers daily fixed-route service for a one dollar per trip between Havre, nearby reservations, and small towns. The service stops at many small towns along the intercity routes, and uses biodiesel to cut down on greenhouse gas emissions.[71] By 2011, it was averaging 1,600 rides a month, far exceeding its projection of 250. A math instructor at a college said about the service: "Not only do I save around a hundred dollars a week taking the bus, but I get to know other people in the community whom I might not otherwise have met."[72]

Since 2017, the BC government has funded an intercity bus service through provincial Crown corporation BC Transit on the Highway of Tears, the notorious stretch of road that Indigenous women in Saskatchewan feared would be the province's fate without proper transit.[73] In the first year of service, five thousand people travelled throughout northern British Columbia via the Bulkley Nechako Regional Transit System.[74] There are also connections to bus routes to smaller towns, all at a fraction of the cost Greyhound had charged.[75] Two-thirds of the operating costs are covered by the province; the rest comes from communities and First Nations.[76] Highway of Tears safety advocate Glady Radek said: "There's always room for improvement, but I'm actually very, very happy with having our own transit system up here."[77]

Tribal transit is offering invaluable service across North America. The Spokane Tribe's Moccasin Express, for example, offers free trips multiple times a day from the reservation in

Washington state to various municipalities in the area; there is also paratransit available for seniors and people with disabilities who are unable to get to the fixed-route bus stop.[78]

Electric buses now boast incredibly long ranges. In 2017 a Proterra model set a world record by driving 1,102 miles on a single charge. In fact, long intercity trips are almost ideal for electric buses, as regular and somewhat lengthy stops allow for charging. There is no technological question remaining about the viability of passenger rail, either. Building up a network of reliable, free trains with dedicated tracks may come with a high upfront capital cost, but it would bring enormous benefits for the climate, economic equality, accessibility, and more. Ideally, these advances should be led by federal and state or provincial governments in order to maximize coordination and improve seamless transfers between services.

But rural transit tends to be expensive for small municipalities to cover, especially if there isn't a large ridership from the get-go. Take the example of Iqaluit, the capital of the Northern territory of Nunavut with a population of 7,740: it ran a transit system in the early 2000s that transported an average of twenty-eight people per day, but shut it down due to the $150,000-per-year cost.[79] Of course, $150,000 isn't much of an expense for cities to incur—it's the price of a manager or two. But the expense can be prohibitive for a town, especially if the system hasn't existed for long enough to build up a constituency of ridership. However, in late 2019 the mayor of Iqaluit said its new transportation master plan would hopefully include a public bus system, with a councillor adding: "Some form of public transportation needs to be undertaken to alleviate congestion and provide alternatives to people in town."[80]

A somewhat clueless article published by *Grist* in 2014 is an example of this funding predicament. Titled "Even Rural America Can Have Good Public Transportation," the piece detailed the shockingly efficient bus system of the 32,000-person region of Aspen, Colorado, including stops within walking distance, frequent service, and buses equipped with bike racks.[81] But as commenters pointed out, Aspen, home of a legendary ski resort, is a very wealthy area and not at all representative of most rural and small towns.

"I live in a poor rural community," an online commenter wrote. "We can't afford good schools, our health care facilities are small and in danger of closing, jobs have always been scarce. How can we fund mass transit?" It was a legitimate point. But it also exemplified the foundational issue keeping rural areas from having quality transit: strong and consistent funding. It's not hyperbolic to suggest that many rural areas across the country could have Aspen-like transit service. Municipalities shouldn't be forced to rely on uneven sources of revenue like property taxes and fares. Rather, as we will explore further in part three, they should be guaranteed funding through income and wealth taxes administered at all levels of government.

Rural areas can attain autonomy for their residents without relying on the whims of ride-hailing companies that might hike fares or go bankrupt next week, building up a public service that people of all ages and abilities can use. So-called micromobility, such as Uber's attempts to replace transit service in small towns, will never be an affordable and environmentally responsible means to fill the gaps. Transit technologies, in contrast, are immediately deployable and accessible to all. There is nothing speculative or imagined about their potential successes. They only require sustained political support and an awareness of what riders require: a sense of comfort, affordability, and reliability. Getting more people into legitimately shared vehicles, owned and operated by a public service, is a critical first step to cutting greenhouse gases, improving equity and accessibility, and allowing communities to plan in smarter, more predictable ways.

These services can also be a gateway into a broader low-carbon transition. Rural areas are especially vulnerable to the impacts of climate change—and offering transportation alternatives is a tangible example of how society can be run differently and more beneficially for all.[82] That's even more needed because of the rapidly aging population, with the number of Americans ages 65 and older expected to almost double by 2060 and the desire for rural seniors to "age in place."[83] Participatory budgeting and more town-hall-style approaches can be powerful tools in this process.[84]

This transformation will not happen overnight. Driving is a cultural foundation of our society, which will take years to change. It can be a challenge to get small-town residents out of their cars as they—often correctly—associate driving with freedom, employment, and ability to socialize. But such norms can be shifted over time, especially if public transportation is provided in a way that feels community-based and predictable enough to schedule your life around.

That doesn't have to only mean full-length buses either: in small rural areas, public transportation can look like minibuses or even minivans. The key is that such vehicles are publicly owned and operated by professional drivers, through a service that prioritizes service for all. A vision of public transportation that encompasses rural areas and small towns is a far more powerful vision of mobility justice and social transformation, one that recognizes existing conditions rather than trying to cram everything into a singular model of urban transit.

Rural transit is only the first step to a more fundamental transformation of space and relations that will decommodify housing and create more equitable and just rural communities. But establishing better transit, now, is a key tool in that process. After all, low-income people living in rural areas need to be able to catch a bus or train to get to a town council meeting or a protest before bigger picture conditions will change. The path forward isn't easy, but it is immensely doable and required. Rural and small-town residents are vital members of society, fully deserving of viable transportation services that improve their access to public services, reduce loneliness and isolation, and create good unionized jobs.

Chapter 9

Walmart on wheels

Labour and unions

Transit workers and unions can collaborate with riders to improve conditions for everyone.

WHO DOES THE WORK?

The rise of neoliberalism in the 1970s and 1980s had calamitous impacts on labour: wages stagnated, union density and militancy plummeted, and precarity returned with outsourcing and offshoring. While official unemployment numbers remain low (the U.S. hit a fifty-year low of 3.5 percent in late 2019), a vast majority of job creation is "alternative work arrangements" like traditional temp or contract work, along with new "gig economy" jobs like TaskRabbit and DoorDash.[1] One of every ten workers in Toronto now participates in the gig economy for some of their income.[2]

No sector is expected to be hit as hard by advanced technologies as transportation. Trucking and taxis have been identified by media outlets as losing millions of jobs due to automation, though that claim has been repeatedly challenged by researchers.[3] Next-generation automobility is about many things, but it remains above all about questions of labour: who performs it, how much they're compensated, their legal categorization, and whether those jobs will even exist in the future.

THREE REVOLUTIONS: IMPACT ON LABOUR

A Driver's Life

The websites of ride-hailing companies are chock full of endorsements of the benefits of driving for them. Uber brags of three reasons why drivers will love the work: the ability to set your own schedule, the possibility to make more money with longer distances and surge pricing, and the opportunity to meet new people (from "long-time residents to first-time tourists, families, small business owners, and more").[4] Lyft includes a similar list of incentives, including keeping all the tips, making more money during peak hours, and being a part of the "Lyft community" of riders and drivers.[5] Testimonies from drivers are quoted prominently on Lyft's website.

The dream as hawked by such companies sees drivers having control over their own lives: being your own boss without having to worry about the logistics of owning a small business, and doing work that seems to help regular people.[6] Another promotional page for Uber boasts of drivers' ability to move to different places without worrying about where they're going to find work.[7]

There's clearly a strong attraction to at least try out work with ride-hailing companies. Around the world, an estimated two to four million people drive for Uber alone, providing an incredible 15 million rides each day.[8] Lyft reports that it uses almost 1.5 million drivers, who have earned over $500 million in tips to date.[9] (Many drivers pull shifts for both Uber and Lyft, although the design of the Uber Partner app discourages users from running both apps at once.)[10] In a world of hard-to-find jobs and ungrateful bosses, the appeal of driving for Uber or Lyft isn't hard to grasp, particularly if you already own a car that's rarely in use.

But the allure of electric, ride-hailing, and autonomous

vehicles to Silicon Valley investors isn't merely to reinvent the taxi with a nifty app and evade regulations imposed on taxis such as limits on the number of vehicles on the road. Rather, financial backers of companies like Uber, Lyft, Waymo, and Tesla are banking on eventually making drivers obsolete—and in the meantime, using the threat of autonomy to discipline the labour force to accept ever-lower compensation and working conditions, and ensuring that politicians don't ruin their future attempts at monopolization by properly funding public transit.

Former Uber CEO Travis Kalanick explained the situation this way: "The reason Uber could be expensive is because you're not just paying for the car—you're paying for the other dude in the car. When there's no other dude in the car, the cost of taking an Uber anywhere becomes cheaper than owning a vehicle."[11]

Ride-hailing companies have fought tooth and nail to ensure that their drivers continue to be considered independent contractors rather than employees. That means almost all costs are downloaded onto the driver—and minimum wage and overtime laws don't apply. The driver covers everything from the price of owning or leasing the vehicle to fuel, maintenance, insurance, and fees. Uber and Lyft say that they only take 25 percent of the fare. But the additional booking fee can increase the cut to upwards of 42 percent, with lower fares resulting in higher effective commissions.[12] Larry Hanley of the ATU equated the situation to "Walmart on wheels," creating artificial downward pressure on the entire sector. "It's an ugly thing," he told me. "It's yet another arm of economically well-endowed capitalists to bring pain to the people at the bottom."

Many estimations have been made of how much Uber and Lyft drivers actually make. Uber claimed in 2014 that drivers earned $74,200 a year in San Francisco and $90,800 a year in New York.[13] A 2015 Uber-funded study estimated that its drivers were making over $19 per hour in earnings in the top twenty markets.[14] But crucially, none of those estimates included Uber's commission or vehicle expenses. Multiple rate cuts have left drivers getting even less than when the company first started operating, representing a total collective loss for drivers of billions of dollars.[15]

A May 2018 study by the Economic Policy Institute found that driver compensation averages $11.77 per hour, after Uber's fees and vehicle expenses. However, once all other costs were covered, including mandatory Social Security and Medicare tax payments and federal taxes, that figure was knocked down to an average of $9.21 per hour.[16] Several other studies agree on an after-cost rate of $10 per hour.[17]

Driving for a ride-hailing company as a woman, trans, or gender non-conforming person has its own risks. As a popular ride-hailing website described it, "If a rider gets a little creepy and spooks the woman for any reason—she's in a very vulnerable spot. Her options are quite limited when compared to traditional public-facing jobs."[18] A twenty-four-year-old single mother of two told *Bloomberg* in late 2018 about her experience driving for Uber: "Every single time, every day that I drive, every night that I drive, there is at least one questionable experience."[19]

Several trans drivers for Uber have been kicked off the platform; if a person is transitioning, the app's Real-Time ID Check that requires a selfie of the driver may not exactly match the photo the company has on file. Janey Webb, an Uber driver in Iowa, was deactivated right before July 4, one of the more profitable days of the year. "A trans person can't be expected to update their license every three months or so just to avoid being deactivated," she said.[20]

Katie Wells of the Kalmanovitz Initiative for Labor and the Working Poor conducted a two-year study about the work lives of forty Uber drivers in the Washington, DC, area.[21] While some drivers are in a stable financial position and do it for fun or supplemental income, many desperately rely on fares for survival. "Their work lives suck," Wells told me.

Wells explains that for many drivers, one extra repair or a car crash can mean that they can't feed their kids and they have to sell things they find in the closet. Yet the rating system discourages drivers from talking about their conditions. Riders rate the quality of service between one and five stars; sustained ratings below 4.6 could resulting in deactivation of a driver's account.[22] "The rating system is this ingenious way to isolate the workers from any kind of relationship building," Wells says.

To keep their ratings up, Uber drivers are expected to offer more and more items to riders: bottled water, candy, Wi-Fi, a charger—all of which cost the driver out of pocket.[23] The rating system requires drivers to be "on" at all times, which is an enormous amount of emotional labour. A 2016 *Harvard Business Review* feature explained that the process "involves actively reshaping a worker's inner emotional life to conform to employers' and customers' expectations of emotional performance."[24] Further, the lack of predictability about what passengers desire in a ride can provoke anxiety and poor morale in drivers who are trying their best.[25]

The Uber app has also been the subject of criticism for the way that it "gamifies" the experience, using psychological tricks to incentivize drivers to keep working longer than they otherwise would. The company has "exploited some people's tendency to set earnings goals," applying similar behavioural

> "Drivers are vulnerable in terms of how much money they're going to make and how much they're going to spend. They're working long hours, they're not making much pay. They're driving sixteen- or eighteen-hour days, seven cups of coffee, really rooting for the public transit system to fail. It's a precarious work life, and it's affecting their home life as well."
>
> —KATIE WELLS, Kalmanovitz Initiative for Labor and the Working Poor

motivations as are found in popular video games and the Netflix autoplay function. Those include constant reminders to the driver of how close they are to meeting a certain earnings goal, as well as "forward dispatching," in which a new ride is assigned before the current one ends, and experimenting with female-sounding voices to encourage male drivers.[26]

Drivers can be logged out of the app or sent warning messages for a low acceptance rate, or for accepting a ride and then immediately cancelling (which, if undetected, helps avoid a low acceptance rate).[27] Companies have stopped deactivating drivers for a low acceptance rate out of concerns that such a policy could contribute to a court categorizing their contractors as employees. But they do send more ride requests to drivers with higher acceptance ratings, so there's an incentive to keep rates up.[28] Those requests sometimes mean driving a long distance for a pickup, at the driver's expense.

Drivers for both leading companies are forced into taking UberPool or Lyft Line rides. The shared trips are berated on driver forums as a waste of time, with multiple pickups that can lead to interpersonal conflicts between random (and potentially inebriated) strangers.[29] Uber's S-1 filing ahead of its 2019 initial public offering revealed that it knew its plan to eliminate additional incentives like weekly bonuses for completing extra trips during busy times would further anger drivers.[30]

Many Lyft drivers who leased vehicles through the company's Express Drive program have ended up in precarious situations. Some live in the $240-per-week car itself, as they can't afford apartments and get paid lower rates than Lyft drivers who own their own vehicles.[31] Uber relaunched its own vehicle leasing program in mid-2019, collaborating with auto loan company Fair to allow drivers without a car to effectively rent one for $185 per week. All but the most basic maintenance costs are downloaded on the driver—a major concern given that Fair offers used vehicles.[32]

Collective Rights

Because they're considered independent contractors, drivers aren't able to force ride-hailing companies to collectively bargain with them. In mid-2019, the U.S. National Labor Relations Board confirmed that Uber's drivers indeed are to be classified as contractors, not employees.[33] Risks to drivers who engage in job actions are extremely high, as Uber has the power to deactivate anyone they suspect of participating. In response to an attempt by Seattle city council to allow ride-hailing drivers to unionize, Uber started notifying drivers via the app of company-produced anti-union podcast episodes.[34]

Seattle city councillor Kshama Sawant told me that her office was hearing from Uber drivers that the company deactivated their app after they were more open about wanting to unionize. "This big corporation is using intimidation tactics to prevent the workers fighting for their rights," she says.

Attempts by ride-hailing drivers to organize strikes have faced serious challenges, especially since the app doesn't allow for drivers to connect to each other and Uber's driver Facebook page has reportedly deleted critical posts.[35] Surge pricing and last-minute promotions can be effective in encouraging drivers to break a strike.[36]

Another impediment to organizing is that many Uber drivers don't see themselves as being in the job for the long haul. This reduces the likelihood that they will risk their employment by struggling for better conditions.[37] Wells told me that many ride-hailing drivers haven't previously held jobs with full-time benefits, so the working conditions are not very different than what they're used to. Constant competition against other drivers for rides encourages them to keep their heads down. "The failures they had to make an income they believed were their own," Wells says. "They internalized the idea that they couldn't figure it out or they feel really sorry for other drivers who can't make it. They know that other people are failing."

The threat of autonomous vehicles is also used to deter drivers from organizing, the equivalent of the self-checkout for fast food workers.[38] Taxi and limo drivers are losing significant market share to Uber and Lyft, so they have to work far more hours to make the same amount of money.[39] Ride-hailing companies have also played direct roles in undermining labour actions by taxi drivers.[40]

Patterns of exploitation and anti-labour practices are found in the offices and factories of the next-generation automobile companies as well. Tesla has been the subject of multiple allegations of racism and unsafe working conditions.[41] Ambulances have been called to Tesla's factory in Fremont, California, hundreds of times since 2014 for workers experiencing health problems and injuries.[42] The factory reportedly lacks clearly marked safety lines because CEO Elon Musk dislikes the colour yellow—and the warning beeps of forklifts.[43] An investigation indicated that Tesla was reporting workplace injuries as "personal medical" cases, so they weren't counted on company reports. The number of work days per worker missed due to injuries and illness doubled at Tesla's Fremont factory in 2018, with two-thirds of injuries from cumulative trauma caused by repetitive stress.[44]

Tesla has also been repeatedly accused of unfair labour practices including illegal surveillance and intimidation to prevent workers organizing to unionize with United Auto Workers, causing the union to file multiple charges with the National Labor Relations Board.[45] In May 2018, the union filed a complaint with the agency over a tweet by Musk that implied unionizing would jeopardize worker stock options.[46] In September 2019, a judge ruled that Musk and other Tesla executives had violated labour laws by interfering with union organizing, including allowing security guards to harass workers distributing union pamphlets and prohibiting workers from wearing pro-union clothing.[47]

Tesla workers have said that "anything union or pro-union is shut down really fast" and that "pro-union people are generally fired for made-up reasons."[48] General Motors CEO Mary Barra said that Tesla's interest in buying one of its closing factories was dropped because Musk didn't want the company's unionized workers.[49] Tesla has opposed the introduction of a clause in California's electric vehicle rebate policy about manufacturers having to be "fair and responsible" in treatment of factory workers, as the company thinks it is part of UAW's plan to unionize its Fremont factory.[50]

Uber's offices have also been plagued with allegations of sexual harassment and systemic discrimination.[51] An internal investigation into sexual harassment claims conducted by Uber in the wake of major allegations resulted in more than twenty employees being fired.[52] In 2017, over 200 claims of sexual harassment or other inappropriate behaviour going back as far as 2012 were investigated by an outside law firm on behalf of the company, but Uber took action on only 58 cases.

In March 2018, Uber agreed to pay $10 million to settle a class-action lawsuit brought by over 400 female engineers and engineers of colour about discrimination in pay and hiring.[53] In July 2018, Uber's head of human resources Liane Hornsey resigned following an internal investigation into allegations of racial discrimination.[54] That same month, it was reported that Barney Harford—Uber's chief operating officer, hired by new CEO Dara Khosrowshahi to "help fix problems" at the company—was the subject of multiple complaints to human resources about incidents considered insensitive toward women and people of colour. Harford left the company a year later.[55]

The Heart of the Project

Chronic exploitation of workers is at the heart of the so-called electric and ride-hailing revolutions. And autonomous vehicles take concerns about labour to a new level: the entire project is an attempt to eradicate labour. Despite there being no immediate pathway to widespread deployment of the technology, Wells told me that all forty Uber drivers whom they interviewed in their research brought up the looming threat of autonomous vehicles on their own accord, unprompted.

It's consistent with the narrative of ride-hailing more generally. In 2016, Uber CEO Travis Kalanick said: "If we are not tied for first, then the person who is in first, or the entity that's in first, then rolls out a ridesharing network that is far cheaper or far higher-quality than Uber's, then Uber is no longer a thing."[56] A report prepared by consulting firm Roland Berger suggested that the erasure of driver costs is the only path to profitability for operators, who would go from a 227 percent loss in non-autonomous business as usual to a 10 percent gain by eliminating the driver and committing autonomous vehicles to both traditional routes and last-mile services.[57]

Yet resistance by drivers to the precarity of next-generation automobility is growing. In May 2019, just before Uber's initial public offering and only months after a similar action in San Francisco and Los Angeles, ride-hailing drivers around the world staged strikes and protests. Veena Dubal—professor of law at the University of California Hastings and a former taxi worker organizer—wrote in *Slate* that while Uber and Lyft didn't immediately raise driver wages or recognize unions as bargaining units, the strike should be considered a "huge, unprecedented victory for service workers in the on-demand platform economy."[58]

California's sweeping legislation, Assembly Bill 5 (AB-5), may force Uber and Lyft to have its workers classified as employees rather than independent contractors.[59] It's unclear what the future of AB-5 is at this point, but Uber has already responded by claiming that drivers aren't a core part of their business model and thus aren't employees.[60] Both Uber and Lyft are dedicating $60 million to fund a 2020 state ballot initiative that would keep drivers classified as less than employees through the creation of a new category for ride-hailing drivers.[61] Some labour unions have also been in talks with the companies to establish a compromise deal that would keep drivers categorized as independent contractors but with additional benefits.[62] Drivers will continue to fight for the right to organize but may be restricted by existing antitrust laws.[63]

Victories such as the strikes and California's AB-5 have been achieved thanks to the hard work by organizations like L.A.'s Rideshare Drivers United, the New York Taxi Workers Alliance, and Gig Workers Rising.[64] But fights against the profiteers of the three revolutions in automobility—whether organizing a union in Tesla's factory or demanding better pay for Uber and Lyft drivers—are extremely difficult to win. These fights will become increasingly difficult to win as the companies attract more investment and win over more milquetoast unions, and autonomous technologies get closer to commercial deployment. These fights must continue, with solidarity from transit riders and drivers. But to address environmental and economic justice, it's imperative that progressives struggle for good unionized transportation work on other fronts as well.

PUBLIC TRANSIT: CHALLENGES AND OPPORTUNITIES

Anti-labour Bias

The rhetoric of cost savings and labour reduction popularized by the "three revolutions" of automobility has wormed its way into communities and transit agencies across North America, exacerbating years of pre-existing austerity measures. Rather than respond to the threats of ride-hailing and autonomous vehicles with a radical increase in funding for public and active transportation, most governments have opted to pressure transit organizations to fight for their lives with the same or less money—which has pushed some into partnerships with the very ride-hailing companies that are destroying their business model.

Hanley told me: "There are threats to the transit system because they've artificially taken the floor out from the wage base and that creates an opportunity for transit agencies who have no conscience to use the lower wages as a way to rid themselves of workers who may have a decent wage. It's a way for transit agencies to disengage with the employment relationships they have by essentially using Uber and Lyft as third-party contractors."

This trend is having serious impacts on the opportunity for jobs and their quality. More ride-hailing cars on the road are worsening congestion, a factor that bus drivers have identified as impeding efficiency and increasing potential for altercations with passengers.[65] The allure of ride-hailing may also be "siphoning off would-be bus drivers," leaving the profession of bus driving in danger if it doesn't undergo a "radical makeover."[66]

Madeline Janis of Jobs to Move America told me that the entry of companies like Uber and Lyft also leads public transit agencies to cut costs when it comes to day-to-day operations such as purchasing new equipment and maintaining existing stock. "Rather than best value and the way they do procurement, it's always cheap," she says. "Maintenance is delayed and people are laid off and there's this push to privatize. There's a defensiveness that public agencies develop as they face the constant attack of everything that has to do with the public sector."

Automation poses additional threats to the future of transit drivers; it has the potential to wipe out tens of thousands of jobs. In 2016, Columbus, Ohio, won a $50 million grant to implement a "smart city" plan that includes automating transit, prompting the transit union local to hold a press conference at the state capitol opposing self-driving buses.[67] Transport Workers Union International president John Samuelsen said at the time that the threat of automation is a "not-so-thinly-veiled attack on the trade union movement."

Self-driving buses are expected to disproportionately affect Black drivers in the U.S. The president of an Ohio union local said, "It would be devastating in the African American community as predominantly the bus drivers are African American."[68] Public transit investments in the U.S. deliver the greatest job benefits for Black people, including construction, operations, and improving access to other employment opportunities.[69] In

Philadelphia, for example, nearly 60 percent of the workers at the city's transit agency are Black.[70]

Ride-hailing has certainly accelerated the assault on unionized transit workers. But such attacks stem from a history of privatized transportation and austerity politics that predate Uber and Lyft, and trace back to the systemic neglect of public forms of mobility. Rail modes like subways and streetcars are often promoted for their ability to carry more people with fewer drivers. Such modes are viewed as a way to challenge private car culture without adding too much to public expenditure. Expanding bus networks, which require more drivers and tend to have smaller capacity but service lower-income or lower-density areas, is a harder sell.

For example, transportation planner Dan Malouff of *BeyondDC* has written that one of the advantages of streetcars is reduced operational costs: "Fewer vehicles means more efficient use of fuel and fewer (unionized and pensioned) drivers to pay."[71] Similarly, Jarrett Walker argued in a 2010 post on the *Human Transit* blog that automation of the Vancouver SkyTrain allowed for high frequencies well into the night, and that requiring a driver would result in service cuts.[72]

These are accurate statements, technically speaking. But they each contain an unfortunate anti-labour bias that implies that the problem is wages and benefits rather than austerity and chronic underfunding. Subways and light rail are the most efficient modes of transportation—but they can't be seen as the only modes worth funding. Buses serve as the backbone of systems that connect low-income and lower-density areas. Light rail projects that result in the reduction of bus service are arguably an especially insidious form of cost-cutting.

In Ottawa, transit agency OC Transpo shut down bus lines, downsizing its bus fleet by 170 buses and laying off 345 staff in anticipation of the opening of its $2.1 billion light rail transit line—which was first proposed in 2012, well before ride-hailing was popularized. Almost all of the staff laid off were bus drivers.[73] Rather than using existing buses and drivers to connect riders to the new rail line, Ottawa sabotaged the effectiveness of the line by using it as an excuse to administer austerity.

The Rank and File

Transit agencies are also not immune to issues of exploitation and racism. In late 2018, the president of the ATU local that represents transit workers in London, Ontario, resigned. The union's members had voted that he step down after fostering a toxic environment and chronic lack of support around workplace harassment and discrimination.[74] Such a situation points to concerning issues within the transit labour movement about protection of abusive management. But it also represents the potential of the kind of workplace democracy that unions offer rank-and-file workers, who can collectively eject leaders who behave contrary to their values. While Uber CEO Travis Kalanick was eventually forced out of the company after a series of catastrophic mistakes, the ability for regular people and workers to fight for their rights and accountability is much greater in publicly owned, operated, and unionized services. In a private corporation, executives are ultimately accountable only to a handful of board members and influential shareholders.

There are many examples of transit unions protecting their members. In 2016, in response to a grievance from ATU Local 113, a provincial arbitrator required Toronto's TTC to create a social media policy to better protect transit workers from targeted harassment on its social media account.[75] Transport Workers Union Local 100 successfully pressured New York's MTA to remove advertisements for the Museum of Sex from the front of buses in mid-2018, as they had allegedly resulted in increased sexual harassment of female bus drivers.[76]

Members of ATU Local 689 refused to service three private Metro rail cars that were to be provided to white nationalists travelling to a Unite the Right rally in Washington, DC, in August 2018.[77] The union said in a statement: "More than 80 percent of Local 689's membership is people of color, the very people that the Ku Klux Klan and other white nationalist groups have killed, harassed and violated. The union has declared that it will not play a role in their special accommodation."

Time after time, transit unions have fought for and often won improvements in wages, benefits, safety, anti-discrimination policies, annual leave, and workplace conditions.[78] As a result, compared to Uber and Lyft drivers, transit workers have better pay, more predictable hours, and (quite obviously) don't have to cover work expenses. Belonging to a union also gives employees the power to take workplace action such as striking if collective bargaining fails to secure a fair deal, something that is inaccessible to non-unionized employees and contractors in the private sector.

Above and Beyond

Transit operators perform many functions that autonomous vehicles are incapable of. There are countless examples of drivers going above and beyond the regular function of operating the vehicle to aid other people.[79]

An Edmonton bus driver, Derek Bailey, saw a man slumped over in a bus shelter in −20°F windchill conditions, brought him on board the bus, and called paramedics for help. "Had he been out there for maybe another hour, two at the most, he would have frozen to death," said Bailey.[80] A New York bus driver grabbed a student's hood as the student was exiting the bus, just as a car sped by that would have hit them.[81] Bus drivers have saved a toddler from wandering alone in freezing conditions, driven passengers to safety in a shooting spree despite being wounded themselves, and administered CPR to pedestrians who have collapsed on the side of the road.[82] Drivers have rescued a young boy with a disability from oncoming traffic, helped an elderly woman carry her groceries from the bus to her home, and blocked other vehicles to ensure that a goose and goslings got across the road safely.[83] These are situations that autonomous vehicles will never be able to replicate.

Transit workers and unions can collaborate with riders

to improve conditions for everyone. Bus drivers in Winnipeg went on a two "fare strikes" in 2019 to protest underfunding, workplace safety, and fare hikes.[84] Inspired by similar actions in Okayama, Japan, and Sydney, Australia, the fare strikes maintained regular bus service but elected not to inform riders of the requirement to pay.[85] Such job actions show a collaborative approach that maintains good relations with passengers and unites drivers' and passengers' struggles.

Free transit is widely understood as being in the interest of driver safety and quality of work.[86] A survey conducted in 2016 by the Amalgamated Transit Union found that 73.6 percent of assaults are the result of fare disputes, while another 35.1 percent are caused by inadequate service.[87] Policing fare collection can be a stressful additional task for bus drivers, who are required to bear the brunt of anger about high fares and unreliable service. It also helps justify the hiring of dozens of transit enforcement officers, using money that could otherwise be used to improve service quality.

In ride-hailing and autonomous vehicle services, users have no control over the price. But transit operators and riders can successfully team up to pressure their local governments to freeze or decrease fares. Hanley told me about organizing between operators and riders: "Frankly, I'm disappointed that we don't do it more often. We encourage and train our local officers to get out there and organize with the riders. Where they do it, they succeed in improving transit." A March 2018 issue of *In Transit,* the ATU's member publication, highlighted several rider groups across North America that the union worked with. It reported collaborating with Clevelanders for Public Transit to fight against fare hikes and service cuts, and with Portland's Bus Riders Unite, which helped win a low-income transit pass and free student transit for two schools in an underserved part of the city.[88]

There is also potential for more organizing between transit operators and drivers for ride-hailing services and taxi companies. After all, it's not enough to tell drivers in already precarious job situations that they're going to lose a work opportunity if Uber or Lyft is banned from a city or congestion pricing prevents cabs from entering the downtown. Efforts to try to unionize ride-hailing drivers are a good example of this—but limited if the drivers can't legally unionize. A more promising struggle may be to include greatly expanded public transportation as part of a sweeping environmental program, with a priority on hiring drivers who are currently working for ride-hailing and taxi companies, including a variety of rural transportation options.

Dubal told me that ride-hailing drivers often think about concepts like the Green New Deal: "When you're in meetings, drivers are constantly talking about the environmental impacts that these companies are making on cities, on roads, traffic congestion, accidents, all that stuff." She adds that a vehicle cap, like the taxi medallion system that restricts the number of for-hire cars on the road, is beneficial for both wages and climate impacts of ride-hailing.

Ride-hailing services and autonomous vehicle fleets are an attempt to dodge and undermine labour rights at every level, with the long-term goal of eradicating the very need for workers. So far, many governments have allowed it to happen without much opposition. But the response to such pressures should not be to cede even more ground to the logic and demands of new automotive companies.

We must work instead to prioritize public transportation as the primary mode of mobility in communities. This would help to provide jobs for such workers, as well as opportunities for "just transition" employment out of the fossil fuel economy and into manufacturing, maintaining, and operating complex machinery like buses, trains, and subways. Such demands can easily include nationalization for the purposes of manufacturing electrified transit vehicles. For example, in response to the announced closure of the General Motors factory in Oshawa, Ontario, labour leaders called for the nationalization of the plant to maintain jobs and manufacture electric vehicles for

Canada Post.[89] There's an excellent precedent for this: in 1971 the Manitoba government nationalized the bus manufacturer that would eventually become New Flyer Industries, the largest bus producer in North America (though the province privatized it in 1986).[90]

This vision slots in perfectly with demands formulating around the proposed Green New Deal, with popular interpretations of the plan including nationalization of fossil fuel companies, electric utilities, and housing.[91] Centring public transportation in this transition as a means to create good unionized work seems particularly intuitive. Such efforts would help provide highly liberatory and ecological job opportunities—with technologies like automation integrated in a way that promotes human well-being and the right to the city, rather than further promoting anti-labour principles.

Part Three

Destination >>> Destination >>> Destination >>> Destination

Chapter 10

Money and the power

The issue has never really been technological. It's a matter of political priorities.

THE STRUGGLE CONTINUES

By now, it should be clear that genuinely public transportation offers a range of existing and potential benefits over the unlikely promises made by boosters of the "three revolutions" in automobility:

> climate and environment
> racial and economic equality
> safer and less congested communities
> accessibility for seniors, people with disabilities, and women, trans, and gender non-conforming people
> data privacy and surveillance
> rural and intercity service
> strengthened labour rights

The existing limitations of public transportation have been acknowledged, and potential solutions identified. On every issue, it is clear what's required to achieve justice and equality in transportation. Together, transit riders and potential riders, transit workers and all workers, need to struggle against the well-funded forces of Tesla, Uber, and Waymo that seek to remake communities to further entrench private capital accumulation, and for public transportation that prioritizes people over profits.

Some progressive transportation advocates hypothesize about nationalizing services like Uber and Lyft, bringing them under democratic control to maximize their potential for public good.[1] One example imagined that "rideshares could be run by national councils of workers and riders, collaborating with public transportation agencies to ensure an efficient and environmentally friendly transit system."[2] It's a very appealing notion. But it also presupposes that such services could continue to exist without outrageously wasteful subsidies from venture capitalists—or that they should continue to exist at all given their incredible spatial inefficiencies, emissions impacts, and slowing down of other modes. There's really nothing to nationalize outside of an app, a brand, and continued automobility.

Outside the largest of municipalities, even attempting to regulate the services can be fraught with difficulties. If we desire safer, denser, and more human-scaled cities and towns, we must seriously recommit to public ownership and operation of communal transportation, along with limiting the usage of private automobiles in all forms. There's no way around it: services like Uber and Lyft should be abolished, replaced with high-quality transit. We must seize this moment of crisis for truly democratic involvement, with transit riders and workers having actual power over planning.

After thirty years of neoliberalization and experiments with P3s, it's time to challenge the mythology that the private sector is intrinsically more efficient or better suited to constructing large-scale infrastructure projects and services. Existing agencies can provide far better service through buses, trains, and smaller vehicles as appropriate.

As Junfeng Jiao of the University of Texas at Austin, who studies food deserts and transportation planning, told me: "Innovation doesn't just belong to the startups. Public transit can also do innovation, and actually have more motivation to do that. We should change our minds about the idea that only Uber and Lyft can use apps. Public companies and government can use innovation as well. As a matter of fact, maybe more."

HOW WILL WE PAY FOR IT?

Austerity has seriously compromised transit systems across the country. The question of funding thus underpins the future of transit and communities. A resistance against privatization, data hoarding, and declining democratic oversight is more than a nice idea. Practically, it means finding an enormous amount of resources to build new infrastructure like bus rapid transit lines, light rail, subways, electric buses, intercity buses, rural transit, and high-speed rail; along with retrofits to existing systems to install elevators in stations, improve ventilation in tunnels, climate-proof transit routes, and ensure up-to-date and easily usable timetables at stops.

There is an immediate need to hire more unionized drivers, cut or eliminate fares, create public transit apps, improve snow clearing on sidewalks, set up adequate bus shelters for both heat and cold, provide training in de-escalation, anti-racism, and conflict resolution for workers and riders, and build out public housing through nationalization and direct ownership.

For many policy wonks, money is the start and the end of the conversation. These ideas could drastically help improve the lives of many people, but who is going to pay for them? How would we actually cover the costs of building the communities that we dream of?

The first thing to remember is that we are already paying an astronomical amount for the existing autocentric transportation system. Individual households are shelling out thousands of dollars a year in car costs, including gas, insurance, maintenance, and parking. Hundreds of dollars more are spent per household in taxes that go directly into road construction and repair, as well as for a wide range of subsidies like income tax exclusions for commuter parking and electric vehicle rebates.

Then there are the short-term and long-term healthcare costs resulting from collisions, air pollution, and mental health impacts resulting from forced isolation. Or consider the tremendous land-use impacts resulting from urban sprawl, highways, and parking, including lack of housing, destruction of wetlands, and road salt runoff. Perhaps the largest cost of all is yet to come: the catastrophic impacts of climate change, which will increase the frequency, intensity, and duration of extreme weather events such as flooding, wildfires, and droughts. All of these impacts hit low-income people the hardest, particularly Black and Indigenous communities.

The narrative that public transportation costs "too much money" ignores the tremendous amount that's currently being shelled out, and that's assumed to be the price we must pay for mobility. In reality, transportation costs have been heavily privatized to individual owners through ownership costs, with the construction and funding of necessary infrastructure like roads and parking lots subsidized by the state.

In 2010, the total economic costs of motor vehicle crashes in the U.S.—including lifetime costs for fatalities, injuries, and damaged vehicles—was $242 billion.[3] When lost quality of life was factored in, that number ballooned to $836 billion. A data tool designed by transportation engineer George Poulos in 2015 to assess Metro Vancouver's transportation costs found that for every $1 a car owner paid to drive, society paid $9.20 in road infrastructure, pollution, crashes, and noise.[4] In comparison, riding the bus only costs society $1.50 for every $1 paid, while cycling costs 8 cents and walking a single cent.[5]

Governments are spending tens of billions of dollars on new highways every year, locking themselves into costly maintenance and repairs for the distant future at an estimated cost, in the U.S., of $24,000 per mile every year.[6] Phasing out—or least seriously curbing—automotive travel would free up significant money for other purposes, including public transportation; while some public transportation will still require roads, the amount of square footage required will inevitably decline.

Some municipalities have tried to impose taxes on ride-hailing services to make them pay for impacts on roads, congestion, and emissions. In June 2018, Washington, DC, voted to increase the tax on ride-hailing receipts from 1 percent to 6 percent, with 83 percent of that revenue going to the Washington Metropolitan Area Transit Authority.[7] Other cities—including New York, San Francisco, and Chicago—have implemented similar taxes to better fund public transportation.[8] These are strong proposals that help expand transit infrastructure over the course of decades. But they also lock a certain amount of ride-hailing into a city, with the transit agency becoming partly dependent for funding on companies that are explicitly attempting to undermine their service. Such tools should be seen as helping to mitigate the increased threat of automobility—but nothing much beyond that.

Congestion pricing—charging each driver a price to enter a specific area, usually a downtown region—is another favoured policy of neoliberal urbanists. A five-pound-per-day congestion price was implemented for central London in 2003 under mayor Ken Livingstone. The primary beneficiary of the revenue was buses: 300 new buses were introduced onto London's streets on the same day that the policy was launched.[9] Daniel Aldana Cohen told me that Livingstone's focus on buses was "very much an equity and social justice story," as buses are how working-class people tend to get around in the city. Entrance of cars into the zone has decreased by 44 percent since its introduction, with cycling up by 66 percent.[10]

Compare that approach to mayor Michael Bloomberg's PlaNYC proposal in 2008.[11] It featured a flagship policy of congestion pricing, but with a far less justice-oriented investment approach; the plan was to put a significant chunk of the revenue into commuter rail service to the downtown Manhattan business district that would primarily serve affluent riders. As a result, Cohen says there was a larger gap in support for congestion pricing between rich and poor residents. "In New York, congestion pricing was very much viewed as a pro-elite option that was going to benefit wealthy New Yorkers and would do nothing for working-class New Yorkers who lived further away," Cohen told me. "They didn't see any prospect for investment helping them."

There are lingering equity concerns with congestion pricing; rich drivers can absorb the costs, while less well-off drivers have to find an alternative or pay a larger proportion of their income. Immediate funding to add buses and trains can offer those alternatives—but if that funding is available, it brings up the question of why a congestion price is needed in the first place.

Paul Mees argued in *Transport for Suburbia* that the benefits of congestion pricing tended to be overhyped. Peak-period car trips to central London had been declining for years before the measure was introduced, and the congestion charge is actually beneficial for wealthy motorists, as streets would be less crowded for those who could afford it. Counterintuitively, he suggested that congestion should be viewed as beneficial: it creates a strong demand for alternatives like dedicated transitways.[12]

Like carbon taxes and other user fees, congestion pricing can create disproportionate political backlash that undermines support for other policies.[13] Transit already tends to be considerably cheaper than driving; the impediment to usage is overwhelmingly poor service, not the price of driving. Adding further cost to the notoriously inelastic sector of transportation fails to provide drivers with a serious alternative.[14]

Other cities around the world are simply banning cars from their downtowns or removing parking spaces. Starting in November 2018, Madrid prohibited all vehicles in its downtown aside from those belonging to residents who live within the area, electric delivery vehicles, taxis, and public transit.[15] Oslo announced plans to ban cars by 2019, but backlash from business interests pressured the city to delay implementation and instead ban parking.[16] These are strong proposals, which will help limit automobile usage and expand transit infrastructure over the course of decades. But if we want to radically and immediately confront the intersecting crises of climate change, racist and classist segregation, lack of accessibility for seniors, people with disabilities, and women, trans, and gender non-conforming people, and ever-increasingly deadly traffic, we'll have to dream much bigger.

DEMOCRATIC CONTROL

The power of transit isn't simply about helping people get from one place to another in a timely and free way—although it is, of course, that. The fight for genuinely public transportation is one for democratic control over communities. The universal right to transportation serves as a foundation of a broader struggle against capitalist commodification and exploitation.

Bus network designs and congestion pricing are fine in theory. But they often keep power in the hands of technocrats and away from communities of low-income riders and transit workers who have the best sense of the limitations that hold systems back. The world under neoliberalism is already intricately planned by capitalists, developers, and landlords. Our struggle is to seize those existing powers and deploy them democratically through planning councils and community organizations populated by transit riders and workers.

It's not enough to rejig a few zoning bylaws and developer regulations, or even pick better routes that serve low-income communities. We have to confront the extreme wealth that holds our governments hostage and deprives transit systems of the funds they need for a rapid escalation in service, access, and affordability. Enormous amounts of money are being hoarded by capitalists and used for their political gain—resources that can and should be used for public transit, housing, social services, and more.

According to a 2018 report by the Economic Policy Institute, the top 1 percent of families in the U.S. earned an average of 26.3 times as much income as the bottom 99 percent; that ratio increases to 44.4 times in New York and 39.5 times in Florida.[17] As of late 2017, the three richest people in the U.S.—Bill Gates of Microsoft, Jeff Bezos of Amazon, and Warren Buffett of Berkshire Hathaway—own the equal amount of wealth as the bottom 160 million people in the country.[18] Bezos's company, Amazon, earned $11.2 billion in profits in 2018 but didn't pay a single dollar in federal income tax, and instead received $129 million in tax breaks and credits.[19] In January 2017, Oxfam reported that two men in Canada—David Thomson of Thomson Reuters and Galen Weston Sr. of George Weston Limited—had the same amount of wealth as the bottom 30 percent of the country.[20]

Trump's Tax Cuts and Jobs Act of 2017 cut the highest tax bracket from 39.6 percent to 37 percent (while also increasing the income threshold), doubling the estate tax deduction and slashing the corporate income tax rate from 35 percent to 21 percent.[21] The bill also cut the rate of corporate income coming back to the U.S. from foreign jurisdictions and exempted foreign income from U.S. tax. At the time, the tax changes were predicted to cost an incredible $2.3 trillion over ten years.[22] Advocates for corporate income tax cuts said the policy would increase investment by companies, in turn creating more jobs and spending. Yet a January 2018 analysis indicated that 36 percent of gains were going to shareholders in the form of share buybacks and dividends, 23 percent to capital expenditure, and only 12 percent to higher worker wages.[23] In August 2018, Goldman Sachs predicted that U.S. companies would hit $1 trillion in share buybacks over the year, calling it "a direct result of tax reform."[24]

As revealed by the Panama Papers—and promptly ignored—an astonishing amount of money is being offshored by the rich; economist Gabriel Zucman pegs the total at a minimum of $7.6 trillion. The organization Tax Justice Network estimates tax haven hoarding at between $21 and $31 trillion.[25]

Unless such incredible inequities are meaningfully addressed, it will be impossible for transit agencies to massively improve their systems at the rate and scope needed to avoid catastrophic climate change and another generation's worth of racist and classist transportation policies. The continued enforced use of automotive modes—including privately owned vehicles, ride-hailing services, and autonomous fleets—represents a further privatization of transportation and dodging of the desperate need to redistribute wealth to build legitimately public transportation.

Extreme concentrations of capital plague cities and towns with rampant gentrification, real estate speculation, uneven development, and violently unpredictable employment patterns that undermine any ability to publicly plan in an effective manner. Ending such destructive chaos requires the decommodification of housing and planning through the mass buildout of public stock and nationalization of key sectors of economies.

"Everybody will agree that we need better transit, but in order for that you need a political and social movement that is demanding that the super wealthy and big business be taxed in order to expand those investments," Kshama Sawant of Seattle City Council told me. "You can't do it on the backs of already burdened working people. We need to tax big business and the wealthy to massively expand public transportation, and to make it affordable or free to everybody, and to make it possible that people don't have to drive their cars every day and not depend on app-based corporations and entirely rely on public transportation. That automatically means putting working people and the environment first, not the interest of Uber's profits."

Governments spend a phenomenal amount of money on institutions such as the military, policing, prisons, and courts. They take up ever-increasing portions of budgets while imposing punishment and surveillance on predominantly low-income communities of colour—the same communities that have the worst access to affordable transportation. A February 2017 report by the Prison Policy Initiative estimated that mass incarceration in the U.S. costs $182 billion per year.[26] Such systems are both extremely cost-intensive and deeply racialized, devastating entire low-income communities of colour with family separation, unemployment, and disenfranchised voting rights. In a cruel twist, New York governor Andrew Cuomo is now expanding transit police powers by spending $249 million over four years to hire an additional five hundred officers, instead of working toward the far cheaper option of abolishing fares and improving service.[27]

We can reallocate massive funding for military and carceral institutions that destroy the lives of people in low-income communities in the Global North and entire countries in the Global South into areas like public transportation. Such a shift would help address long-standing racial and class-based oppressions. It would also drastically reduce greenhouse gas emissions, which have the greatest impacts on such communities.

These issues have the potential to bring together many different struggles. *Rights in Transit* author Kafui Attoh says that the most successful transit campaigns have been those that knit together labour groups, environmental organizations, and community members.[28] Attoh told me: "The ecological crisis and economic crisis are collective action problems. The solution lies in cooperation. Solving the ecological crisis means we have to cooperate with other nations and other people to solve something that goes beyond our borders and households. Public transit represents the ethos that is required to solve those problems, as well as a practical solution: more buses rather than cars. I feel like it captures everything."

Yet the class implications of transit policies aren't always obvious to the public. Cohen says that community members looking to organize around such issues need to become "way more interested" in building compelling narratives and class-based coalitions. Sawant says Seattle's increasing of the minimum wage to $15 per hour by 2021, following community organizing by fast food workers, unions, and political groups, is an example of how to "build to struggle against a billionaire class and political establishment that is hostile to working people and environmental goals."

There is plenty of desire for this kind of shift. In an early 2019 poll, the proposal by Rep. Alexandria Ocasio-Cortez to tax incomes above $10 million at a rate of 70 percent received support from 59 percent of registered voters.[29] Similar support is present in Canada: 69 percent of respondents to a 2019 federal poll think that the rich should be taxed more—and only 27 percent believe that corporations are paying a fair share.[30] At a far more fundamental level, the collection of any profits in the first place depends on the theft of surplus value from workers, environmental destruction, and maintaining of colonial dispossession of Indigenous peoples from their lands. Viewing the world through such a lens, "fair taxation" isn't nearly enough—we need to dream far bigger.

No matter how good our plans are for a just transition from fossil fuels, the ideas won't matter unless we can take genuinely public control of the production and distribution of industries, including transportation, housing, and energy. Consumption "choices" like driving and suburban living are available in a capitalist system only because automobiles,

> "There are ways to build public transit in ways that are more equitable, but the root of the issue is that cities are essentially just machines of capital at this point, and they're not really meant as livable communities. Until we solve the root of that problem, there's never going to be an adequately built public transit network because that's not the point of cities according to the people running them."
>
> —P.E. MOSKOWITZ, author, *How to Kill a City*

suburban homes, and the resources required to fuel them are profitable to produce.[31]

Some busy transit lines may be profitable—but many are not, especially feeder lines from low-income and low-density neighbourhoods. Politicians looking for excuses to privatize or close down transit services can erode the remaining profitability over time. The response to this trend should not be to argue for transit on the merits of potential moneymaking; that is buying into the logic of capitalism that prioritizes exchange over use value. Our struggles should be grounded in the decommodification of society, funding programs and services with resources expropriated from rich households and corporations.

ORGANIZING AND SOLIDARITY

To respond to these realities, we must expand what constitutes transit activism and ground it in struggles by organized (or organizing) labour. Though the neoliberal onslaught has left it weakened and often compromised, organized labour remains one of the most powerful vehicles for change in society. As *Lifeblood* author Matthew Huber and others have observed, labour unions have long fought for environmental and social gains. For example, the Oil, Chemical and Atomic Workers Union agitated in the 1960s for the Occupational Health and Safety Administration that helped limit the spread of toxic chemicals into both workers and communities.[32]

Labour organizer Jane McAlevey has written extensively about the importance of "whole-worker organizing" that attempts to integrate the issues facing workers in every aspect of their communities.[33] By "bargaining for the common good," workers in different sectors—healthcare, education, government, hospitality—can include demands for improved transit service, accessibility, and funding when they negotiate contracts or threaten strike action.

For non-transit workers, organizing and solidarity work

with transit unions is the most obvious step, supporting protracted contract negotiations or calls for mass strikes and free transit.[34] But workers in all sectors can agitate for better transit to their workplaces and communities. In turn, organized labour can "raise the floor" for everyone, regardless of whether they work in the same industry—or work at all. For example, United Teachers Los Angeles won more green spaces on school properties from their 2019 strike, an environmental benefit that may not be immediately associated with the interests of teachers.[35] The teachers also won a series of anti-carceral demands, including an end to "random" searches of students and an immigrant defence fund with a dedicated hotline and attorney.[36]

Class-based campaigns for better transit must be organized alongside other unions and organizations fighting for public housing, food justice, and harm reduction. The struggle will take place at city council meetings, picket lines, union halls, community boards, and bus stops. Activism is often inflated, or caricatured, into something far grander than it needs to be. It means talking to people, using tools like petitions, panel discussions, postering, and elections to give ambitious ideas a platform and connect people's daily lives with policy changes. More than anything, it's about helping people realize their own power.

Community-organized town-hall-style meetings can be excellent places to give working-class residents an opportunity to voice their perspectives about transportation issues. It isn't always easy: many such meetings are overwhelmingly attended by affluent residents. As author Steven Higashide put it: "Some of these actors can be persuaded or bargained with. More often, transit reformers have to outmaneuver, out-organize, and outvote them."[37] But with some basic organizing techniques and a commitment to struggling over years or decades with fellow transit riders and workers, such skills can be developed and political ground can be gained. Transit riders' unions winning lower fares and increased service hours are proof of this. It just takes work.

Activists can also push for programs such as free twelve-month transit passes to drivers who trade in their old inefficient clunkers, like those available in Montreal and British Columbia.[38] Gun buyback programs can serve as inspirations for such a transition, seeking to remove dangerous items from the public in exchange for cash or other incentives. If New Zealand can pay out over $60 million in compensation for 56,000 prohibited weapons, why can't we do the same for automobiles?[39] Canada's "Retire Your Ride" program that ran between 2009 and 2011 sets a similar precedent, removing 120,000 vehicles with a model year 1995 or earlier from the roads in exchange for cash, car-sharing credits, commuter bike discounts, or rebates toward a new vehicle.[40] A future iteration could frame a buyback as a phasing out of automobility, not simply an opportunity to buy a newer model.

Orienting struggles around fare-free transit and demanding that transportation be recognized as a universal service is another way to knit together movements for climate, economic equality, accessibility, and more. But lower or free fares can only truly be appealing if reliable service is guaranteed. That requires a radical reconfiguration of road space and funding to prioritize collective forms of transportation: less highway funding, more transit spending.[41]

Transit success is a virtuous cycle: it can difficult for people to imagine the benefits of a dedicated bus lane or an all-door boarding system until it's implemented. Every small success is a step in that direction. Projects can't just be one-off pilots: the focus must be on building a scalable and coordinated system of transit service. Such campaigns should also emphasize the massive potential for good, unionized work resulting from transit expansion, whether it's manufacturing electric buses and trains, driving the vehicles, or maintaining and cleaning them.[42] Public transit is about far more than transportation:

it contains the possibility of communal prosperity, unionized work, and control over our own labour.

PUBLIC SOLUTIONS FOR THE PUBLIC GOOD

The rise of ride-hailing services like Uber and Lyft and autonomous vehicles like Waymo and General Motors' Cruise isn't the result of technical superiority. All of the solutions are already out there, in the form of buses, streetcars, light rail, subways, commuter trains, motor coaches, intercity rail (with dedicated tracks), bicycles, and sidewalks. Technology can always be improved, but the issue has never really been technological. It's a matter of political priorities—who has the power and control to shape their own communities and destinies.

Over the decades, politicians at every level of government have fallen in line with the narrative that communities should be built around the personal vehicle, an intentional process tracing back to the start of the twentieth century, one that rendered other forms of transportation far less viable due to sprawling communities and more dangerous roads. It resulted in racial segregation, food deserts, lack of access to employment and other critical services, destruction of entire communities and ecosystems, the spewing of greenhouse gases and air pollution, millions of deaths and serious injuries, a profound sense of alienation from our communities—and much more.

Ride-hailing services like Uber and Lyft can't fix these problems. Tighter regulations around labour practices, wages, environmental impact, and congestion can help limit the worst excesses of the glorified taxi services—but the existence of such companies presupposes the continuation of many of those very conditions. They will lobby heavily against governments to resist changes. Ride-hailing services must be fought at every opportunity, whether it's defending communities from their entrance in the first place or, if it's too late, implementing geo-fencing, vehicle caps, and other regulations with the end goal of removing them entirely.

It's unclear if these companies even have a future. Given the fundamental inefficiencies of the service, there's no way they can make a profit without massive hikes in fares. But regardless of how long they last, they continue to inflict massive damages on communities, further extending the life of automobility and convincing policymakers to opt for austerity over transit.

As far as autonomous vehicle companies go, there are already major warning signs: a rabid focus on private data collection and monetization, a refusal to handing over safety information to regulators, a tendency to blame anyone but themselves for accidents, a failure to guarantee accessibility for people with disabilities, the buying up of hybrid vehicles instead of full electrics to maximize profits, the moralizing by advocates that pedestrians will have to "learn" not to jaywalk, and no clear indication of long-term plans about how they expect to ensure that vehicles are primarily shared. These technologies fail to confront some of the most serious impacts of automobility.

Autonomous vehicles are being designed by some of the biggest and most profitable companies in the world, including Google, General Motors, Ford, Uber, and Tesla. The motivations of these companies and financial interests are not to benefit residents of low-income communities that have suffered decades of transportation-related discrimination. After all, they're the same players that, via automotive lobby groups, helped inflict such devastation in the first place. Their obligations are to investors and shareholders, not to the public good.

These companies view our communities as sites of capital accumulation, not of collective well-being. While autonomous vehicles could feasibly make advances in some areas and benefit some riders, the costs will likely be far greater, especially if they further destroy their ultimate competitor of public transportation. Zipcar co-founder Robin Chase often speaks of the "heaven" or "hell" scenario when it comes to autonomous vehicles. It's clearly intended as a metaphor. But the hell scenario could well manifest literally, accelerating the planet into catastrophic climate change, ending society as we know it—with the worst effects in countries in the Global South and low-income communities of colour in the Global North. The racist horrors of Hurricanes Katrina and Maria would only be the beginning.

There would be no second chance. Catastrophic climate change would be the end of the line for many communities. And as the seas rise and the forests burn, private companies would have unprecedented quantities of our personal data to help usher in even greater surveillance and advertising, which they would then subject us to as we try to get around what remains of the world. Why take that risk, leaving the fate of humanity in the same financial and political hands that helped bring us to this point?

Incredible amounts of resources and talent are being poured into designing a technology without clear socially beneficial purpose. Its purpose is only to beat out competitors, eradicate human labour, and make already unfathomably wealthy people far more money. If investments continue, something close to full autonomy will likely be perfected in the decades to come. But technology is deeply political; this time and energy could be spent on many other things, like painting bus lanes, expanding social housing, installing elevators, leading workshops on anti-racist and conflict resolution, and restoring wetlands.

THE FUTURE AWAITS

Public transportation works. It's immediately deployable. Entire communities can be overhauled in a few short years to reorient around free transportation. Municipalities can slash greenhouse gas emissions, reduce congestion, convert previously busy streets into wider sidewalks and cycle tracks, decrease fatalities, greatly improve accessibility for seniors and people with disabilities, and reduce assault and harassment of women, trans, and gender non-conforming people in public spaces. The strengthening of public transportation can be combined with many other social movements: communities struggling for housing rights, minimum wage increases, unionized and dignified work, abolition of policing and incarceration, better healthcare, and improved community safety and resiliency. Along the way, genuine alternatives to ride-hailing and taxis can be supported by public transit agencies.

Transit is most importantly a source of political and social power. Wresting it back from the brink of privatization and partnerships with Silicon Valley–backed demagogues will be an incredible challenge. But it will be a first step into more livable, collective, genuinely public social relations. The bigger and more geographically wide the demands are, the better service we can win. Transit systems thrive on coordination and easy transfers between systems, which can only be accomplished with collective planning.

This movement will likely require the same tools as social movements have used in the past: door-knocking, petitioning and canvassing, direct actions, strikes and other militant labour struggle, lawsuits, research, marches, educational sessions, expressions of mutual aid. As Cohen and others have argued, it's less about having the right technical facts for a debate than about painting a vision of a better, more equitable and environmentally sustainable society (although having the right facts certainly helps, and provides opportunities for nerdy researchers to get involved).[43] That vision is one of shared power: among workers, tenants, bus riders, migrants, people with disabilities, youth, and seniors. We can debate the specifics in the process, like whether we prefer a trolleybus or light rail on a particular street, or which highway should be prioritized for depaving and restoration. The foundational principle of radical transit politics is one of togetherness—which in turn means a coherent opposition to white supremacy, anti-migrant xenophobia, ableism, and union-busting.

Communities have been fighting for truly public transportation for many decades. Back in the 1920s, that meant rallying against the incursion of automobiles in their cities. Rosa Parks's refusal in 1955 to move to the back of a racially segregated bus in Montgomery, Alabama, which triggered the Montgomery bus boycott, was a pivotal moment in civil rights history but should also be remembered as a form of transit justice.[44] Jane Jacobs faced off against Robert Moses over the Lower Manhattan Expressway in the 1960s, highway revolts stopped or slowed new freeway construction, ADAPT rolled into traffic in the 1970s, Barbara Lott-Holland and Eric Mann organized the Bus Riders Union in Los Angeles in the 1990s, and ongoing Google bus blockades in San Francisco kicked off in 2013.[45] Transit organizing is rapidly picking up momentum around the world as a response to the climate emergency, including by young organizers pairing it with the Youth Climate Strike.[46]

Transit riders' unions are resisting attempts by neoliberal politicians to further decimate transit, while courageous transit unions are going on fare strikes to demand better working conditions.[47] Indigenous activists across Canada are demanding reliable intercity transit.[48] Countless more efforts have occurred in communities across the U.S. and Canada. Not all of them resulted in victory. There have been setbacks and disappointments. But they are all inspiring attempts by communities to struggle for better conditions—something that, outside of a purely defensive position to hold back the technologies' worst excesses, simply can't be done with ride-hailing and autonomous vehicles. We need to build the alternatives to fill the void that allowed these monstrosities to emerge in the first place.

This book started with an acknowledgement of the dire shape that public transit is in. There's no use denying that reality. At almost every turn, politicians across the U.S. and Canada have failed to make the necessary funding and prioritization to massively improve public transportation—and they're now taking advantage of electric cars, ride-hailing services, and autonomous vehicles as excuses to never make those investments. They're also sustaining the mirage of fiscal responsibility by further privatizing what should be public services.

There are many existing flaws in the systems, especially those that have been successfully disciplined by capital to orient their service around profits, real estate values, private employers, and political gain. That can change. It must change, if we want to live in places committed to addressing climate change, environmental destruction, air pollution, and urban sprawl; that oppose invasive surveillance, data hoarding, and racist discrimination; that reject precarious work and privatized services; that see alternatives to traffic fatalities, isolated rural communities, and inaccessible infrastructure. Public transit can't be the only focus; related issues include wages, housing, harm reduction, healthcare—and the entire capitalist, colonial economic order that runs and ruins our society. But transit is an essential part of the struggle.

A future of ecological, reliable, free, and accessible public transportation awaits us. It will require years of committed fighting against the forces of austerity, white supremacy, and automotive dominance in both old and new forms. But it's a struggle that we must win to survive—and to build a much more beautiful world.

Acknowledgements

This book is the product of conversations with dozens of experts who generously took time to speak with a random journalist from Winnipeg. These participants are listed in full on the next page. Additionally, I relied heavily on the invaluable published writings and research of the following journalists: Angie Schmitt, Laura Bliss, Andrew J. Hawkins, Johana Bhuiyan, Amir Efrati, Alissa Walker, Oliver Moore, Aaron Gordon, Ben Spurr, Eric Jaffe, and Noam Scheiber.

Paris Marx's *Radical Urbanist* newsletter was a frequent source of inspiration; Paris frequently helped me wrap my head around new transportation technologies and fads. Many others have been leading advocates of better transit for long before my time, and I learned a great deal from their works: Mimi Sheller, Paul Mees, Jarrett Walker, Jonathan English, Samuel Schwartz, Christof Spieler, Todd Litman, and Robert Cervero. The twin forces of Bruce Schaller and Hubert Horan have played an enormous and undervalued role, which I am deeply grateful for, in dismantling the tech-journalist-created hype about ride-hailing companies.

This book wouldn't have happened without all the incredible people at Between the Lines Books: Amanda Crocker, who first reached out about the idea, as well as Renée Knapp and David Bush. Tilman Lewis was a truly incredible editor to work with, who greatly improved the quality of the work with a genuine kindness and investment in the subject. Many thanks to Danesh Mohiuddin for his remarkable work on the cover art, which many people have expressed a love of.

Countless friends in Winnipeg and across Canada also worked to keep me excited and invested in this book at the times that felt especially overwhelming. That includes all my friends on Twitter, most of whom I haven't had the pleasure of meeting yet in person (you know who you are).

ACKNOWLEDGEMENTS

Endless thanks to my supervisor, Jonathan Peyton, for his constant support, encouragement, and flexibility while I worked on a giant project that wasn't my master's thesis. Massive love to my parents, Brenda and Garth, and my sister, Rachel, for always being there for me. And most importantly, for my partner and my love, Emily, who has been there for the extreme highs and lows of this project: always there to tell me that I do know what I'm talking about, and no it's not a waste of time, and yes people will read it (I needed to be told these things far more often than I'd like to admit). And thanks to our two cats—Stokely and Muggsy—for always being around to cuddle or play when I needed a break from writing.

This book is ultimately dedicated to all transit workers—the drivers, mechanics, janitors, and administrators—who serve riders and communities through often worsening conditions of austerity and privatization. Following the examples of labour unions and transit rider organizations across the continent, we can collectively fight for better service and working conditions that benefit everyone. Thanks to all who are already doing that work. If we fight, we can win.

Interviews

LLOYD ALTER, design editor of TreeHugger.com; phone interview on December 20, 2018

KAFUI ATTOH, assistant professor of urban studies at the City University of New York and author of *Rights in Transit: Public Transportation and the Right to the City in California's East Bay* (2019); phone interview on June 6, 2018

ELENI BARDAKA, assistant professor in the department of civil, construction and environmental engineering at North Carolina State University studying socio-economic impacts of urban rail; phone interview on July 6, 2018

CONNOR BEATON, journalist and activist in Scotland; phone interview on January 18, 2019

ALEX BIRNEL, advocacy manager at MOVE Texas; phone interview on June 10, 2018

DEEPA CHANDRAN, graduate of master of urban planning at University of Manitoba with expertise in transit accessibility in Winnipeg, Manitoba; phone interview on June 14, 2018

DANIEL ALDANA COHEN, assistant professor of sociology at the University of Pennsylvania and co-author of *A Planet to Win: Why We Need a Green New Deal* (2019); phone interview on June 19, 2018

HANA CREGER, environmental equity co-ordinator at Greenlining Institute; phone interview on June 6, 2018

ASHLEY DAWSON, professor of English at the City University of New York and author of *Extreme Cities: The Peril and Promise of Urban Life in the Age of Climate Change* (2017); phone interview on June 28, 2018

VEENA DUBAL, associate professor of law at the University of California Hastings College of the Law and expert in the intersections of law, technology, and labour; phone interview on August 15, 2019

YVES ENGLER, activist and co-author of *Stop Signs: Cars and Capitalism on the Road to Economic, Social and Ecological Decay* (2011); phone interview on December 23, 2018

STEPHANIE FARMER, associate professor of sociology at Roosevelt University and author of 2011 research article "Uneven Public Transportation Development in Neoliberalizing Chicago, USA"; phone interview on August 1, 2018

BILLY FIELDS, associate professor of political science at Texas State University and co-editor of *Transport Beyond Oil: Policy Choices for a Multi-modal Future* (2013); phone interview on December 20, 2018

YONAH FREEMARK, doctoral candidate in urban studies at MIT and founder of the *Transport Politic*; phone interview on June 28, 2018

AHMED EL-GENEIDY, professor of urban planning at McGill University; phone interview on June 29, 2018

LAWRENCE HANLEY, international president of the Amalgamated Transit Union; phone interview on May 31, 2018

STEVEN HIGASHIDE, director of research at TransitCenter and author of *Better Buses, Better Cities: How to Plan, Run, and Win the Fight for Effective Transit* (2019); phone interview on June 15, 2018

STEVEN HILL, journalist and author of *Raw Deal: How the "Uber Economy" and Runaway Capitalism Are Screwing American Workers* (2015); phone interview on July 13, 2018

MATTHEW HUBER, associate professor of geography at Syracuse University and author of *Lifeblood: Oil, Freedom, and the Forces of Capital* (2013); phone interview on January 10, 2019

MADELINE JANIS, executive director and founder of Jobs to Move America; phone interview on June 4, 2018

CRYSTAL JENNINGS, housing and transit co-ordinator at Pittsburghers for Public Transit; phone interview on June 11, 2018

JUNFENG JIAO, assistant professor in the community and regional planning program and founding director of Urban Information Lab at University of Texas at Austin; phone interview on July 3, 2018

NICOLE KALMS, associate professor of design and founding director of Monash University's XYX Lab; phone interview on June 12, 2018

STEFAN KIPFER, associate professor in environmental studies at York University and researcher of urban politics and public transit; phone interview on May 29, 2018

PAUL LANGAN, founder of High Speed Rail Canada; phone interview on July 5, 2018

STEVEN LAPERRIÈRE, vice-president of Regroupement des activistes pour l'inclusion au Québec (RAPLIQ); phone interview on June 8, 2018

MATTHEW LEWIS, climate and energy policy consultant in Berkeley; phone interview on July 6, 2018

GREG LINDSAY, director of applied research at NewCities and co-author of *Aerotropolis: The Way We'll Live Next* (2011); phone interview on July 2, 2018

TODD LITMAN, founder and executive of Victoria Transport Policy Institute; phone interview on July 5, 2018

AMY LUBITOW, assistant professor of sociology at Portland State University and co-author of 2017 research article "Transmobilities: Mobility, Harassment, and Violence Experienced by Transgender and Gender Nonconforming Public Transit Riders in Portland, Oregon"; phone interview on July 9, 2018

ANGELLA MACEWEN, senior economist at the Canadian Labour Congress (now senior economist at the Canadian Union of Public Employees); phone interview on July 11, 2018

PARIS MARX, journalist and curator of the *Radical Urbanist* newsletter; phone interview on June 8, 2018

MOATAZ MOHAMED, assistant professor of civil engineering at McMaster University and expert in electrification of transit systems; phone interview on January 11, 2019

DAVID MOSCROP, postdoctoral researcher at the University of Ottawa; phone interview on August 22, 2018

P.E. MOSKOWITZ, journalist and author of *How to Kill a City: Gentrification, Inequality and the Fight for the Neighborhood* (2017); phone interview on May 30, 2019

PETER NORTON, associate professor of history at the University of Virginia and author of *Fighting Traffic: The Dawn of the Motor Age in the American City* (2008); phone interview on June 1, 2018

KIM PERROTTA, executive director of Canadian Association of Physicians for the Environment; phone interview on June 13, 2018

SIMON PIRANI, senior visiting research fellow at the Oxford Institute for Energy Studies and author of *Burning Up: A Global History of Fossil Fuel Consumption* (2018); phone interview on December 23, 2018

SHELAGH PIZEY-ALLEN & VINCENT PUHAKKA, executive director and member of TTCriders; phone interview on June 29, 2018

THEA RIOFRANCOS, assistant professor of political science at Providence College and author of *Resource Radicals: From Petro-Nationalism to Post-Extractivism in Ecuador* (2020); phone interview on May 6, 2019

TOBY SANGER, senior economist at Canadian Union of Public Employees (now executive director of Canadians for Tax Fairness); phone interview on June 21, 2018

KSHAMA SAWANT, council member of Seattle City Council and member of Socialist Alternative; phone interview on August 3, 2018

TERESA SCASSA, Canada Research Chair in information law and policy at the University of Ottawa Faculty of Law; phone interview on July 4, 2018

MIMI SHELLER, professor of sociology at Drexel University and author of *Mobility Justice: The Politics of Movement in an Age of Extremes* (2018); phone interview on December 20, 2018

MARTA VICIEDO, director and founding partner of Urban Impact Lab and chair of Transit Alliance Miami; phone interview on July 26, 2018

HARSHA WALIA, author of *Undoing Border Imperialism* (2013) and co-founder of the Vancouver chapter of No One Is Illegal; phone interview on June 26, 2018

JARRETT WALKER, transit consultant and author of *Human Transit: How Clearer Thinking about Public Transit Can Enrich Our Communities and Our Lives* (2011); phone interview on May 24, 2018

KATIE WELLS, postdoctoral fellow at Georgetown University's Kalmanovitz Initiative for Labor and the Working Poor; phone interview on July 8, 2018

Notes

INTRODUCTION

1. "Transportation in Science Fiction," *Technovelgy.com*, www.technovelgy.com.

2. Laura Bliss, "The Attainable Wonders of Wakandan Transit," *CityLand*, February 21, 2018, www.citylab.com; Andrew J. Hawkins, "Black Panther's Wakanda Is a Transportation Utopia with a Dash of Reality," *Verge*, February 23, 2018, www.theverge.com; Gersh Kuntzman, "'Black Panther' Succeeds as Urban Utopia: There Are No Cars in Wakanda," *Newsweek*, February 22, 2018, www.newsweek.com.

3. The film even featured a BART-specific inside joke in the dialogue. (Katie Dowd, "There's Apparently a Deep-Cut BART joke in 'Black Panther,'" *SFGate*, February 28, 2018, www.sfgate.com.)

4. J. Robert Subrick, "The Political Economy of Black Panther's Wakanda," in *Superheroes and Economics*, ed. Brian O'Roark and Rob Salkowitz (New York City: Routledge, 2019), 68.

5. Janette Sadik-Khan, Twitter post, February 21, 2018, 3:23 p.m., https://twitter.com/jsadikkhan/.

6. Kriston Capps, "The 'Namewashing' of Public Transit," *CityLab*, November 25, 2019, www.citylab.com.

7. Hawkins, ""Black Panther's Wakanda Is a Transportation Utopia"; Bliss, "The Attainable Wonders of Wakandan Transit."

8. William J. Mallett, *Trends in Public Transportation Ridership: Implications for Federal Policy* (Washington, DC: Congressional Research Service, 2018), www.fas.org; Eric Jaffe, "2 Notes of Caution on America's 'Record' Mass Transit Year," *CityLab*, March 10, 2015, www.citylab.com.

9. Yonah Freemark, "U.S. Transit Systems Are Shedding Riders: Are They under Threat?," *Transport Politic*, May 18, 2018, www.thetransportpolitic.com.

10. Skip Descant, "2018 Was the Year of the Car, and Transit Ridership Felt It," *Government Technology*, April 30, 2019, www.govtech.com. The downward trend across all transit modes accelerated especially between 2016 and 2017 in cities including Milwaukee (13.6 percent decrease), Charlotte (11.6 percent), Cleveland (10.8 percent) and Miami (8.7 percent). (Christopher Yuen, "Why Does Ridership Rise or Fall?: Lessons from Canada?," *Human Transit*, April 19, 2018, www.humantransit.org.)

11. Faiz Siddiqui, "Falling Transit Ridership Poses an 'Emergency' for Cities, Experts Fear," *Washington Post*, March 24, 2018.

12. "Annual Subway Ridership," Metropolitan Transportation Authority, http://web.mta.info; "Annual Bus Ridership by Route," Metropolitan Transportation Authority, http://web.mta.info.

13. Chicago's system dropped by 3.2 percent, Washington, DC's by 3.4 percent, and the Philadelphia area's by 7.3 percent. (Yuen, "Why Does Ridership Rise or Fall?")

14. Siddiqui, "Falling Transit Ridership Poses an 'Emergency.'"

15. Matthew Dickens, *Public Transportation Ridership Report: First Quarter 2019* (Washington, DC: American Public Transportation Association, 2019), www.apta.com.

16. Justin McElroy, "'So Much Appetite': TransLink Ridership Soars to Record 437 Million Boardings," *CBC News*, April 25, 2019, www.cbc.ca.

17. Freemark, "U.S. Transit Systems Are Shedding Riders."

18. Katherine Savage, "Results from the 2016 Census: Commuting within Canada's Largest Cities," Statistics Canada, May 29, 2019, www.statcan.gc.ca.

19. Feargus O'Sullivan, "Breaking Down the Many Ways Europe's City-Dwellers Get to Work," *CityLab*, October 18, 2017, www.citylab.com.

20. Renate van der Zee, "How Amsterdam Became the Bicycle Capital of the World," *Guardian*, May 5, 2015, www.theguardian.com; Adele Peters, "These Historical Photos Show How Amsterdam Turned Itself into a Bike Rider's Paradise," *Fast Company*, November 3, 2015, www.fastcompany.com.

21. Every year of the operation of ride-hailing services in a market results in a 1.3 percent loss of heavy rail ridership and a 1.7 percent loss of bus ridership; after eight years, that means a massive 12.7 percent loss in bus riders. (Michael Graehler, Jr., Richard Alexander Mucci, and Gregory D. Erhardt, "Understanding the Recent Transit Ridership Decline in Major US Cities: Service Cuts or 2 Emerging Modes?," 98th Annual Meeting of the Transportation Research Board, November 14, 2018, www.usa.streetsblog.org.)

22. Yonah Freemark, "Too Little, Too Late?: A Decade of Transit Investment in the U.S.," *Transport Politic*, January 7, 2020, www.thetransportpolitic.com.

23. Skip Descant, "2018 Was the Year of the Car, and Transit Ridership Felt It," *Government Technology*, April 30, 2019, www.govtech.com.

24. Leon Drolet, "Leon Drolet: Transit Is Fading as Transportation Options Shift," *Crain's Detroit Business*, September 22, 2019, www.crainsdetroit.com.

25. "4 Things for Transit Agencies to Remember in a World of Driverless Car Hype," TransitCenter, May 3, 2018, http://transitcenter.

org. Similarly, London mayoral candidate Zac Goldsmith once said in a radio interview that "within two or three years there will be no point having bus lanes" because everyone would be driving electric vehicles. (Jon Stone, "Mayor of London Tory Candidate Zac Goldsmith Says There'll Be 'No Point' in Having Bus Lanes in Two to Three Years Because We'll All Be Driving Electric Cars," *Independent*, November 20, 2015, www.independent.co.uk.)

26. Samantha Craggs and Dan Taekema, "Ontario Cancels Hamilton LRT in Chaotic Announcement: Mayor Calls It a 'Betrayal,'" *CBC News*, December 16, 2019, www.cbc.ca; "Doug Ford Announces $40M for Ontario Auto Sector Plan," *Canadian Press*, February 14, 2019, www.cbc.ca.

27. Jarrett Walker, *Human Transit: How Clearer Thinking about Public Transit Can Enrich Our Communities and Our Lives* (Washington, DC: Island Press, 2012), 23.

28. Christof Spieler, *Trains, Buses, People: An Opinionated Atlas of US Transit* (Washington, DC: Island Press, 2018), 2–3.

29. "Failure to Restore and Modernize U.S. Public Transit Results in a Loss of $340 Billion in Business Revenue, According to APTA Study," American Public Transportation Association, May 17, 2018, www.apta.com; Dana Rubinstein, "Sources: MTA Tells Task Force That System-Wide Repairs Could Run $60B," *Politico*, October 25, 2018, www.politico.com; Adam Vaccaro, "MBTA Puts Price Tag for Fixing the System at $10 Billion," *Boston Globe*, May 13, 2019.

30. Leah Libresco, "How Often D.C.'s Metro Catches on Fire," *FiveThirtyEight*, May 16, 2016, https://fivethirtyeight.com; Katie Wells, Kafui Attoh, and Declan Cullen, "Uber, the 'Metropocalypse,' and Economic Inequality in DC," *Working-Class Perspectives*, February 5, 2018, www.workingclassstudies.wordpress.com; "The Economic Cost of Failing to Modernize Public Transportation," American Public Transportation Association, May 2018, www.apta.com.

31. Paul Mees, *Transport for Suburbia: Beyond the Automobile Age* (London: Earthscan, 2010).

32. Freemark, "U.S. Transit Systems Are Shedding Riders."

33. Laura Bliss, "Behind the Gains in U.S. Public Transit Ridership," *CityLab*, January 13, 2020, www.citylab.com.

34. Steven Higashide, *Better Buses, Better Cities: How to Plan, Run, and Win the Fight for Effective Transit* (Washington, DC: Island Press, 2019), 2.

35. Gains can be won, like California's AB-5 and New York's vehicle cap and minimum wage. But the likes of Uber, Tesla, and Waymo are constantly lobbying and undermining the rules. Any victory must be considered temporary—and a mere stopgap that doesn't advance the much bigger project of building excellent transit.

36. Jon Porter, "The Uber for Helicopters Is Now Uber," *Verge*, June 6, 2019, www.theverge.com.

37. Rob Pegoraro, "An Elegy for Car2Go, the Smarter Zipcar Rival That Lost Its Way," *Fast Company*, December 21, 2019, www.fastcompany.com.

38. Yonah Freemark, "Is Transit Ridership Loss Inevitable?: A U.S.-France comparison," *Transport Politic*, September 9, 2019, www.thetransportpolitic.com.

39. Mees, *Transport for Suburbia*, xi.

40. Mengphin Ge, Johannes Friedrich, and Thomas Damassa, "6 Graphs Explain the World's Top 10 Emitters," World Resources Institute, November 25, 2014, www.wri.org.

41. It's worth noting at the outset that the U.S. and Canada have different legislative and funding contexts—and that the focus of this book is not on interrogating those nuances; other more technical texts are a better source for that. (Simply put, Canada's transit agencies tend to rely much more heavily on passenger fares than their U.S. counterparts, which use a combination of sales taxes and subsidies.)

42. Hubert Horan, "Uber's Path of Destruction," *American Affairs* 3, no. 2 (2019): 108–33.

43. "The right to the city is, therefore, far more than a right of individual access to the resources that the city embodies: it is a right to change ourselves by changing the city more after our heart's desire," Harvey wrote. "It is, moreover, a common rather than an individual right since this transformation inevitably depends upon the exercise of a collective power to reshape the processes of urbanization." (David Harvey, "The Right to the City," *New Left Review* 53 (2008).)

44. Mimi Sheller, *Mobility Justice: The Politics of Movement in an Age of Extremes* (New York City: Verso Books, 2018).

45. Spieler, *Trains, Buses, People*, 6.

46. Jonathan Watts, "We Have 12 Years to Limit Climate Change Catastrophe, Warns UN," *Guardian*, October 8, 2018, www.theguardian.com.

47. Jane McAlevey, *No Shortcuts: Organizing for Power in the New Gilded Age* (Oxford: Oxford University Press, 2016).

48. James Wilt, "Free Transit Is Just the Beginning," *Briarpatch*, November 29, 2019, www.briarpatchmagazine.com.

CHAPTER 1 > OFF THE RAILS

1. Aarian Marshall, "Elon Musk Reveals His Awkward Dislike of Mass Transit," *Wired*, December 14, 2017, www.wired.com.

2. Rich Sampson, "What Elon Musk Doesn't Understand about

Public Transit Hurts Everyone," *Quartz*, December 26, 2017, www.qz.com.

3. David Z. Morris, "Elon Musk Calls Transit Expert 'an Idiot' and Says Public Transport 'Sucks,'" *Fortune*, December 16, 2017, www.fortune.com.

4. Jeff Sparrow, "The Great Acceleration," *Overland* 236 (Spring 2019), www.overland.org.au.

5. Mees, *Transport for Suburbia*, 10; Richard F. Weingroff, "Federal Aid Road Act of 1916: Building the Foundation," *Public Roads* 60, no. 1 (1996), www.fhwa.dot.gov.

6. Sparrow, "The Great Acceleration."

7. Joseph Stromberg, "Highways Gutted American Cities: So Why Did They Build Them?," *Vox*, May 11, 2016, www.vox.com.

8. Mees, *Transport for Suburbia*, 16.

9. Erin Blakemore, "How the GI Bill's Promise Was Denied to a Million Black WWII Veterans," *History*, June 21, 2019, www.history.com. Between 1940 and 1970, the percentage of the U.S. population living in a suburban area increased from 13.4 percent to 37.1 percent; that increased to 51 percent by 2010. (Becky Nicolaides and Andrew Wiese, "Suburbanization in the United States after 1945," *Oxford Research Encyclopedias* (Oxford: Oxford University Press, 2017).)

10. Stromberg, "Highways Gutted American Cities."

11. "Interstate Frequently Asked Questions," U.S. Department of Transportation Federal Highway Administration, www.fhwa.dot.gov; Stromberg, "Highways Gutted American Cities."

12. Mees, *Transport for Suburbia*, 19.

13. Doug Monroe, "Where It All Went Wrong," *Atlanta*, August 1, 2012; Johnny Miller, "Roads to Nowhere: How Infrastructure Built on American Inequality," *Guardian*, February 21, 2018, www.theguardian.com.

14. Nicolaides and Wiese, "Suburbanization in the United States."

15. Spieler, *Trains, Buses, People*, 8.

16. Kevin O'Leary, "The Legacy of Proposition 13," *Time*, June 27, 2009.

17. Doron Levin, "Here Are Some of Worst Car Scandals in History," *Fortune*, September 26, 2015, https://fortune.com.

18. Gaming of fuel economy standards resulted in European drivers paying an extra 150 billion euros in fuel since 2000 (equivalent to about US$175 billion). (Damian Carrington, "Carmakers' Gaming of Emissions Tests 'Costing Drivers Billions,'" *Guardian*, August 29, 2018, www.theguardian.com.)

19. Mark Stevenson, "Automakers Spent $49 Million in 2017 Lobbying Washington to Make Cars Dirty Again," *CarBuzz*, February 7, 2018, https://carbuzz.com; Joseph White and David Shepardson,

"Donald Trump Proposes Rollback of Vehicle Emission Rules, Fewer Electric Vehicle Sales," *Reuters*, August 2, 2018, https://globalnews.ca.

20. Gregory H. Shill, "Should Law Subsidize Driving?," *New York University Law Review* (forthcoming).

21. Catherine Lutz, "The U.S. Car Colossus and the Production of Inequality," *American Ethnologist* 41, no. 2 (2014).

22. English, "How America Killed Transit."

23. William S. Morrow, Jr., "Urban Mass Transportation Acts," *Encyclopedia.com*, 2004, www.encyclopedia.com; English, "How America Killed Transit."

24. English, "How America Killed Transit"; Robert Cervero, *The Transit Metropolis: A Global Inquiry* (Washington, DC: Island Press, 1998), 37.

25. Mark Ellis, "Bus Services under Privatisation Have Been a Failure Say Campaigners," *Mirror*, October 26, 2016, www.mirror.co.uk. The Railways Act of 1993 established the framework for the privatization of British Rail, which took place over the next several years. The infrastructure of British Rail was turned into a publicly traded company called Railtrack. By the end of the century, over forty people had been killed and hundreds more injured in three major crashes. (Stephen Smith, "Why Britain's Railway Privatization Failed," *CityLab*, September 27, 2012, www.citylab.com.) The U.K. rail system has been plagued by late, expensive, and overcrowded trains in which "private companies reap the benefits, while passengers bear the costs." ("The Guardian View on Rail Privatisation: Going off the Tracks," *Guardian*, December 5, 2017, www.theguardian.com.) U.K. commuters pay six times as much of their salaries on rail fares compared to other European countries with publicly owned railways. ("UK Commuters Spend up to Six Times as Much of Their Salary on Rail Fares as Other European Passengers," Trades Union Congress, 2019, www.tuc.org.uk.) Connor Beaton, a journalist and former national secretary for the Scottish Socialist Party, told me that the privatization of Scotland's railways—bought in 2015 by Abellio, owned by the Dutch rail operator Nederlandse Spoorwegen—have resulted in constant crew and carriage shortages, train cancellations, and worsening quality of service. The London Underground also underwent a similarly catastrophic privatization in the early 2000s, with New Labour contracting out the upgrading and maintenance of the historic system to Metronet and Tube Lines. By 2010, Metronet had gone into insolvency and Tube Lines was bought out by the Transport for London. (Yonah Freemark, "London Underground's Privatization Experiment Dead as Remaining PPP Is Bought Out," *Transport Politic*, May 11, 2019, www.thetransportpolitic.com.) A report by the National Audit Office found that the failure of Metronet

cost the public between £170 million and £410 million. (Dan Milmo, "Collapse of Tube Contractor Metronet Could Cost Taxpayer £410m," *Guardian*, June 5, 2009, www.theguardian.com.)

26. Oliver Moore, "Metrolinx Settles Lawsuit with Builders of $5.4-Billion Crosstown Light-Rail Project," *Globe and Mail*, September 6, 2018, www.theglobeandmail.com.

27. Moore, "Metrolinx Settles Lawsuit."

28. David Kennedy, "Metrolinx Doled Out Extra $237M to Keep Eglinton Crosstown on Schedule," *On-Site*, December 10, 2018, www.on-sitemag.com.

29. Tracey Lindeman, "Will Ottawa Ever Get Its Light Rail?," *CityLab*, April 19, 2019, www.citylab.com.

30. Josh Pringle, "LRT Will Be 'Stabilized' in New Year: Hubley," *CTV News*, December 5, 2019, www.ottawa.ctvnews.ca.

31. Michael Sainato, "Public Transit System in Washington DC Struggles with Privatization," *Guardian*, December 15, 2018, www.theguardian.com.

32. Bill Bradley, "The Streetcar Boondoggle Continues, This Time in Detroit," *CityLab*, May 16, 2017, www.citylab.com.

33. Kelly Weill, "Elon Musk Hyperloop Dreams Slam into Cold Hard Reality," *Daily Beast*, March 29, 2019, www.thedailybeast.com.

34. John Greenfield, "Cheer up Clevelanders, the O'Hare Express Is Dead, and You Can Kill the Hyperloop," *StreetsBlog Chicago*, December 16, 2019, www.chi.streetsblog.org.

35. Adrian Morrow, "Government-Managed Projects Could Save Ontario Money: Auditor-General," *Globe and Mail*, December 9, 2014; Keith Reynolds, *Public-Private Partnerships in BC: Update 2018* (Vancouver: Columbia Institute, 2018), www.columbiainstitute.ca; John Loxley, *Wrong Turn: Is a P3 the Best Way to Expand Edmonton's LRT?* (Edmonton: Parkland Institute, 2013), www.parklandinstitute.ca.

36. "Canada Line Foreign Workers Treated Unfairly, Tribunal Rules," *CBC News*, December 3, 2008, www.cbc.ca; Keven Drews, "Canada Line Workers Get Money Five Years after Human Rights Tribunal Decision," *Vancouver Sun*, April 2, 2013; Krystle Alarcon, "Imported Workers Fight Back," *Tyee*, January 8, 2013, https://thetyee.ca.

37. "Canada Infrastructure Bank Loaning $1.28-Billion to Montreal Electric Rail Project," *Canadian Press*, August 22, 2018; Taylor C. Noakes, "How a New Transit System Could Hobble Montreal," *Next City*, March 12, 2018, https://nextcity.org.

38. Erika Stark and Erin Sylvester, "Updated: Calgary Transit Cancels Connect Card, Vows Legal Action to Recover Money," *Calgary Herald*, July 1, 2015, www.calgaryherald.com.

39. Spieler, *Trains, Buses, People*, 14.

40. Douglas Hanks, "Miami's Big Transit Showdown: Modernized Bus or Metrorail for South Dade?," *Miami Herald*, July 18, 2018. In 2017, a poll of Miami-Dade residents about the idea of increasing the sales tax to 1 percent from 0.5 percent for transit funding was supported by 48 percent, with 50 percent opposing it. (Douglas Hanks, "Pursuing a Rail Expansion, Miami-Dade Mayor Polls Voters on Increasing Transit Tax," *Miami Herald*, March 23, 2017.) In August 2018, a lawsuit was launched against Miami-Dade and Mayor Carlos Gimenez over the sales tax. (Douglas Hanks, "Lawsuit: County Squandered $1.5 Billion of Transit Tax Promised for Metrorail Growth," *Miami Herald*, August 13, 2018.) A few weeks later, the Citizens' Independent Transportation Trust board passed a resolution that forces commissioners to stop using the tax revenue to balance the budget. (K. Barrett Bilali, "Citizen's Group Moves to Hold County Accountable on Transit," *Miami Times*, August 30, 2018.) The same has happened in other cities, with Phoenix's city council taking the first step in August 2018 to divert billions of dollars toward roads that was previously allocated for transit in a referendum. (Angie Schmitt, "Phoenix City Council Moves to Hijack Transit Money for Roads," *Streetsblog USA*, August 31, 2018, https://usa.streetsblog.org.)

41. Jesse Scheckner, "New Mobility World Coming to South Dade Transitway," *Miami Today*, October 1, 2019, www.miamitodaynews.com.

42. The tax amounted to $250 million per year or $2.5 billion over ten years. (Lisa Johnson and Tamara Baluja, "Transit Referendum: Voters Say No to New Metro Vancouver Tax, Transit Improvements," *CBC News*, July 2, 2015, www.cbc.ca; Seth Klein, Marc Lee, and Iglika Ivanova, "Why We're Voting YES to New Transit and Transportation Funding," *Policy Note*, March 2, 2015, www.policynote.ca.)

43. Hiroko Tabuchi, "How the Koch Brothers Are Killing Public Transit Projects around the Country," *New York Times*, June 19, 2018, www.nytimes.com.

44. "Your Bus Is on Time: What Does That Even Mean?," TransitCenter, August 27, 2018, https://transitcenter.org.

45. Aparita Bhandari, "Better Bus Service Could Help Solve Scarborough's Transit Troubles," *Discourse*, June 4, 2019, www.thediscourse.ca.

46. Until recently, the province provided a $1.50 subsidy for discounted fares for people using both services in the same trip, but that was cancelled by Ontario's Conservative government that was elected in 2018. "Ford Government Cuts Subsidy for Discounted GO Transit, TTC Fares," *Canadian Press*, July 9, 2019, www.toronto.citynews.ca.

47. Leah Binkovitz, "New Study Examines How Historic Racism Shaped Atlanta's Transportation Network," Kinder Institute for Urban Research, February 8, 2017, https://kinder.rice.edu.

48. Thomas W. Sanchez, "The Connection between Public Transit and Employment," *Journal of the American Planning Association* 65, no. 3 (1999).

49. Yonah Freemark, "Housing Arguments over SB 50 Distort My Upzoning Study: Here's How to Get Zoning Changes Right," *Frisc*, May 22, 2019, https://thefrisc.com.

50. Stefan Kipfer, "Free Transit and Beyond," *Bullet*, December 3, 2012, https://socialistproject.ca.

51. Abdallah Fayyad, "The Criminalization of Gentrifying Neighborhoods," *Atlantic*, December 20, 2017, www.theatlantic.com.

52. Kayla McLean, "'There Will Be No Little Jamaica': Toronto Neighbourhood Threatened by LRT Construction," *Global News*, December 23, 2019, www.globalnews.ca. In response to criticism from business owners in Toronto's Little Jamaica, Metrolinx said that it's not responsible for building affordable housing to protect communities.

53. Daniel C. Vock, "Buses, Yes Buses, Are 'the Hottest Trend in Transit,'" *Governing*, September 2017, www.governing.com; Meagan Flynn, "No Easy Ride: What Using METRO's New Bus Network Is Like in a Low-Income Community [updated]," *Houston Press*, September 3, 2015, www.houstonpress.com; Olivia Kelly, "'False Information' about Dublin Bus Redesign Slated by Planner," *Irish Times*, July 23, 2018, www.theirishtimes.com.

54. Danielle Sweeney, "Hard Lessons from Baltimore's Bus Redesign," *CityLab*, January 14, 2019, www.citylab.com.

55. Sweeney, "Hard Lessons from Baltimore's Bus Redesign."

56. Eric Goldwyn and Alon Levy, "A Fantasy Map for Brooklyn's Buses That's Grounded in Reality," *CityLab*, November 19, 2018, www.citylab.com.

CHAPTER 2 > MANUFACTURING AUTOMOBILITY

1. Tom Krishner, "US New-Vehicle Sales in 2018 Rise Slightly to 17.27 Million," *Associated Press*, January 3, 2019, www.foxnews.com.

2. William J. Mallett, *Trends in Public Transportation Ridership: Implications for Federal Policy* (Washington, DC: Congressional Research Service, 2018), https://fas.org; Daniel C. Vock, "More Poorer Residents Are Driving Cars, Presenting New Issues for Transit Agencies," *Governing*, April 9, 2018, www.governing.com.

3. Aaron Short, "Trump Shifts Obama Transit Funding to Roads," *Streetsblog USA*, November 13, 2019, www.usa.streetsblog.org.

4. "Where the Energy Goes: Gasoline Vehicles," U.S. Department of Energy, www.fueleconomy.gov.

5. Fred Lambert, "Even Electric Cars Powered by the Dirtiest Electricity Emit Fewer Emissions Than Diesel Cars, Says New Study," *Electrek*, November 1, 2017, https://electrek.co.

6. Julianne Beck and Amanda Morris, "Electric Vehicle Adoption Improves Air Quality and Climate Outlook," *Phys.org*, April 12, 2019, https://phys.org; Jamie Doward, "New Law to Tackle Electric Cars' Silent Menace to Pedestrians," *Guardian*, May 6, 2018, www.theguardian.com.

7. Zachary Shahan, "Tesla Model 3 = 60% of US Electric Vehicle Market," *CleanTechnica*, April 7, 2019, https://cleantechnica.com.

8. "Why Zipcar Became an Acquisition Instead of an Acquirer," *Boston Business Journal*, January 2, 2013, www.bizjournals.com; Mansoon Iqbal, "Uber Revenue and Usage Statistics (2019)," *Business of Apps*, May 10, 2019, www.businessofapps.com; "Uber's $82 Billion Valuation Underwhelms in Most-Anticipated IPO since Facebook," *VentureBeat*, May 10, 2019, https://venturebeat.com.

9. Robin Chase, "Will a World of Driverless Cars Be Heaven or Hell?," *CityLab*, April 3, 2014, www.citylab.com.

10. "SAE International Releases Updated Visual Chart for Its 'Levels of Driving Automation' Standard for Self-Driving Vehicles," Society of Automotive Engineers International, December 11, 2018, www.sae.org.

11. David Beard, "This Is the Tech Fully Autonomous (Level 5) Cars Will Need to Have," *Car and Driver*, October 3, 2017, www.caranddriver.com; Sandeep Sovani, "Top 3 Challenges to Produce Level 5 Autonomous Vehicles," *ANSYS*, December 13, 2018, www.ansys.com.

12. "40+ Corporations Working on Autonomous Vehicles," CB Information Services, August 28, 2019, www.cbinsights.com.

13. Anthony Mirhaydari, "Uber vs. Waymo in $2.8T Battle for 'Robotaxis,'" *PitchBook*, May 18, 2018, https://pitchbook.com. In 2018, Morgan Stanley analysts estimated that Waymo may already be worth $175 billion in value. (Alan Ohnsman, "Why Waymo Is Worth a Staggering $175 Billion Even before Launching Its Self-Driving Cars," *Forbes*, August 7, 2018, www.forbes.com.)

14. David Z. Morris, "Driverless Cars Will Be Part of a $7 Trillion Market by 2050," *Fortune*, June 3, 2017, https://fortune.com.

15. Adrienne Lafrance, "The High-Stakes Race to Rid the World of Human Drivers," *Atlantic*, December 1, 2015.

16. "Uber's $82 Billion Valuation," *VentureBeat*; Rebecca Ungarino, "Lyft Went Public at a $24 Billion Valuation: Here's How That Compares to Other High-Profile Tech Companies Dating Back to

the Dotcom Bubble," *Business Insider*, April 7, 2019, https://markets. businessinsider.com.

17. Paayal Zaveri and Deirdre Bosa, "Uber's Growth Slowed Dramatically in 2018," *CNBC*, February 15, 2019, www.cnbc.com. The year prior, in 2017, Uber lost $2.2 billion. In the second quarter of 2019 alone, Uber lost $5.2 billion, its largest-ever quarterly loss. (Dominic Rushe, "Uber Sees Biggest-Ever Quarterly Loss: $5bn in Three Months," *Guardian*, August 8, 2019, www.theguardian.com.)

18. "Lyft Reveals It Doubled Revenue to $2.2B in 2018 as It Files to Go Public," *CBC News*, March 1, 2019, www.cbc.ca.

19. Lauren Feiner, "Uber CEO Says He's Building the Next Amazon, Even Though Growth Is Slowing," *CNBC*, May 10, 2019, www.cnbc.com.

20. Melanie Zanona, "Uber Tripled Its Lobbying Efforts in 2016," *Hill*, January 23, 2017, https://thehill.com. That year, Uber had 370 active lobbyists in 44 states, more than Amazon, Microsoft and Walmart combined. (Avi Asher-Schapiro, "Trump Administration Fights Effort to Unionize Uber Drivers," *Intercept*, March 26, 2018, https://theintercept.com.) Between 2013 and 2016, the company spent $3.3 million on lobbyists in New York at both the state and city level. (Olivia Solon, "How Uber Conquers a City in Seven Steps," *Guardian*, April 12, 2017, www.theguardian.com.)

21. Anna Sanders, "Ride-Sharing Companies Spent Over $1M Lobbying in NYC," *New York Post*, August 4, 2018, https://nypost.com.

22. Sanders, "Ride-Sharing Companies."

23. Horan, "Uber's Path of Destruction."

24. Johana Bhuiyan, "Valerie Jarrett, One of President Obama's Longest-Serving Aides, Is Joining Lyft's Board," *Vox*, July 31, 2017, www.vox.com.

25. Bill Ruthhar and Hal Dardick, "Former Obama Aide Fined $90,000 for Illegally Lobbying Emanuel on Uber's Behalf," *Chicago Tribune*, February 16, 2017. Emanuel himself had served as White House chief of staff between 2008 and 2010.

26. Andrew J. Hawkins, "Meet the Self-Driving Car Industry's Most Important Lobbyist," *Verge*, April 27, 2016, www.theverge.com.

27. Alex Samuels, "Uber, Lyft Return to Austin as Texas Gov. Abbott Signs Ride-Hailing Measure into Law," *Texas Tribune*, May 29, 2017, www.texastribune.org. Similarly, in September 2017, London, England, banned Uber for failing to comply with regulations including reporting criminal offences, ensuring background checks on drivers, and its use of "Greyball" to secretly deny service to government regulators. ("What Does London's Uber Ban Mean?," *BBC*, September 22, 2017, www.bbc.com.) But the company successfully regained a probationary licence via a court challenge. (Tom McKay, "Uber

Regains Temporary License to Operate in London after Promising to Stop Being Terrible," *Gizmodo*, June 26, 2018, https://gizmodo.com.)

28. Joy Borkholder, Mariah Montgomery, Miya Saika Chen, and Rebecca Smith, *Uber State Interference: How Transportation Network Companies Buy, Bully, and Bamboozle Their Way to Deregulation* (Oakland: Partnership for Working Families, 2018), 6.

29. Solon, "How Uber Conquers a City."

30. Horan, "Can Uber Ever Deliver? Part One: Understanding Uber's Bleak Operating Economics," *Naked Capitalism*, November 30, 2016, www.nakedcapitalism.com.

31. Brian O'Keefe and Marty Jones, "How Uber Plays the Tax Shell Game," *Fortune*, October 22, 2015, https://fortune.com.

32. Noam Scheiber, "How Uber's Tax Calculation May Have Cost Drivers Hundreds of Millions," *New York Times*, June 5, 2017, www.nytimes.com.

33. Laura Bliss, "To Measure the 'Uber Effect,' Cities Get Creative," *CityLab*, January 12, 2018, www.citylab.com.

34. Regina R. Clewlow and Gouri Shankar Mishra, *Disruptive Transportation: The Adoption, Utilization, and Impacts of Ride-Hailing in the United States* (Davis: University of California, October 2017), 30.

35. "Global Survey of Autonomous Vehicle Regulations," *Synced*, March 15, 2018, https://medium.com.

36. "Autonomous Vehicles: Self-Driving Vehicles Enacted Legislation," National Conference of State Legislatures, September 18, 2019, www.ncsl.org.

37. Andrew J. Hawkins, "California Green Lights Fully Driverless Cars for Testing on Public Roads," *Verge*, February 26, 2018, www.theverge.com.

38. Andrew J. Hawkins, "The Self-Driving Car War between Arizona and California Is Heating Up," *Verge*, March 2, 2018, www.theverge.com.

39. Angie Schmitt, "Self-Driving Cars Are Coming: Will They Serve Profit or the Public?," *In These Times*, July 6, 2018; Jack Stilgoe and Alan Winfield, "Self-Driving Car Companies Should Not Be Allowed to Investigate Their Own Crashes," *Guardian*, April 13, 2018, www.theguardian.com.

40. Casey Tolan, "Feinstein Slams Brakes on AV Deregulation Bill," *East Bay Times*, March 15, 2018, www.govtech.com.

41. Andrew J. Hawkins, "Congress Takes Another Stab at Passing Self-Driving Car Legislation," *Verge*, July 28, 2019, www.theverge.com.

42. Ryan Johnston, "Autonomous Vehicle Rules Fought 'My Way or the Highway' by Lobbyists, says Indiana Lawmaker," *StateScoop*, April 10, 2018, https://statescoop.com.

43. Johnston, "Autonomous Vehicle Rules Fought."

44. Chris Brooks, "How New York Taxi Workers Took On Uber and Won," *LaborNotes*, August 23, 2018, www.labornotes.org.

45. Tom Warren, "Uber Loses Its London License as Regulator Cites a 'Pattern of Failures,'" *Verge*, November 25, 2019, www.theverge.com; Gwyn Topham, "Uber Loses London Licence after TfL Finds Drivers Faked Identity," *Guardian*, November 25, 2019, www.theguardian.com.

46. See chapter 9 for more on AB-5.

47. Paris Marx, "Uber Finally Admits It's Taking on Buses," *Radical Urbanist*, February 15, 2018, https://medium.com.

48. James Thorne, "Uber Sees Rapid Adoption for New Bus Service as It Recruits for 'High Capacity Vehicles Team' in Seattle," *GeekWire*, April 3, 2019, www.geekwire.com.

49. Leslie Hook, "Uber's New CEO Plans Expansion into Buses, Bikes," *Financial Times*, February 14, 2018, www.ft.com.

50. Tim Redmond, "Uber's Plans Include Attacking Public Transit," *48hills*, May 6, 2019, www.48hills.org.

51. Redmond, "Uber's Plans Include Attacking Public Transit."

52. Bruce Schaller, *The New Automobility: Lyft, Uber and the Future of American Cities* (New York City: Schaller Consulting, 2018), www.schallerconsult.com.

53. Alison Griswold and Dan Kopf, "After Uber, Americans Spent More on Taxis and Less on Public Transit," *Quartz*, September 25, 2019, https://qz.com.

54. Clewlow and Mishra, *Disruptive Transportation*, 2. The study showed that between 49 to 61 percent of ride-hailing trips replaced walking, biking, transit, or not making the trip at all.

55. Steven R. Gehrke, Alison Felix, and Timothy Reardon, *A Survey of Ride-Hailing Passengers in Metro Boston*, (Boston: Metropolitan Area Planning Council, 2018), 12, www.mapc.org.

56. Martin E. Comas, "Need a Ride?: Altamonte Springs Will Help Pay Your Uber trip within Its City," *Orlando Sentinel*, March 4, 2016, www.orlandosentinel.com.

57. Spencer Woodman, "Welcome to Uberville: Uber Wants to Take Over Public Transit, One Small Town at a Time," *Verge*, September 1, 2016, www.theverge.com.

58. Ben Spurr, "Small Ontario Town's Uber Partnership Could Signal Shift for Canadian Public Transit," *Toronto Star*, April 15, 2018.

59. Andrew J. Hawkins, "Texas Town Ditches Its Bus Service for Ride-Sharing App Via," *Verge*, March 12, 2018, www.theverge.com.

60. Spencer Woodman, "Welcome to Uberville," *Verge*, September 1, 2016, www.theverge.com.

61. Woodman, "Welcome to Uberville."

62. Woodman, "Welcome to Uberville."

63. Colin Horgan, "Uber Wants in to Public Transit: Cities Should Proceed with Caution," *Maclean's*, May 19, 2017, www.macleans.ca.

64. Spurr, "Small Ontario Town's Uber Partnership." Transit subsidies range from $0.78 per ride in Toronto, to $1.62 per ride in Vancouver, to $4.49 per ride in the York Region. (Jennifer Palisoc, "How Does the TTC's Funding Compare to Other Transit Agencies?," *Global News*, November 13, 2014, https://globalnews.ca.)

65. Laura Bliss, "'Uber Was Supposed to Be Our Public Transit,'" *CityLab*, April 29, 2019, www.citylab.com.

66. Jeff Sparrow, "The Great Acceleration," *Overland* 236 (Spring 2019), www.overland.org.au.

CHAPTER 3 > RUNNING ON EMPTY

1. "Sources of Greenhouse Gas Emissions: Transportation Sector Emissions," United States Environmental Protection Agency, www.epa.gov; "Use of Oil," U.S. Energy Information Administration, September 28, 2018, www.eia.gov; Christopher Mims, "More Americans Die from Car Pollution Than Car Accidents," *Quartz*, October 15, 2013, https://qz.com.

2. "5-Year Anniversary Remarks from Uber CEO Travis Kalanick," Uber, June 4, 2015, www.uber.com.

3. "Cars, Trucks, Buses and Air Pollution," Union of Concerned Scientists, July 19, 2018, www.ucsusa.org; Annette Dubreuil, "Air Pollution Is Costing Us Dearly," Ecofiscal Commission, November 29, 2017, https://ecofiscal.ca.

4. David Reichmuth, "New Data Show Electric Vehicles Continue to Get Cleaner," Union of Concerned Scientists, March 8, 2018, https://blog.ucsusa.org.

5. David Shepardson and Nick Carey, "U.S. Vehicle Fuel Economy Rises to Record 24.7 mpg: EPA," *Reuters*, January 11, 2018, www.reuters.com.

6. Irvin Dawid, "Gov. Jerry Brown Signs 16 Bills to Spur Sales of New and Used Electric Vehicles," *Planetizen*, September 20, 2018, www.planetizen.com.

7. "Lyft Climate Impact Goals," Lyft, June 15, 2017, https://blog.lyft.com.

8. Lewis Fulton, Jacob Mason, and Dominique Meroux, *Three Revolutions in Urban Transportation* (Davis: University of California, 2017), 2, https://ncst.ucdavis.edu.

9. Paris Marx, "The Electric Vehicle Revolution Will Be Dirty and Unequal," *Radical Urbanist*, June 14, 2019, https://medium.com.

10. Jeff Desjardins, "Here Are the Raw Materials We Need to Fuel

the Electric Car Boom," *Business Insider*, October 27, 2016, www. businessinsider.com. The projected demand for lithium-ion batteries shows a growth rate of 21.7 percent annually.

11. Desjardins, "Here Are the Raw Materials."

12. "Leading Scientists Set Out Resource Challenge of Meeting Net Zero Emissions in the UK by 2050," Natural History Museum, June 5, 2019, www.nhm.ac.uk.

13. Mark Burton and Eddie Van Der Walt, "Electric Vehicles Shake Up the Biggest Metals Markets," *Globe and Mail*, August 3, 2017.

14. Todd C. Frankel, "The Cobalt Pipeline," *Washington Post*, September 30, 2016; "CBS News Finds Children Mining Cobalt for Batteries in the Congo," *CBS News*, March 5, 2018, www.cbsnews.com.

15. Peter Whoriskey, "In Your Phone, in Their Air," *Washington Post*, October 2, 2016.

16. Elsa Dominish, Sven Teske, and Nick Florin, *Responsible Minerals Sourcing for Renewable Energy* (Sydney: University of Technology Sydney's Institute for Sustainable Futures, 2019), https:// earthworks.org.

17. Glenn Greenwald, "Watch: Glenn Greenwald's Exclusive Interview with Bolivia's Evo Morales, Who Was Deposed in a Coup," *Intercept*, December 16, 2019, www.theintercept.com.

18. Joey Gardiner, "The Rise of Electric Cars Could Leave Us with a Big Battery Waste Problem," *Guardian*, August 10, 2017, www. theguardian.com.

19. Mitch Jacoby, "It's Time to Get Serious about Recycling Lithium-Ion Batteries," *Chemical & Engineering News*, July 14, 2019, https://cen.acs.org.

20. Dominish, Teske, and Florin, *Responsible Minerals Sourcing*, ii.

21. Jacoby, "It's Time to Get Serious."

22. Steph Willems, "As Pedestrian Deaths Spike, Safety Group Puts the Spotlight on SUVs," *Truth about Cars*, February 28, 2019, www. thetruthaboutcars.com.

23. Kelly Waldron, "How Many Miles Do You Drive Each Day?," *New Jersey 101.5*, April 18, 2015, https://nj1015.com; "Range of Electric Vehicles," EnergySage, January 2, 2019, www.energysage. com.

24. Patrick McGee, "Electric Cars' Green Image Blackens Beneath the Bonnet," *Financial Times*, November 7, 2017, www.ft.com.

25. David Roberts, "Electric Buses Are Coming, and They're Going to Help Fix 4 Big Urban Problems," *Vox*, April 28, 2018, www.vox.com.

26. Frank Kelly, "Electric Cars Are Not the Answer to Air Pollution, Says Top UK Adviser," *Guardian*, August 4, 2017, www.theguardian. com; Roy Harrison, "Viewpoint: Why EVs Aren't a Silver Bullet

for the Particulate Problem," *Engineer*, November 22, 2017, www.theengineer.co.uk..

27. Rosanna Xia, "The Biggest Likely Source of Microplastics in California Coastal Waters?: Our Car Tires," *Los Angeles Times*, October 2, 2019, www.latimes.com.

28. James H. Gawron et al., "Life Cycle Assessment of Connected and Automated Vehicles: Sensing and Computing Subsystem and Vehicle Level Effects," *Environ. Sci. Technol* 52, no. 5 (2018): 3249–56.

29. Gabrielle Coppola and Esha Dey, "Driverless Cars Are Giving Engineers a Fuel Economy Headache," *Bloomberg*, October 11, 2017, www.bloomberg.com.

30. Zeke Hausfather, "Factcheck: How Electric Vehicles Help to Tackle Climate Change," *CarbonBrief*, May 13, 2019, www.carbonbrief.org.

31. F. Todd Davidson, Dave Tuttle, Joshua D. Rhodes, and Kazunoria Nagasawa, "Is America's Power Grid Ready for Electric Cars?," *CityLab*, December 7, 2018, www.citylab.com.

32. "What Is U.S. Electricity Generation by Energy Source?," U.S. Energy Information Administration, March 1, 2019, www.eia.gov; Kristi Anderson et al., *A Costly Diagnosis: Subsidizing Coal Power with Albertans' Health* (Calgary: Pembina Foundation for Environmental Research and Education, 2013), https://ab.lung.ca; Ed Osann and Becky Hayat, *Protecting Our Waters from Toxic Power Plant Discharges and Reducing Water Use in the Process* (New York City: Natural Resources Defense Council, 2014), www.nrdc.org; Anthony J. Marchese and Dan Zimmerle, "The US Natural Gas Industry Is Leaking Way More Methane Than Previously Thought: Here's Why That Matters," *Conversation*, July 2, 2018, https://theconversation.com; "We Must Stop New York's 'Peaker Plants' Choking Marginalized Communities," New York Lawyers for the Public Interest, February 11, 2019, https://nylpi.org.

33. Zeke Hausfather, "Factcheck: How Electric Vehicles Help to Tackle Climate Change," *CarbonBrief*, May 13, 2019, www.carbonbrief.org.

34. James Temple, "At This Rate, It's Going to Take Nearly 400 Years to Transform the Energy System," *MIT Technology Review*, March 14, 2018, www.technologyreview.com.

35. Sladjana Djunisic, "IEA Flags 'Deeply Worrying' Stagnation in Renewable Energy Growth," *Energy Mix*, May 9, 2019, https://theenergymix.com.

36. Tom Krishner, "US New-Vehicle Sales in 2018 Rise Slightly to 17.27 Million," *Associated Press*, January 3, 2019, www.foxnews.com; Julia Pyper, "US Electric Vehicle Sales Increased by 81% in 2018,"

Greentech Media, January 7, 2019, www.greentechmedia.com. The Tesla Model 3 represented almost 40 percent of electric sales.

37. Aaron Gordon, "EV Credits Mostly Go towards Rich People Who Would Buy EVs Anyway: Study," *Jalopnik*, June 4, 2019, https://jalopnik.com.

38. "U.S. New-Vehicle Sales in 2018 Rise Slightly to 17.27 Million, with Trucks and SUVs Leading the Way," *Los Angeles Times*, January 4, 2019; Shill, "Should Law Subsidize Driving?," 68.

39. Joseph White, "GM, Doubling Down on Big Suvs, Unveils Longer Chevy Tahoe, Suburban," *Reuters*, December 10, 2019, www.reuters.com.

40. Alessandro Innocenti, Patrizia Lattarulo, and Maria Grazia Pazienza, "Car Stickiness: Heuristics and Biases in Travel Choice," *Transport Policy* 25 (2013): 158–68.

41. "U.S. Households Are Holding On to Their Vehicles Longer," U.S. Energy Administration, August 21, 2018, www.eia.gov.

42. Chris Nelder, interview with Costa Samaras, Energy Transition Show, podcast audio, August 8, 2018, https://xenetwork.org.

43. David Keith and Christopher R. Knittel, "Why Reducing Carbon Emissions from Cars and Trucks Will Be So Hard," *Conversation*, May 6, 2019, https://theconversation.com.

44. Peter Slowik, Lina Fedirko, and Nic Lutsey, "Assessing Ride-Hailing Company Commitments to Electrification," International Council on Clean Transportation, February 20, 2019, www.theicct.org.

45. Andrew J. Hawkins, "Uber Will Start Paying Some Drivers to Switch to Electric Cars," *Verge*, June 19, 2018, www.theverge.com.

46. Johana Bhuiyan, "Uber Powered Four Billion Rides in 2017: It Wants to Do More—and Cheaper—in 2018," *Vox*, January 5, 2018, www.vox.com. Uber has pledged to help almost half its drivers in London transition to electric vehicles by 2021 with grants—but that was a decision forced by the city after it chose not to renew the company's licence to operate, and the grants only represent a small portion of the costs that a driver is required to incur for a new vehicle. (Gwyn Topham, "Uber to Introduce Clean Air Fee to All London Rides," *Guardian*, October 23, 2018, www.theguardian.com.)

47. Peter Slowik, "Why Aren't Uber and Lyft All-Electric Already?," International Council on Clean Transportation, March 22, 2019, www.theicct.org.

48. Slowik, Fedirko, and Lutsey, "Assessing Ride-Hailing Company Commitments."

49. "Lyft Offers Electric Vehicle Options for Riders, Drivers," *Associated Press*, February 6, 2019, www.cbc.ca.

50. Robinson Meyer, "Your Lyft Ride Is Now Carbon-Neutral: Your Uber Isn't," *Atlantic*, April 19, 2018, www.theatlantic.com.

51. Kevin Anderson, "The Inconvenient Truth of Carbon Offsets," *Nature*, April 4, 2012, www.nature.com.

52. Laura Bliss, "Uber and Lyft Could Do a Lot More for the Planet," *CityLab*, April 30, 2018, www.citylab.com.

53. Andrew J. Hawkins, "Not All of Our Self-Driving Cars Will Be Electrically Powered—Here's Why," *Verge*, December 12, 2017, www.theverge.com; Ryan Felton, "Google's Mass-Purchase of Chrysler Pacifica Hybrids Could Mean $465 Million in Federal Tax Credits," *Jalopnik*, June 4, 2018, https://jalopnik.com.

54. Andrew J. Hawkins, "Waymo's Fleet of Self-Driving Minivans Is About to Get 100 Times Bigger," *Verge*, May 31, 2018, www.theverge.com.

55. Joseph Wildey, "Waymo's Vans Rack Up Test Miles, but Charging and Emissions Remain Opaque," *Medium*, September 1, 2018, https://medium.com; Alexis C. Madrigal, "Finally, the Self-Driving Car," *Atlantic*, December 5, 2018, www.theatlantic.com.

56. Tim Higgins and Chester Dawson, "Waymo Orders Up to 20,000 Jaguar SUVs for Driverless Fleet," *Wall Street Journal*, March 27, 2018.

57. Michael Martinez, "Hybrids Are Better for Autonomy, Ford says," *Automotive News*, December 11, 2017, www.autonews.com.

58. Jim Farley, "Optimizing Our Self-Driving Vehicle to Better Serve You," *Medium*, December 6, 2017, https://medium.com.

59. Hawkins, "Not All of Our Self-Driving Cars."

60. Lewis Fulton, Jacob Mason, and Dominique Meroux, *Three Revolutions in Urban Transportation* (Davis: University of California, 2017), 2, https://ncst.ucdavis.edu.

61. Fulton, Mason, and Meroux, *Three Revolutions in Urban Transportation,* 2.

62. Brian McKenzie, *Who Drives to Work?: Commuting by Automobile in the United States, 2013* (Suitland: United States Census Bureau, August 2015), 2, www.census.gov. Some cities are doing better than others—there is a 13.5 percent carpool rate in Phoenix and 11.6 percent in San Antonio—but others are far worse than average, such as the 5.1 percent rate in Washington, DC. (Laura Bliss, "Carpooling Is Totally Coming Back This Time, We Swear," *CityLab*, September 15, 2017, www.citylab.com.)

63. Jacques Leslie, "Will Self-Driving Cars Usher in a Transportation Utopia or Dystopia?," *Yale Environment 360*, January 8, 2018, https://e360.yale.edu.

64. Brooke Crothers, "Tesla's Elon Musk: Car Can Drive Itself Across Country in Two Years," *Forbes*, January 10, 2016, www.forbes.com.

65. Matthew Rocco, "Chrysler, Waymo Explore Selling Self-Driving Cars to Consumers," *Fox Business*, May 31, 2018, www.foxbusiness.com.

66. Schaller, *The New Automobility*, 2.

67. Sidney Fussell, "I Tried Uber's New 'Pool Express' Service and Honestly, Just Take a Bus," *Gizmodo*, February 21, 2018, https://gizmodo.com.

68. Mark Southerland, *Evaluation of Ecological Impacts from Highway Development* (Rockville: Dynamac Corporation, April 1994), 14.

69. Greg Breining, "We're Pouring Millions of Tons of Salt on Roads Each Winter: Here's Why That's a Problem," *Ensia*, November 6, 2017, https://ensia.com.

70. Michael Linse and Zach Barasz, "Urban Transportation Will Go All-Electric Sooner Than You Think," *TechCrunch*, May 29, 2015, https://techcrunch.com.

71. Linse and Barasz, "Urban Transportation Will Go All-Electric"; Daniel Gross, "Compared to Cars, Electric Buses Could Accelerate Pollution Reduction, Fuel Savings," *Chicago Tribune*, September 8, 2014.

72. Gross, "Compared to Cars."

73. *2019 Public Transportation Fact Book* (Washington, DC: American Public Transportation Association, 2019), 16, www.apta.com.

74. "Global Warming Potentials," Government of Canada, February 18, 2019, www.canada.ca.

75. Ben Spurr, "TTC Subway System 10 Times More Polluted Than Outside, Study Shows," *Toronto Star*, April 25, 2017, www.thestar.com; Lauren Pelley, "Ride the GO Train?: You Could Be Breathing in Diesel Fumes, Researchers Say," *CBC News*, February 7, 2017, www.cbc.ca. London Underground riders experience eight times the exposure to fine particulate matter compared to levels outside. (Patrick Grafton-Green, "People Who Use Tube 'Exposed to Eight Times More Air Pollution Than Those Who Drive to Work,'" *Evening Standard*, February 14, 2017, www.standard.co.uk.)

76. Brad Aaron, "Bus Depots a Symptom of Environmental Injustice," *Streetsblog NYC*, April 17, 2007, https://nyc.streetsblog.org.

77. Don Mitchell, "Noise from Toronto's Public Transit Could Lead to Long-Term Hearing Loss: Study," *Global News*, November 23, 2017, https://globalnews.ca. Low-income communities of colour suffer the worst impacts of this kind of noise pollution, which the World Health Organization has identified as second only to air pollution as the most harmful environmental problem to human health, contributing to hearing loss, heart disease, strokes, and sleep disturbance. ("Traffic Noise Health Impacts Second Only to Air

Pollution, New WHO Report Says," Transport & Environment, March 30, 2011, www.transportenvironment.org; Joan A. Casey, Peter James, and Rachel Morello-Frosch, "Urban Noise Pollution Is Worst in Poor and Minority Neighborhoods and Segregated Cities," *Conversation*, October 5, 2017, https://theconversation.com.)

78. *An Analysis of Transit Bus Axle Weight Issues* (Winnipeg: MORR Transportation Consulting, November 2014), iii, www.trb.org.

79. Marcy Lowe, Bengu Aytekin, and Gary Gereffi, *Public Transit Buses: A Green Choice Gets Greener* (Durham: Duke University Global Value Chains Center, 2009), 4, www.gvcc.duke.edu.

80. J. Riley Edwards, "Train Energy, Power and Traffic Control," University of Illinois Board of Trustees, 2010, www.engr.uky.edu.

81. Todd Litman, *Evaluating Public Transit Benefits and Costs: Best Practices Guidebook* (Victoria: Victoria Transport Policy Institute, 2019), 56, www.vtpi.org.

82. Spurr, "TTC Subway System 10 Times More Poluted"; Raneem Alozzi, "Let TTC Subway Workers Use Face Masks Over Air Quality Concerns, Transit Unions Say," *Toronto Star*, August 1, 2019, www.thestar.com; Adam Carter, "Rare Private Prosecution Charges Levied against TTC over Subway Air Quality," *CBC News*, November 29, 2019, www.cbc.ca. Similarly, the researchers who tested the air quality of the London Underground noted that new airtight trains with closed windows offer major improvements for the amount of particulate matter that riders are exposed to, with better ventilation offering even more improvements. (Grafton-Green, "People Who Use Tube 'Exposed to Eight Times More Air Pollution.'")

83. Pelley, "Ride the GO Train?"; Bryan Passifiume, "On the Move: Metrolinx Pushes GTA Transit Plan Forward," *Toronto Sun*, January 6, 2019, https://torontosun.com. Transport for London announced an £86.1 million ($110 million USD) program in 2017 to retrofit some 5,000 of the city's buses with exhaust systems to cut down air pollution like nitrogen dioxide and particulate matter by up to 95 percent. (Will Date, "£86.1 Million London Bus Retrofit Programme Announced," *Air Quality News*, June 28, 2017, https://airqualitynews.com.)

84. Michael Glotz-Richter and Hendrick Koch, "Electrification of Public Transport in Cities (Horizon 2020 ELIPTIC Project)," *Transportation Research Procedia* 14 (2016): 2614–19.

85. Alaric Nightingale, "Forget Tesla, It's China's E-Buses That Are Denting Oil Demand," *Bloomberg*, March 19, 2019, www.bloomberg.com.

86. Linse and Barasz, "Urban Transportation Will Go All-Electric."

87. "Proterra Catalyst Electric Vehicles Achieve Up to 25 MPGe," Proterra, www.proterra.com.

88. This comparison especially holds true if autonomous vehicles

continue to use extremely high levels of energy, requiring even larger batteries to operate on a regular basis.

89. Skip Descant, "Electric Buses Are Not Only Clean but Less Costly to Run," *Government Technology*, December 4, 2018, www.govtech.com.

90. Aarian Marshall, "Why Electric Buses Haven't Taken Over the World—Yet," *Wired*, June 7, 2019, www.wired.com.

91. Kyle Field, "Could Buses Be the Perfect Vehicle-to-Grid Mobile Battery for Cities?," *CleanTechnica*, May 24, 2018, www.cleantechnica.com.

92. Paige St. John, "Stalls, Stops and Breakdowns: Problems Plague Push for Electric Buses," *Los Angeles Times*, May 20, 2018; Joshua Panas, "City of Albuquerque, BYD Reach Settlement after Fallout Over ART Project," *KOB-TV*, May 31, 2019, www.kob.com.

93. Alon Levy, Josh Fairchild, and James Aloisi, "Kicking the Tires on Battery-Electric Buses," *CommonWealth*, May 25, 2019, https://commonwealthmagazine.org.

94. Andy Darrell, "New Electric Buses Are a Holiday Gift for New York City," Environmental Defense Fund, December 23, 2019, www.blogs.edf.org.

95. China, in comparison, has added approximately 80,000 new electric buses to its fleets. In late 2017, Shenzhen became the first city in the world to electrify its entire fleet with 16,359 buses, which required the construction of 510 charging stations and 8,000 charging poles across the city. Of the 385,000 electric buses in the world, 99 percent are now in China. (Linda Poon, "How China Took Charge of the Electric Bus Revolution," *CityLab*, May 8, 2018, www.citylab.com; Han Ximin, "All Shenzhen Public Buses Now Electric," *EyeShenzhen*, December 28, 2017, https://mp.weixin.qq.com.)

96. Levy, Fairchild, and Aloisi, "Kicking the Tires on Battery-Electric Buses."

97. Eric Doherty, "Battery Trolleybuses Ready for Heavy Duty Climate Action," *National Observer*, December 19, 2018, www.nationalobserver.com.

98. "Everett Bus Lane: The Little Pop-Up That Could," TransitCenter, January 2, 2018, http://transitcenter.org.

99. "Buses, Trains, and Hurricanes: Transit and Natural Disasters," Canadian Urban Transit Association, October 24, 2017, http://cutaactu.ca.

100. Jennifer Temmer and Henry David Venema, *Building a Climate-Resilient City: Transportation infrastructure* (Winnipeg: International Institute for Sustainable Development, April 2017);

"Smart Growth and Climate Change," United States Environmental Protection Agency, www.epa.gov.

1. Nathan Bomey, "Why Buying a New Car Is More Expensive Than Ever," *USA Today*, September 12, 2019, www.usatoday.com. The range is from $7,110 for a small sedan to $10,840 for a pickup truck. The average new vehicle depreciated by $3,330 in 2019.

2. Ryan Felton, "Americans Owe a Record $1.1 Trillion in Car Loans," *Jalopnik*, September 18, 2017, https://jalopnik.com; Higashide, *Better Buses, Better Cities*, 6. This debt load increased by 75 percent between 2009 and 2018. In addition to the 17.2 million vehicles bought in 2018, another 40 million used vehicles were exchanged.

3. Adie Tomer, *Transit Access and Zero-Vehicle Households* (Washington, DC: Brookings Institution, 2011), www.brookings.edu; "Household, Individual, and Vehicle Characteristics," Bureau of Transportation Statistics, May 20, 2017, www.bts.gov.

4. "Car Access United States," National Equity Atlas, https://nationalequityatlas.org. Only 6.5 percent of white households don't have a vehicle.

5. "Household Expenditures and Income," Pew Charitable Trusts, March 30, 2016, www.pewtrusts.org.

6. Alana Semuels, "No Driver's License, No Job," *Atlantic*, June 15, 2016, www.theatlantic.com.

7. David C. Phillips, *Do Low-Wage Employers Discriminate against Applicants with Long Commutes?: Evidence from a Correspondence Experiment* (Notre Dame: University of Notre Dame, 2018), 3, https://poverty.ucdavis.edu.

8. Higashide, *Better Buses, Better Cities*, 5.

9. Paula Dutko, Michele Ver Ploeg, and Tracey Farrigan, *Characteristics and Influential Factors of Food Deserts* (Washington, DC: United States Department of Agriculture, 2012), 13, www.ers.usda.gov.

10. Imran Cronk, "The Transportation Barrier," *Atlantic*, August 9, 2015, www.theatlantic.com.

11. Emily Badger, "The Suburbanization of Poverty," *CityLab*, May 20, 2013, www.citylab.com.

12. "Drive Clean in the San Joaquin," San Joaquin Valley Air Pollution Control District, www.valleyair.org; "Replace Your Ride," South Coast Air Quality Management District, https://xappprod.aqmd.gov/RYR.

13. Dani Burlison, "Making EVs Possible for Low-Income

Drivers," *Sustainable America*, November 30, 2018, https://sustainableamerica.org.

14. BlueLA, https://www.bluela.com.

15. Alissa Walker, "When Electric Isn't Good Enough: Sacramento Is the Staging Ground for a Fight to Make Drivers Spend Less Time on the Road," *Curbed*, October 24, 2018, www.curbed.com.

16. Laura Bliss, "Rural California Awaits Its 'Uber,'" *CityLab*, September 21, 2017, www.citylab.com.

17. Patricia Leigh Brown, "The Anti-Uber," *New York Times*, June 17, 2017, www.nytimes.com.

18. Malak Abas, "The Winnipeg Women Ridesharing to Keep Each Other Safe," *Vice*, February 1, 2019, www.vice.com.

19. Edu Bayer, "Inside the Dollar Van Wars," *New York Times*, June 8, 2018, www.nytimes.com.

20. Brown, "The Anti-Uber."

21. Laura Bliss, "Lyft Is Reaching L.A. Neighborhoods Where Taxis Wouldn't," *CityLab*, June 29, 2018, www.citylab.com.

22. Bliss, "Lyft Is Reaching L.A. Neighborhoods"; Will Livesley-O'Neill, "Ridehail Revolution: Groundbreaking ITS Dissertation Examines Discrimination and Travel Patterns for Lyft, Uber, and Taxis," UCLA Institute of Transportation Studies, June 27, 2018, www.its.ucla.edu.

23. Dara Kerr, "Lyft Pledges $1.5M to Give Free Rides to Low-Income People," *CNET*, May 2, 2018, www.cnet.com; "Expanding 'Wheels for All' to Help Those in Need," Lyft Blog, May 2, 2018, https://blog.lyft.com.

24. Elise Herron, "Portlanders in Food Deserts Can Soon Take a Lyft to the Grocery Store for the Same Price as a Bus Ticket," *Willamette Week*, May 30, 2019, www.wweek.com; Travis Robinson, "Health Leaders, Lyft Team Up to Help Indianapolis Food Desert," *WISH*, June 4, 2019, www.wishtv.com.

25. Ashley Nunes, "If Driverless Cars Are Going to Change the World, They Have to Be Affordable," *Guardian*, March 12, 2019, www.theguardian.com.

26. "Saving on Fuel and Vehicle Costs," Office of Energy Efficiency & Renewable Energy, www.energy.gov.

27. "How Much Do Electric Cars Cost?," EnergySage, January 2, 2019, www.energysage.com.

28. Jack Stewart, "Tesla's $7,500 Tax Credit Goes Poof, But Buyers May Benefit," *Wired,* January 2, 2019, www.wired.com.

29. Molly F. Sherlock, *The Plug-In Electric Vehicle Tax Credit* (Washington, DC: Congressional Research Service, 2019), 2, https://fas.org.

30. Joe Cortright, "Electric Vehicle Subsidies: Inefficient & Inequitable," *City Observatory*, June 5, 2019, http://cityobservatory.org.

31. Sean O'Kane, "GM Will Be the Second Automaker to Lose the EV Tax Credit, While Bolt Sales Stumble," *Verge*, January 3, 2019, www.theverge.com; Sean Szymkowski, "Trump's Proposed 2020 Budget Would End Electric-Car Tax Credits," *Car Connection*, March 12, 2019, www.thecarconnection.com. Congressional Research Service calculated that maintaining the tax credit will cost a total of $7.5 billion between 2018 and 2022 in forgone revenue. (Sherlock, *The Plug-In Electric Vehicle Tax Credit*, 2.)

32. Ellen Edmonds, "AAA: Ride-Hailing Twice the Cost of Car Ownership," AAA, August 21, 2018, https://newsroom.aaa.com.

33. Tim Dunne, "Ride-Hailing Services: The Price Better Be Right," J.D. Power, February 21, 2018, www.jdpower.com; Megan Leonhardt, "Uber and Lyft Are Costing 20-Somethings an Insane Amount of Money in the Long Term," *Business Insider*, February 9, 2018, www.businessinsider.com.

34. People with a household income over $200,000 per year account for close to 45 trips per person annually, compared to under 15 per year for households that earn between $50,000 and $100,000, and closer to 5 for households that earn under $50,000. (Schaller, *The New Automobility*, 12.)

35. Hubert Horan, "Can Uber Ever Deliver? Part Three: Understanding False Claims about Uber's Innovation and Competitive Advantages," *Naked Capitalism*, December 2, 2016, www.nakedcapitalism.com.

36. Matthew Daus, *The Expanding Transportation Network Company "Equity Gap": Adverse Impacts on Passengers with Disabilities, Underserved Communities, the Environment & the On-Demand Workforce* (New York City: University Transportation Research Center, 2018), 20.

37. Todd Litman, *Autonomous Vehicle Implementation Predictions: Implications for Transport Planning* (Victoria: Victoria Transportation Policy Institute, 2019), 9, www.vtpi.org.

38. Daus, *The Expanding Transportation Network*, 32.

39. Hana Creger, "Public Transit: Uber's Next Casualty?," Greenlining Institute, August 3, 2017, http://greenlining.org.

40. Anne E. Brown, "Op-Ed: L.A.'s Taxi Industry Discriminates against Black Riders: If We Don't Force Them to Change, They Won't," *Los Angeles Times*, August 12, 2018, www.latimes.com.

41. Compared to passengers with white-sounding names, passengers with African American–sounding names experience 35 percent longer waiting times and twice as frequent cancellation rates. (Yanbo Ge, Christopher R. Knittel, Don MacKenzie, and Stephen

Zoepf, *Racial and Gender Discrimination in Transportation Network Companies* (Cambridge: National Bureau of Economic Research, October 2016), 2, www.nber.org.)

42. Rebekah Sanders, "Uber and Lyft Are Making It Harder for Arizona Seniors to Get Around," *Arizona Republic*, June 12, 2018.

43. Daus, *The Expanding Transportation Network*, 40.

44. "Mobile Fact Sheet," Pew Research Center, February 5, 2018, www.pewresearch.org.

45. David Roberts, "Here's the Real Nightmare Scenario for Self-Driving Cars," *Vox*, April 20, 2018, www.vox.com.

46. Adrienne Lafrance, "How Self-Driving Cars Will Threaten Privacy," *Atlantic*, March 21, 2016, www.theatlantic.com.

47. "The Most and Least Affordable Cities for Public Transit," *ValuePenguin*, March 2017, www.valuepenguin.com. This average is based on a survey of 73 cities.

48. Higashide, *Better Buses, Better Cities*, 15.

49. "Transit Deserts & Hulchanski's Three Cities," Martin Prosperity Institute, 2010, www.martinprosperity.org; "Stranded without Transit?: U of T Researchers Say One Million Urban Canadians Suffer from 'Transport Poverty,'" *U of T News*, January 9, 2019, www.utoronto.ca/news.

50. Deepa Chandran, "Transportation Inclusion and Community Wellbeing: Exploring Public Transit Accessibility of Winnipeg's North End Neighbourhoods," master's thesis (University of Manitoba, 2017), 80.

51. White members made up 88 percent of MPO boards in 2006, while representing only 61 percent of the population. Only 3 percent of board members were Hispanic, despite making up 17 percent of the population; and Black people made up 7 percent of boards though they represented 15 percent of the population. (Angie Schmitt, "How Structural Racism at Regional Planning Agencies Hurts Cities," *Streetsblog USA*, January 5, 2018, https://usa.streetsblog.org.)

52. "Deliberations are primarily technocratic, with the majority of substantive discussion occurring among specialists within technical committees who arrive at a consensus to serve to the elected officials on MPO boards." (Thomas W. Sanchez, *An Inherent Bias?: Geographic and Racial-Ethnic Patterns of Metropolitan Planning Organization Boards* (Washington, DC: Brookings Institution, 2006), 6, www.brookings.edu.)

53. Cameron MacLeod, Patricia Wood, Matthew Whittier, and Benjamin Wert, *Mixed Signals: Toronto Transit in a North American Context* (Toronto: CodeRedTO, 2018), www.coderedto.com.

54. Higashide, *Better Buses, Better Cities*, 11, 19.

55. Josh Cohen, "Seattle Raises the Equity Bar on Transit-Oriented Development," *Next City*, May 8, 2018, https://nextcity.org.

56. "Community Benefits Agreements," Toronto and York

Region Labour Council, January 2013, www.labourcouncil.ca/community_benefits.

57. Carlito Pablo, "Vancouver Plan to Mass Rezone 67,000 Single-Family Lots for Duplexes up for Public Hearing," *Georgia Straight*, August 23, 2018, www.straight.com; Sarah Mervosh, "Minneapolis, Tackling Housing Crisis and Inequity, Votes to End Single-Family Zoning," *New York Times*, December 13, 2018.

58. Adam Brinklow, "Poll: Two-Thirds of California Voters Back SB 50 Housing Bill," *Curbed*, May 17, 2019, https://sf.curbed.com; Matthew Yglesias, "Gavin Newsom Promised to Fix California's Housing Crisis: Here's a Bill That Would Do It," *Vox*, December 7, 2018, www.vox.com. The bill has popular support, but it was delayed for voting until 2020.

59. Samuel Stein, "The Zone Defense," *Jacobin*, June 4, 2019, www.jacobinmag.com.

60. Kipfer, "Free Transit and Beyond."

61. Zach Dubinsky and Valerie Ouellet, "Who's behind the Smiling Faces of Some Airbnb Hosts?: Multimillion-Dollar Corporations," *CBC News*, April 30, 2019, www.cbc.ca.

62. Samuel Stein, "Tenants Won This Round," June 18, 2019, www.jacobinmag.com.

63. Ryan Reft, "From Bus Riders Union to Bus Rapid Transit: Race, Class, and Transit Infrastructure in Los Angeles," *KCET*, May 14, 2015, www.kcet.org.

64. Scott Miller, "The Los Angeles Bus Riders Union," *Against the Current* 69 (1997), www.solidarity-us.org; Daniel B. Wood, "No-Seat, No-Fare Campaign Moves L.A. Buses into Gear," *Christian Science Monitor*, September 14, 1998, www.csmonitor.com.

65. Matthew Roth, "FTA Won't Fund BART Airport Connector, $70 Million to Go to Transit Ops," *Streetsblog SF*, February 12, 2010, https://sf.streetsblog.org.

66. Minerva Perez, "Stockton Is Building an All-Electric Bus Rapid Transit Route," *StreetsBlog CAL*, August 10, 2017, https://cal.streetsblog.org.

67. "Our Accomplishments," TTCriders, www.ttcriders.ca.

68. "Transit Users Launch Petition Calling for Affordable Fares on New Union Pearson Line," Our Union Pearson Coalition, November 24, 2014, www.ttcriders.ca.

69. Aurelio Perri, "City of Calgary Sells 70K Sliding-Scale Low-Income Transit Passes in First 3 Months," *Global News*, September 6, 2017, https://globalnews.ca.

70. Roberta Altstadt, "TriMet Moves Forward on Launch of Low-Income Fare Program Aimed for July 1, 2018," TriMet, January 24, 2018, http://news.trimet.org.

71. J. David Goodman, "Of 800,000 Poor New Yorkers, Only 30,000 Can Get the New Half-Priced MetroCards," *New York Times*, January 4, 2019, www.nytimes.com.

72. Dellheim, Judith, and Jason Prince, eds., *Free Public Transit: And Why We Don't Pay to Ride Elevators* (Montreal: Black Rose Books, 2018), 4. In mid-2018, Estonia announced that it was expanding free public transit from its capital Tallinn to the entire country for bus travel to rural municipalities and other regions. (Feargus O'Sullivan, "Estonia Will Roll Out Free Public Transit Nationwide," *CityLab*, May 17, 2018, www.citylab.com.) The French city of Dunkirk introduced free transit in late 2018, making it the largest municipality in Europe to do so; a month after its launch, the city's mayor reported up to an 85 percent increase on some routes. (Kim Willsher, "'I Leave the Car at Home': How Free Buses Are Revolutionising One French City," *Guardian*, October 15, 2018, www.theguardian.com.)

73. Eric Jaffe, "How Free Transit Works in the United States," *CityLab*, March 6, 2013, www.citylab.com; David Erickson, "Mountain Line Bus Rides to Remain 'Zero Fare' through at Least 2020," *Missoulian*, October 13, 2017, https://missoulian.com; Angie Schmitt, "How Tampa Tripled Ridership on Its Streetcar," *Streetsblog USA*, April 8, 2019, https://usa.streetsblog.org.

74. Richard Zussman, "City of Victoria Proposes Free Public Transit, Province Not Willing to Foot the Bill," *Global News*, April 26, 2019, www.globalnews.ca; Laura Bliss, "Why Kansas City's Free Transit Experiment Matters," *CityLab*, December 13, 2019, www.citylab.com.

75. Blair Stenvick, "TriMet Board Members Say They're Considering a Fareless System," *Portland Mercury*, December 11, 2019, www.portlandmercury.com.

76. Wojciech Kębłowski, "Public Transport Can Be Free," *Jacobin*, August 24, 2018, www.jacobinmag.com.

77. Dellheim and Prince, *Free Public Transit*, xix–xx.

78. "French City of Dunkirk Tests Out Free Transport—and It Works," *France24*, August 31, 2019, www.france24.com.

79. "2019 Preliminary Operating Budget: Transit Department," City of Winnipeg, March 7, 2019, www.winnipeg.ca.

80. Brooks, "How New York Taxi Workers Took On Uber."

81. Jose Martinez, "MTA Looks to Lure Dollar Van Passengers Back," *Spectrum News*, August 28, 2018, www.ny1.com.

1. Daniel Golson, Joey Capparella, and Laura Sky Brown, "Check Out Every Car Commercial from Super Bowl LIII 2019," *Car and Driver*, February 4, 2019, www.caranddriver.com.

2. Lee Morgan, "The Effects of Traffic Congestion," *USA Today*, https://traveltips.usatoday.com.

3. Phil LeBeau, "Traffic Jams Cost US $87 Billion in Lost Productivity in 2018, and Boston and DC Have the Nation's Worst," *CNBC*, February 12, 2019, www.cnbc.com.

4. Benjamin Schneider, "CityLab University: Induced Demand," *CityLab*, September 6, 2018, www.citylab.com.

5. Higashide, *Better Buses, Better Cities*, 5.

6. Paul Barter, "'Cars Are Parked 95% of the Time': Let's Check!" Reinventing Parking, February 22, 2013, www.reinventingparking.org.

7. Higashide, *Better Buses, Better Cities*, 3.

8. Mikhail Chester et al., "Parking Infrastructure: A Constraint on or Opportunity for Urban Redevelopment?: A Study of Los Angeles County Parking Supply and Growth," *Journal of the American Planning Association* 81, no. 4 (2015): 268–86; Joe Linton, "18.6 Million Spaces and Still Rising: Study Puts L.A. Parking in Perspective," *Streetsblog LA*, December 1, 2015, https://la.streetsblog.org; Laura Bliss, "Mapping L.A. County's 'Parking Crater,'" *CityLab*, January 11, 2016, www.citylab.com.

9. Tony Dutzik, Elizabeth Berg, Alana Miller, and Rachel Cross, *Who Pays for Parking?: How Federal Tax Subsidies Jam More Cars into Congested Cities, and How Cities Can Reclaim Their Streets* (Santa Barbara: Frontier Group, September 2017), 21, www.frontiergroup.org.

10. "Abolish Parking Minimums," TransitCenter, March 13, 2019, http://transitcenter.org.

11. "Vehicle Deaths Estimated at 40,000 for Third Straight Year," National Safety Council, 2019, www.nsc.org.

12. "Road Traffic Injuries," World Health Organization, December 7, 2018, www.who.int.

13. Richard Florida, "The Geography of Car Deaths in America," *CityLab*, October 15, 2015, www.citylab.com; "Maximum Posted Speed Limits by State," Insurance Institute for Highway Safety, 2019, www.iihs.org.

14. "Distracted Driving 2015," U.S. Department of Transportation, March 2017, https://crashstats.nhtsa.dot.gov.

15. "Vehicle Deaths Estimated at 40,000," National Safety Council.

16. This is the highest percentage since 1985. ("Fatality Facts 2017: State by State," Insurance Institute for Highway Safety, www.iihs.org;

Angie Schmitt, "The Unequal Toll of Pedestrian Deaths," *StreetsBlog USA*, January 10, 2017, https://usa.streetsblog.org.)

17. *Dangerous by Design 2019* (Washington, DC: Smart Growth America, 2019), smartgrowthamerica.org, 2.

18. Angela Laguipo, "Pedestrian Wheelchair Users 36 Percent More Likely to Die in Car Crashes," *Tech Times*, November 27, 2015, www.techtimes.com; Susan Perry, "Pedestrian Wheelchair Users Are at Increased Risk of Dying in Road Collisions, Study Finds," *MinnPost*, November 20, 2015, www.minnpost.com.

19. Schmitt, "The Unequal Toll of Pedestrian Deaths."

20. Anna Lusk, "You Can't Design Bike-Friendly Cities without Considering Race and Class," *CityLab*, February 8, 2019, www.citylab.com.

21. "Building Equity: Race, Ethnicity, Class, and Protected Bike Lanes: An Idea Book for Fairer Cities," PeopleForBikes and Alliance for Biking & Walking, 2014, https://peopleforbikes.org; *Dangerous by Design*, 21.

22. Shill, "Should Law Subsidize Driving?"

23. Ryan Briggs, "City Streets Safer Than Suburban Roads, Study Finds," *Plan Philly*, May 21, 2019, http://planphilly.com; "Road Safety–Speed," World Health Organization, www.who.int.

24. Also, between 2009 and 2016, pedestrian deaths caused by a crash involving an SUV increased by 81 percent. (Erin D. Lawrence, Nathan Bomey, and Kristi Tanner, "Death on Foot: America's Love of SUVs Is Killing Pedestrians," *Detroit Free Press*, July 1, 2018, www.freep.com.)

25. Toby Hagon, "New Tesla Cybertruck Could Put Other Road Users at Risk," *News.com.au,* November 26, 2019, www.news.com.au.

26. Michael Gushulak, "Tesla's Cybertruck: A Rolling Tank against Cyclists & Pedestrians?," *BikeRumor*, November 25, 2019, www.bikerumor.com.

27. "Shared Mobility Principles for Livable Cities," www.sharedmobilityprinciples.org.

28. Corey D. Harper, Chris T. Henderickson, and Constantine Samaras, "Cost and Benefit Estimates of Partially Automated Vehicle Collision Avoidance Technologies," *Accident Analysis & Prevention* 95 (October 2016): 104–15.

29. Raluca Budiu, "Tesla's Touchscreen UI: A Case Study of Car-Dashboard User Interface," Nielsen Norman Group, May 19, 2019, www.nngroup.com.

30. Tamra Johnson, "New Vehicle Infotainment Systems Create Increased Distractions behind the Wheel," AAA, October 5, 2017, www.newsroom.aaa.com.

31. Topham, "Uber to Introduce Clean Air Fee."

32. Danny King, "Zipcar Says Its 1 Million Members Have Taken 400,000 Vehicles off the Road," *Autoblog*, September 9, 2016, www.autoblog.com.

33. Andrew J. Hawkins, "Lyft Will Pay You $550 to Ditch Your Car for a Month," *Verge*, July 31, 2018, www.theverge.com; Jonathon Ramsey, "Lyft Asks for Volunteers to Ditch Their Cars for a Month, 150,000 Sign Up," *Autoblog*, October 8, 2018, www.autoblog.com. Lyft reported that 52 percent of applicants said they found driving stressful, while 57 percent of the 2,000 participants used their personal vehicles less after ditching their car for the month. Next to the reason of going out and drinking (46.1 percent) and time pressures (39.9 percent), the difficulty and expense of parking represented the main reason for why people choose a ride-hailing option (33.1 percent). ("Why 130,000 Lyft Passengers Were Ready to Ditch Their Personal Cars in Less Than 24 Hours," Lyft, December 13, 2018, https://blog.lyft.com.)

34. Mike Ramsey, "Self-Driving Cars Could Cut Down on Accidents, Study Says," *Wall Street Journal*, March 5, 2015.

35. "2018 Self-Driving Safety Report," General Motors, www.gm.com.

36. Steven Higashide, "4 Things for Transit Agencies to Remember in a World of Driverless Car Hype," TransitCenter, May 3, 2018, http://transitcenter.org.

37. Alejandro Henao, "Impacts of Ridesourcing—Lyft and Uber—on Transportation Including VMT, Mode Replacement, Parking, and Travel Behavior" (PhD diss., University of Colorado, 2017).

38. Gehrke, Felix, and Reardon, *A Survey of Ride-Hailing Passengers*, 12.

39. Andrew J. Hawkins, "Uber and Lyft Are the 'Biggest Contributors' to San Francisco's Traffic Congestion, Study Says," *Verge*, May 8, 2019, www.theverge.com.

40. Roger Rudick, "Supervisor Shocked to Hear Uber and Lyft Violate Bike and Transit Lanes," *Streetsblog SF*, September 26, 2017, https://sf.streetsblog.org.

41. Eric Scott, "Column: The Increasing Number of Uber, Lyft Drivers Need to Stay in Their Lane," *Pioneer Press*, November 7, 2018, www.twincities.com.

42. Andrew J. Hawkins, "Cars with High-Tech Safety Systems Are Still Really Bad at Not Running People Over," *Verge*, October 4, 2019, www.theverge.com.

43. Andrew Weber, "Ride-Hailing Hasn't Reduced Drunk Driving-Related Traffic Fatalities, Study Says," *KUT News*, July 28, 2016, www.kut.org.

44. Charlotte Jee, "Uber and Lyft Are behind a Sharp Rise in US

Traffic Deaths," *MIT Technology Review*, October 25, 2018, www. technologyreview.com.

45. Laura Bliss, "Uber and Lyft's Link to Traffic Fatalities," *CityLab*, October 26, 2018, www.citylab.com.

46. "Consumer Reports: 1000s of Uber, Lyft Drivers' Vehicles Have Outstanding Recalls for Deadly Defects," *Associated Press*, May 21, 2019, https://sanfrancisco.cbslocal.com.

47. Litman, *Autonomous Vehicle Implementation Predictions*, 10.

48. Litman, *Autonomous Vehicle Implementation Predictions*, 14.

49. David R. Baker, "How Self-Driving Cars Could Become Weapons of Terror," *San Francisco Chronicle*, October 10, 2016, www. sfchronicle.com.

50. Connie Loizos, "Uber Has Settled with the Family of the Homeless Victim Killed Last Week," *TechCrunch*, March 29, 2018, www.techcrunch.com.

51. Fred Lambert, "Understanding the Fatal Tesla Accident on Autopilot and the NHTSA Probe," *Electrek*, July 1, 2016, https:// electrek.co; Andrew J. Hawkins, "Tesla Didn't Fix an Autopilot Problem for Three Years, and Now Another Person Is Dead," *Verge*, May 17, 2019, www.theverge.com; Michael Grothaus, "Report: Apple Engineer Who Died in Tesla Crash Had Warned about Autopilot Errors," *Fast Company*, March 29, 2018, www.fastcompany.com; Fred Lambert, "Tesla Driver Arrested for Drunk Driving after Blaming Autopilot for Crashing into a Fire Truck," *Electrek*, August 25, 2018, https://electrek.co; Paris Marx, "Tesla on Autopilot Slammed into (Another) Truck," *Radical Urbanist*, May 22, 2019, https:// medium.com.

52. Hawkins, "Tesla Didn't Fix an Autopilot Problem."

53. Matt Drange, "Studies Don't Support Elon Musk's Autopilot Safety Claims," *Information*, May 29, 2019, www.theinformation.com.

54. Nidhi Kalra and Susan M. Paddock, *Driving to Safety: How Many Miles of Driving Would It Take to Demonstrate Autonomous Vehicle Reliability?* (Santa Monica: Rand Corporation, 2016), 10, www.rand.org.

55. Kirsten Korosec, "Waymo's Self-Driving Cars Hit 10 Million Miles," *TechCrunch*, October 10, 2018, https://techcrunch.com.

56. Kalra and Paddock, *Driving to Safety*, 10.

57. Andrew J. Hawkins, "Self-Driving Car Crashes Put a Dent in Consumer Trust, Poll Says," *Verge*, May 22, 2018, www.theverge.com.

58. Stephen Edelstein, "Consumers Have Become More Apprehensive about Self-Driving Cars, Study Says," *Drive*, August 16, 2018, www.thedrive.com.

59. Simon Romero, "Wielding Rocks and Knives, Arizonans Attack Self-Driving Cars," *New York Times*, December 31, 2018; Julia Carrie

Wong, "Rage against the Machine: Self-Driving Cars Attacked by Angry Californians," *Guardian*, March 6, 2018, www.theguardian.com.

60. Faiz Siddiqui, "Silicon Valley Pioneered Self-Driving Cars: But Some of Its Tech-Savvy Residents Don't Want Them Tested in Their Neighborhoods," *Washington Post*, October 3, 2019, www.washingtonpost.com.

61. Jeremy Kahn, "To Get Ready for Robot Driving, Some Want to Reprogram Pedestrians," *Bloomberg*, August 16, 2018, www.bloomberg.com.

62. Angie Schmitt, "Self-Driving Car Makes Prepare to Blame 'Jaywalkers,'" *Streetsblog USA*, August 17, 2018, https://usa.streetsblog.org.

63. Amir Efrati, "Waymo's Big Ambitions Slowed by Tech Trouble," *Information*, August 28, 2017, www.theinformation.com.

64. Russell Brandon, "Self-Driving Cars Are Headed toward an AI Roadblock," *Verge*, July 3, 2018, www.theverge.com.

65. Rodney Brooks, "Bothersome Bystanders and Self Driving Cars," Rodney Brooks, July 4, 2018, https://rodneybrooks.com.

66. Charlie Sorrel, "Self-Driving Mercedes Will Be Programmed to Sacrifice Pedestrians to Save the Driver," *Fast Company*, October 13, 2016, www.fastcompany.com.

67. Johannes Himmelreich, "The Everyday Ethical Challenges of Self-Driving Cars," *Conversation*, March 27, 2018, https://theconversation.com.

68. Sigal Samuel, "A New Study Finds a Potential Risk with Self-Driving Cars: Failure to Detect Dark-Skinned Pedestrians," *Vox*, March 6, 2019, www.vox.com.

69. Angie Schmitt, "Self-Driving Cars Are Coming: Will They Serve Profit or the Public?," *In These Times*, July 6, 2018, http://inthesetimes.com.

70. Angie Schmitt, "Uber Got Off the Hook for Killing a Pedestrian with its Self-Driving Car," *Streetsblog USA*, March 8, 2019, https://usa.streetsblog.org.

71. Timothy B. Lee, "How Terrible Software Design Decisions Led to Uber's Deadly 2018 Crash," *Ars Technica*, November 6, 2019, www.arstechnica.com.

72. Ashley Nunes and Kristen Hernandez, "The Cost of Self-Driving Cars Will Be the Biggest Barrier to Their Adoption," *Harvard Business Review*, January 31, 2019, https://hbr.org.

73. Andrew J. Hawkins, "A Day in the Life of a Waymo Self-Driving Taxi," *Verge*, August 21, 2018, www.theverge.com; Steve LeVine, "What It Really Costs to Turn a Car into a Self-Driving Vehicle," *Quartz*, March 5, 2017, https://qz.com.

74. Adam Millard-Ball, "The Autonomous Vehicle Parking Problem," *Transport Policy* 75 (March 2019): 99–108.

75. Brent Skorup, "Driverless Cars Need Just One Thing: Futuristic Roads," *Wired*, October 10, 2016, www.wired.com.

76. Jeff Davis, "Is the Federal-Aid Highway Program Compatible with the 'Green New Deal?,'" Eno Center for Transportation, January 25, 2019, www.enotrans.org.

77. The gas tax has stagnated at 18.4 cents per gallon since 1993. If the rate had been indexed for inflation, the current tax on gasoline would be about 31 cents per gallon and on diesel fuel about 42 cents. (Aarian Marshall, "How the Humble Gas Tax Became an American Bogeyman," *Wired*, May 9, 2017, www.wired.com; Tony Dutzik, Gideon Weissman, and Phineas Baxandall, *Who Pays for Roads?: How the "Users Pay" Myth Gets in the Way of Solving America's Transportation Problems* (Boston: Frontier Group, 2015), 10, https://frontiergroup.org.)

78. "What Is the Highway Trust Fund, and How Is It Financed?," Tax Policy Center, www.taxpolicycenter.org.

79. Dutzik, Weissman, and Baxandall, *Who Pays for Roads?*, 2.

80. Shill, "Should Law Subsidize Driving?"; Joe Cortright, "There's No Such Thing as a Free-Way," *City Observatory*, May 13, 2015, http://cityobservatory.org.

81. Lynn Anderson Davy and Morgan Kelly, "Houston's Urban Sprawl Increased Rainfall, Flooding during Hurricane Harvey," Princeton University, November 15, 2018, www.princeton.edu.

82. John Vidal, "As Flood Waters Rise, Is Urban Sprawl as Much to Blame as Climate Change?," *Guardian*, September 3, 2017, www.theguardian.com.

83. Sean Marshall, "Cars Take Up Too Much Space on King Street," *Torontoist*, February 18, 2017, https://torontoist.com.

84. "King Street Transit Pilot," City of Toronto, 2019, www.toronto.ca.

85. "King Street by the Numbers," Ryerson City Building Institute, April 3, 2019, www.citybuildinginstitute.ca.

86. Sam Schwartz, *14th Street Transit & Truck Priority Pilot Project* (New York City: Sam Schwartz Transportation Consultants, 2019).

87. Tamar Harris, "Some Businesses Give an Icy Middle Finger to King St. Pilot," *Toronto Star*, January 17, 2018, www.thestar.com.

88. "Transportation Fatalities by Mode," Bureau of Transportation Statistics, www.bts.gov.

89. While drivers or passengers of private automobiles experienced 7.28 deaths per billion passenger-miles between 2000 and 2009, bus passengers—including transit, intercity, school and charter buses—only accounted for 0.11 deaths. Urban mass transit rail such as subways and light rail results in an average of 0.24 deaths per billion

passenger-miles, while commuter rail and Amtrak average 0.43. (Ian Savage, "Comparing the Fatality Risks in United States Transportation Across Modes and Over Time," *Research in Transportation Economics: The Economics of Transportation Safety* 43, no. 1 (2013): 29.)

90. John Metcalfe, "A Good Way to Avoid Injuries on the Road: Ride the Bus," *CityLab*, January 27, 2017, www.citylab.com.

91. Angie Schmitt, "The Best Tool for Reducing Traffic Deaths?: More Transit!," *Streetsblog USA*, August 29, 2018, https://usa. streetsblog.org; Sommer Mathis, "What If the Best Way to End Drunk Driving Is to End Driving?," *CityLab*, June 4, 2014, www.citylab.com.

92. "Amtrak Train Derailment," *Seattle Times*, May 22, 2019, www. seattletimes.com; Jeffrey Cook et al., "South Carolina Amtrak Crash Is the Latest in a String of Accidents over the Past Few Years," *ABC News*, February 5, 2018, https://abcnews.go.com.

93. Trevor Pritchard, "What We Still Don't Know about the fatal Ottawa Bus Crash," *CBC News*, January 13, 2019, www.cbc.ca.

94. Paul Mackie, "Transit Is 10-Times Safer Than Driving—and Makes Communities Safer, Says New APTA Report," *Mobility Lab*, September 8, 2016, https://mobilitylab.org; Schmitt, "The Best Tool for Reducing Traffic Deaths?"

95. Todd Litman, *Safer Than You Think!: Revising the Transit Safety Narrative* (Victoria: Victoria Transport Policy Institute, July 24, 2018).

96. Michael Mui, "1,235 People Have Died on Canadian Subway and Rail Tracks since 2007: Why Don't We Have Safety Barriers?," *Toronto Star*, August 19, 2018, www.thestar.com.

97. Mui, "1,235 People Have Died."

98. Neil deMause, "Can New York Plug All Its Subway Holes Before the Next Storm Hits?," *Gizmodo*, December 12, 2019, www.earther. gizmodo.com.

99. Athlyn Cathcart-Keays, "Why Copenhagen Is Building Parks That Can Turn into Ponds," *CityLab*, January 22, 2016, www. citylab.com.

100. Christopher Robbins, "Gentrified Aquarium: De Blasio's Streetcar and the Tale of Two Waterfronts," *Village Voice*, September 13, 2016, www.villagevoice.com.

101. Joseph Stromberg, "The Real Reason American Public Transportation Is Such a Disaster," *Vox*, August 10, 2015, www. vox.com.

102. Mees, *Transport for Suburbia*, 5.

103. Kim Parker, Juliana Menasce Horowitz, Anna Brown, Richard Fry, D'Vera Cohn and Ruth Igielnik, "1. Demographic and Economic Trends in Urban, Suburban and Rural Communities," Pew Research Center, May 22, 2018, www.pewsocialtrends.org.

104. David L.A. Gordon, "Canadians Increasingly Live in the

Auto-Dependent Suburbs," *Building*, October 10, 2018, https://building.ca. Between 2006 and 2016, 83 percent of population growth in the Toronto census metropolitan area was in suburbs or exurban areas, with only 12 percent in "active cores."

105. Dwyer Gunn, "Why Poverty Is Skyrocketing in the Suburbs," *Pacific Standard*, June 26, 2017, https://psmag.com.

106. A 2018 study by the Brookings Institute reported that the fastest population growth in 2016 and 2017 is happening in exurbs and emerging suburbs, with the growth rate in urban cores cut in half since 2012. (William H. Frey, "US Population Disperses to Suburbs, Exurbs, Rural Areas, and 'Middle of the Country' Metros," Brookings Institute, March 26, 2018, www.brookings.edu.)

107. Rachelle Younglai and Chen Wang, "How Canada's Suburban Dream Became a Debt-Filled Nightmare," *Globe and Mail*, September 13, 2016, www.theglobeandmail.com; Angie Schmitt, "Sprawl Costs the Public More Than Twice as Much as Compact Development," *Streetsblog USA*, March 5, 2015, https://usa.streetsblog.org.

108. Mees, *Transport for Suburbia*, 65.

109. Mees, *Transport for Suburbia*, 8.

110. Sylvia Menezes Roberts, "A Suburban Model for Incremental Transit Improvement," Strong Towns, November 28, 2018, www.strongtowns.org.

111. While ridership in Toronto only increased by 0.1 percent in 2016, Brampton's spiked by 9.2 percent. (Sean Marshall, "The Secret behind Brampton's Transit Success," *TVO*, January 8, 2018, www.tvo.org.)

112. Yonah Freemark, "Calgary's Soaring Transit Use Suggests High Ridership Is Possible Even in Sprawling Cities," *Transport Politic*, December 10, 2014, www.thetransportpolitic.com; Andrew Jeffrey, "Reduced Hours and Longer Waits: How Budget Cuts Will Affect Calgary Transit," *Star Calgary*, August 9, 2019, www.thestar.com.

113. Christina Hernandez Sherwood, "Q&A: Ellen Dunham-Jones on Retrofitting Suburbia," *ZDNet*, March 11, 2013, www.zdnet.com.

114. Mees, *Transport for Suburbia*, 66.

CHAPTER 6 › EXPANDING ACCESS

1. *2017 Disability Statistics Annual Report* (Durham: Institute on Disability, 2018), 2, https://disabilitycompendium.org.

2. Elizabeth A. Courtney-Long, Dianna D. Carroll, Qing C. Zhang, Alissa C. Stevens, Shannon Griffin-Blake, Brian S. Armour, and Vincent A. Campbell, "Prevalence of Disability and Disability Type Among Adults—United States, 2013," *Morbidity and Mortality Weekly Report* 64, no. 29 (2015): 777–83; Martha Ross and Nicole Bateman,

"Disability Rates among Working-Age Adults Are Shaped by Race, Place, and Education," Brookings Institute, May 15, 2018, www.brookings.edu.

3. Joseph Shapiro, "The Sexual Assault Epidemic No One Talks About," *National Public Radio*, January 8, 2018, www.npr.org; Rachel Gilmore, "Women with Disabilities More at Risk of Sexual Assault: Statistics Canada," *iPolitics*, March 15, 2018, https://ipolitics.ca.

4. Sandy E. James, Jody L. Herman, Susan Rankin, Mara Keisling, Lisa Mottet, and Ma'ayan Anafi, *The Report of the 2015 U.S. Transgender Survey* (Washington, DC: National Center for Transgender Equality, 2016), 5, https://transequality.org.

5. "Violence against Trans and Non-Binary People," National Resource Center on Domestic Violence, https://vawnet.org.

6. "Accessibility at Uber," Uber, May 20, 2019, https://accessibility.uber.com.

7. Rahul Bijor and Ann Bordetsky, "Driving Customers to Businesses with UberCENTRAL," Uber Newsroom, July 28, 2016, www.uber.com.

8. Darrell Etherington, "Uber Launches Uber Health, a B2B Ride-Hailing Platform for Healthcare," *TechCrunch*, March 1, 2018, https://techcrunch.com.

9. Dara Khosrowshahi, "An Improved Experience for Riders in Wheelchairs," Uber Newsroom, November 20, 2018, www.uber.com.

10. Rina Raphael, "How Free Lyft Rides Can Dramatically Improve Life for Senior Citizens," *Fast Company*, October 2, 2018, www.fastcompany.com.

11. Tanya Snyder, "Uber, but for Grandma," *Politico*, September 27, 2017, www.politico.com.

12. Ida Mojadad, "Rideshare App for Women Emerges amid Chilling Oakland Ride," *SF Weekly*, September 6, 2018.

13. "Protect Your Safety While Riding with Uber," Uber, www.uber.com.

14. Ashley Halsey III and Michael Laris, "Blind Man Sets Out Alone in Google's Driverless Car," *Washington Post*, December 13, 2016.

15. Barbara Merrill, "Disabled Americans Deserve the Benefits of Self-Driving Cars," *Hill*, September 19, 2018, https://thehill.com.

16. Ashley Halsey III, "Driverless Cars Promise Far Greater Mobility for the Elderly and People with Disabilities," *Washington Post*, November 23, 2017.

17. Stamp Siripanich, "Travel with Trust: Designing for Women's Safety in Autonomous Rideshares," Teague Labs, March 28, 2018, https://medium.com.

18. Nina Strochlic, "Uber: Disability Laws Don't Apply to Us," *Daily Beast,* May 21, 2015, www.thedailybeast.com.

19. Jonathan Stempel, "Uber Is Sued over Lack of Wheelchair-Accessible Cars in NYC," *Reuters*, July 18, 2017, www.reuters.com; Dara Kerr, "Uber Discriminates against People in Wheelchairs, Lawsuit Says," *CNET*, February 28, 2018, www.cnet.com.

20. Andrew J. Hawkins, "Uber and Lyft Are Terrible at Providing Wheelchair-Accessible Service, and Here's the Proof," *Verge*, May 23, 2018, www.theverge.com.

21. Matthew Flamm, "Uber, Lyft and Via Sue to Block Wheelchair-Accessibility Mandate," *Crain's New York Business*, April 13, 2018, www.crainsnewyork.com.

22. Stephen Nessen, "Uber, Lyft, Via Sue City over Wheelchair Requirements," *WNYC News*, April 13, 2018, www.wnyc.org.

23. Nessen, "Uber, Lyft, Via Sue City."

24. Bérénice Magistretti, "As It Speeds toward IPO, Lyft Faces Federal Lawsuit for Disability Discrimination," *Forbes*, March 20, 2019, www.forbes.com.

25. Molly Taft, "Why Can't Uber and Lyft Be More Wheelchair-Friendly?" *CityLab*, December 11, 2018, www.citylab.com.

26. Daus, *The Expanding Transportation Network*, 27.

27. Sarah Emerson, "'GoGoGrandparent' Is Overcharging Seniors for Uber Rides, and Drivers Are Pissed," *Motherboard*, April 13, 2017, www.vice.com.

28. Jamie L. LaReau, "Ford Program Offered Rides to Doctor's Offices: Why They're Ending It," *Detroit Free Press*, December 6, 2019, www.freep.com.

29. Andrew J. Hawkins, "Ford's On-Demand Bus Service Chariot Is Going Out of Business," *Verge*, January 10, 2019, www.theverge.com.

30. Bret Hauff, "Self-Driving Cars Should Be Designed for People with Disabilities," *Motherboard*, May 24, 2017, www.vice.com.

31. Bev Betkowski, "Race to Market Self-Driving Cars Leaving People with Disabilities Behind," *Folio*, February 28, 2019, www.folio.ca.

32. Leila McNeill, "Before Cities Become Smart, They Must Become Accessible," *Mobility Management*, March 1, 2019, https://mobilitymgmt.com.

33. Sara Ashley O'Brien et al., "CNN Investigation: 103 Uber Drivers Accused of Sexual Assault or Abuse," *CNN*, April 30, 2018, https://money.cnn.com.

34. "Uber Received More Than 3,000 Reports of Sexual Assaults in U.S. in 2018," *CBC News*, December 5, 2019, www.cbc.ca.

35. Dara Kerr, "More Than 120 Uber, Lyft Drivers Said to Have Sexually Assaulted Riders," *CNET*, May 1, 2018, www.cnet.com.

36. Katie Roof, "Uber Dealt with Class Action Lawsuit Alleging

Assault by Drivers," *TechCrunch*, November 14, 2017, https://techcrunch.com.

37. Cara Kelly and Tricia L. Nadolny, "Rape, Assault Allegations Mount against Lyft in What New Suit Calls 'Sexual Predator Crisis,'" *USA Today*, September 4, 2019, www.usatoday.com.

38. Johana Bhuiyan, "Uber Filed a Motion to Compel Alleged Sexual Assault Victims to Settle Some Claims under Arbitration," *Vox*, May 15, 2018, www.vox.com.

39. Rebecca Joseph, "Uber Installs Panic Button for Riders to Curb Sexual Assault," *Global News*, May 29, 2018, https://globalnews.ca.

40. Greg Bensinger, "When Rides Go Wrong: How Uber's Investigations Unit Works to Limit the Company's Liability," *Washington Post*, September 26, 2019, www.washingtonpost.com.

41. "Nearly a Quarter of Women Have Turned In Uber Drivers for Uncomfortable Behavior," National Council for Home Safety and Security, December 12, 2018, www.alarms.org.

42. Alice Yin, "'Is This Going to Be My Last Ride?': Female Ride-Share Users Share Concerns—and Safety Tips—after Student's Slaying," *Chicago Tribune*, April 15, 2019.

43. Alex Dalbey, "This Woman Perfectly Explains Why Lying to Male Uber Drivers Is OK," *Daily Dot*, October 10, 2018, www.dailydot.com.

44. Amelia Tait, "'I Got Out and Ran': With One Attack a Week in London, Is Using Uber Safe for Women?," *New Statesman*, March 11, 2018, www.newstatesman.com.

45. Robyn Kanner, "Here's One Small Way Uber Could Finally Support Trans People Like Me," *Mic*, March 14, 2017, www.mic.com.

46. Giles K. Bailey, "Improving Public Transit Safety for Women and the Impact of Ride-Hailing Services," *Metro*, June 28, 2018, www.metro-magazine.com.

47. Nick Van Mead, Harvey Symons, and Aghnia Adzkia, "Access Denied: Wheelchair Metro Maps versus Everyone Else's," *Guardian*, September 21, 2017, www.theguardian.com

48. Jill L. Bezyak, Scott A. Sabella, and Robert H. Gattis, "Public Transportation: An Investigation of Barriers for People with Disabilities," *Journal of Disability Policy Studies* 28, no. 1 (2017), 52–55. The median breakdown for an elevator in the New York subway is nearly four hours.

49. "Toward Universal Mobility: Charting a Path to Improve Transportation Accessibility," Metropolitan Planning Council, December 2019, www.scribd.com.

50. Sasha Blair-Goldensohn, "New York Has a Great Subway, if You're Not in a Wheelchair," *New York Times*, March 29, 2017.

51. Blair-Goldensohn, "New York Has a Great Subway."

52. James Barron, "For Disabled Subway Riders, the Biggest Challenge Can Be Getting to the Train," *New York Times*, July 26, 2018.

53. Van Mead, Symons, and Adzkia, "Access Denied"; Barron, "For Disabled Subway Riders."

54. Lauren O'Neil, "Someone Created a TTC Subway Map with Only Accessible Stations," *blogTO*, November 2018, www.blogto.com.

55. Oliver Moore, "Transit Accessibility for All Remains a Dream Unfulfilled across Canada," *Globe and Mail*, December 29, 2017, www.theglobeandmail.com.

56. "Wheelchair Charging Stations Need to Be Rolled Out Nationwide," *SpinalCord.com*, February 28, 2019, www.spinalcord.com.

57. Andrew Bowen, "Disability Lawsuit Targets San Diego over Dockless Scooters," *KPBS*, February 19, 2019, www.kpbs.org.

58. Elyse Wanshel and Lena Jackson, "New York City's Public Transit Is a Nightmare for People with Disabilities," *HuffPost US*, October 9, 2018, www.huffingtonpost.ca.

59. Joseph Stromberg, "Once Seniors Are Too Old to Drive, Our Transportation System Totally Fails Them," *Vox*, June 12, 2015, www.vox.com.

60. John Rieti, "Toronto Wheel-Trans Riders Singing the Blues over Delays, Irregular Service," *CBC News*, June 22, 2017, www.cbc.ca.

61. Bezyak, Sabella, and Gattis, "Public Transportation," 56.

62. Chantal Braganza, "Why We Need to Treat Public Washrooms as a Human Right," *TVO*, May 29, 2018, www.tvo.org.

63. Stromberg, "Once Seniors Are Too Old to Drive."

64. "In 6 Short Years, Sexual Assault Prevention Now a Priority for Translink," Battered Women's Support Services, July 13, 2018, www.bwss.org.

65. Sexual assaults reported on the London Underground increased by 42 percent between 2015–16 and 2018–19. ("Reports of Sexual Assaults on London Underground Soar," *Guardian*, September 23, 2019, www.theguardian.com.) In mid-2019, a lesbian couple were assaulted by four teens on a London bus after kissing, sparking global outrage; the attackers were later charged for committing an aggravated hate crime. (Linda Givetash, "Four Teens Charged in Attack on Lesbian Couple on London Bus," *NBC News*, July 26, 2019, www.nbcnews.com.)

66. Amy Lubitow, JaDee Carathers, Maura Kelly, and Miriam Abelson, "Transmobilities: Mobility, Harassment, and Violence Experienced by Transgender and Gender Nonconforming Public Transit Riders in Portland, Oregon," *Gender, Place & Culture* 24 (2017): 1398–418.

67. "Sexual Harassment on Public Transport Is a Problem We Must

Solve," Battered Women's Support Services, November 9, 2015, www. bwss.org.

68. Danika Worthington, "Meet ADAPT, the Disabled Activists from Denver Who Changed a Nation," *Denver Post*, July 5, 2017, www. denverpost.com.

69. Janine Jackson, "Disability Rights Activists Are Even Invisible Getting Arrested on Capitol Hill," *FAIR*, May 6, 2011, https://fair.org; Amanda Michelle Gomez and Ryan Koronowski, "ADAPT Activists Put Their Bodies on the Line to Gain Support for Disability Integration Act," *ThinkProgress*, May 24, 2018, https://thinkprogress.org.

70. Blair-Goldensohn, "New York Has a Great Subway."

71. David Gutman, "Settlement: Seattle to Build Thousands of Sidewalk Curb Ramps over Next 18 Years," *Seattle Times*, July 17, 2017.

72. Jonathan Stempel, "U.S. Sues New York City Subway Operator over Disabled Access," *Reuters*, March 13, 2018, www.reuters.com.

73. Sarah Lu, "Class Action Lawsuit by People with Disabilities Authorized against Montreal Public Transit," Rights Watch Blog, December 6, 2017, http://rightswatch.ca; "People with Disabilities Sue BART for Discrimination," Disability Rights Advocates, April 5, 2017, https://dralegal.org.

74. Ben Yakas, "Disability Rights Activists Disrupt MTA Talk, Demanding Subway Accessibility," *Gothamist*, April 27, 2018, http:// gothamist.com.

75. Tyler Olsen, "Audits Find Abbotsford Bus Drivers Breaching Human Rights Agreement by Not Calling Out Stops," *Abbotsford News*, May 4, 2019, www.abbynews.com.

76. "Toward Universal Mobility: Charting a Path to Improve Transportation Accessibility," Metropolitan Planning Council, December 2019, www.scribd.com.

77. Aarian Marshall, "Want to Boost Transit Ridership?: Try Making Women Feel Safer," *Wired*, January 23, 2019, www.wired.com.

78. Toula Drimonis, "Rethinking Public Transit to Meet Women's Needs," *Ricochet,* February 17, 2016, https://ricochet.media.

79. "Sexual Harassment on Public Transport," Battered Women's Support Services.

80. Eric Jaffe, "Public Transportation's Hidden Gender Imbalance," *CityLab*, February 1, 2012, www.citylab.com; Toula Drimonis, "Rethinking Public Transit to Meet Women's Needs," *Ricochet*, February 17, 2016, www.ricochet.media.

81. Anna Kramer, "Good Public Transit Is a Feminist Issue," TTCriders, March 6, 2019, www.ttcriders.ca.

82. Kramer, "Good Public Transit Is a Feminist Issue."

83. Roger Rudick, "Women Account for 15 Percent of

Transportation Workforce," *Streetsblog SF*, February 12, 2019, https://sf.streetsblog.org.

84. Oliver Moore, "Mind the Gender Gap: Transit Agencies Hiring More Women, but Front Lines Lag," *Globe and Mail*, September 5, 2017, www.theglobeandmail.com.

85. A 2018 report said that the transit board in Washington, DC, for example, is made up of thirteen men and two women and Toronto's TTC board is nine men and two women. These boards tend to be overwhelmingly white as well, with Montreal's RTM made up of 17 white people and zero Black, Indigenous, and people of colour while Vancouver's was 11 white people and zero Black, Indigenous, and people of colour. These statistics do not reflect class representation, such as income, wealth, and housing situation. (MacLeod, Wood, Whittier, and Wert, *Mixed Signals*, 53.)

CHAPTER 7 > DATA MINECRAFT

1. Sharmila Nair, "Gartner: 1.5 Billion Smartphones Were Sold in 2017," *Star Online*, February 25, 2018, www.thestar.com.

2. Ben Gilbert, "Elon Musk Just Revealed More Video Games Coming to Tesla Cars—Here's the Full List So Far," *Business Insider*, June 13, 2019, www.businessinsider.com; Shaunacy Ferro, "Tesla Drivers Now Have Access to a Library of Fart Sounds in Their Car," *Mental Floss*, December 17, 2018, www.mentalfloss.com.

3. Joann Muller, "What Tesla Knows about You," *Axios*, March 13, 2019, www.axios.com.

4. Cyrus Farivar, "Why Cops Won't Need a Warrant to Pull the Data off Your Autonomous Car," *Ars Technica*, February 3, 2018, www.arstechnica.com.

5. Jake Holmes, "Kia, MIT to Show a Car Interior That Adapts to Your Mood at CES," *Road Show*, December 20, 2018, www.cnet.com.

6. "Audi to Exhibit New In-Car Entertainment Technologies at CES 2019," Audi MediaCenter, December 12, 2018, www.audi-mediacenter.com.

7. Chris Nelson, "Inside the Cocoon: What to Expect from Automated-Vehicle Interiors," *Automobile*, January 29, 2019, www.automobilemag.com.

8. Gary Silberg, Thomas Mayor, Todd Dubner, Jono Anderson, and Leila Shin, *The Clockspeed Dilemma: What Does It Mean for Automotive Innovation?* (Chicago: KPMG, 2015), 20.

9. Michele Bertoncello, Gianluca Camplone, Paul Gao, Hans-Werner Kaas, Detlev Mohr, Timo Moller, and Dominik Wee, *Monetizing Car Data: New Service Business Opportunities to Create New Customer Benefits* (Milan: McKinsey & Company, 2016), 7, www.mckinsey.com.

10. Peter Nowak, "With Cars Tracking Your Driving Habits, Insurance Industry Changes Lanes," *Globe and Mail*, October 30, 2017, www.theglobeandmail.com.

11. Alex Bozikovic, "Google's Sidewalk Labs Signs Deal for 'Smart City' Makeover of Toronto's Waterfront," *Globe and Mail*, October 17, 2017.

12. Brian Krzanich, "Data Is the New Oil in the Future of Automated Driving," Intel Newsroom, November 15, 2016, https://newsroom.intel.com.

13. Krzanich, "Data Is the New Oil."

14. John R. Quain, "Cars Suck Up Data About You: Where Does It All Go?," *New York Times*, July 27, 2017, www.nytimes.com.

15. Bryson Bort, "How to Protect What Your Car Knows about You," *Parallax*, April 3, 2018, https://the-parallax.com.

16. "Gartner Says by 2020, a Quarter Billion Connected Vehicles Will Enable New In-Vehicle Services and Automated Driving Capabilities," Gartner, January 26, 2015, www.gartner.com.

17. Luis F. Alvarez León, "Eyes on the Road: Surveillance Logics in the Autonomous Vehicle Economy," *Surveillance & Society* 17, no. 1/2 (2019): 198–204.

18. Sarah A. Seo, "How Cars Transformed Policing," *Boston Review*, June 3, 2019, www.bostonreview.net.

19. Lucas Mearian, "Once Your Car's Connected to the Internet, Who Guards Your Privacy?," *Computerworld*, September 18, 2014, www.computerworld.com.

20. Jim Edwards, "Ford Exec: 'We Know Everyone Who Breaks the Law' Thanks to Our GPS in Your Car," *Business Insider*, January 8, 2014, www.businessinsider.com.

21. Sam Frizell, "What Is Uber Really Doing With Your Data?," *Time*, January 8, 2014, https://time.com.

22. Johana Bhuiyan and Charlie Warzel, "'God View': Uber Investigates Its Top New York Executive for Privacy Violations," *Buzzfeed News*, November 18, 2014, www.buzzfeednews.com.

23. Richard Morgan, "Uber Settles Federal Probe over 'God View' Spy Software," *New York Post*, August 15, 2017, https://nypost.com.

24. Dustin Volz, "Uber to End Post-Trip Tracking of Riders as Part of Privacy Push," *Reuters*, August 29, 2017, www.reuters.com.

25. Johana Bhuiyan, "Here's the Letter Alleging Uber Spied on Individuals for Competitive Intelligence," *Vox*, December 15, 2017, www.vox.com.

26. Bhuiyan, "Here's the Letter Alleging Uber Spied."

27. Kif Leswing, "Uber Used Former CIA Officers Posing as Businessmen to Collect Trade Secrets and Other Intel, Explosive

Letter Claims," *Business Insider*, December 16, 2017, www.businessinsider.com.

28. Amir Efrati, "Uber's Top Secret 'Hell' Program Exploited Lyft's Vulnerability," *Information*, April 12, 2017, www.theinformation.com.

29. Eric Newcomer, "Uber Paid Hackers to Delete Stolen Data on 57 Million People," *Bloomberg*, November 21, 2017, www.bloomberg.com.

30. Amir Efrati, "Lyft Investigates Allegation That Employees Abused Customer Data," *Information*, January 25, 2018, www.theinformation.com.

31. Erin Heffernan, "St. Louis Uber Driver Has Put Video of Hundreds of Passengers Online: Most Have No Idea," *St. Louis Post-Dispatch*, July 24, 2018, www.stltoday.com.

32. Erin Heffernan, "Uber Evaluating Policies in Response to Story on St. Louis Driver's Secret Livestream," *St. Louis Post-Dispatch*, July 24, 2018, www.stltoday.com.

33. Jim Salter, "Uber Guideline Now Prohibits Broadcasting Passenger Images," *Associated Press*, November 8, 2018, www.thestar.com; Scott Davis, "Ottawa Senators Players Caught Ripping Assistant Coach, Team Performance while Being Secretly Recorded in an Uber," *Business Insider*, November 6, 2018, www.businessinsider.com.

34. Kelly Egan, "Egan: Posting Senators Video 'Dumbest Decision' of My Life, Says Fired Uber Driver," *Ottawa Citizen*, November 9, 2018.

35. Paris Marx, "Don't Be Fooled: Uber Doesn't Care about Transit," *Radical Urbanist*, February 14, 2019, https://medium.com/radical-urbanist.

36. Colin Lecher, "Amazon, Microsoft, and Uber Are Paying Big Money to Kill a California Privacy Initiative," *Verge*, June 15, 2018, www.theverge.com.

37. Andrew J. Hawkins, "Uber Received Over 400 Data Requests from US Law Enforcement in Just Six Months," *Verge*, April 12, 2016, www.theverge.com.

38. Cara Tabachnick, "Uber Wants to Get the Law on Its Side," *Bloomberg Businessweek*, April 23, 2019, www.bloomberg.com; Beau Zimmer, "App Helps Law Enforcement Use Uber Data to Solve Crimes," *10News WTSP*, March 1, 2018, www.wtsp.com.

39. Erica Evans, "How Police Might Access Your Lyft, Tinder and Google Accounts in a Criminal Investigation," *Deseret News*, July 28, 2019, www.deseret.com.

40. Larry Neumeister, "Judge: Ads Can Run in Uber, Lyft Vehicles in New York City," *Phys.org*, February 23, 2018, https://phys.org.

41. Danielle Furfaro, "Your Ride Home from Uber, Lyft Is About to Get a Lot More Annoying," *New York Post*, March 8, 2018, https://nypost.com.

42. Adrienne Lafrance, "How Self-Driving Cars Will Threaten Privacy," *Atlantic*, March 21, 2016, www.theatlantic.com.

43. Sarah Holder, "Car-Mounted Ads Take a New Direction: Data Collection," *CityLab*, November 20, 2019, www.citylab.com.

44. Josh O'Kane, "Sidewalk Labs' Toronto Deal Sparks Data, Innovation Concerns," *Globe and Mail*, August 1, 2018, www.theglobeandmail.com.

45. Paris Marx, "Uber's Massive Data Play," *Medium Business*, September 20, 2018, https://medium.com.

46. In 2017, Metrolinx received 64 requests from law enforcement and complied with 30; in 2018, Metrolinx granted 35 of 94 requests. (Ben Spurr, "Metrolinx Has Been Quietly Sharing Presto Users' Information with Police," *Toronto Star*, June 3, 2017, www.thestar.com; Ben Spurr, "Metrolinx Gave Presto Users' Personal Info to Police 30 Times Last Year," *Toronto Star*, March 1, 2018, www.thestar.com; Ben Spurr, "Metrolinx Continues to Share Presto Users' Data without Requiring Warrants," *Toronto Star*, February 4, 2019, www.thestar.com.)

47. Kieran Delamont, "Metrolinx and the Surveillance State," *Torontoist*, June 17, 2017, https://torontoist.com.

48. "Mass Transit System or Tool for Mass Surveillance?," Beauceron, February 15, 2019, www.beauceronsecurity.com.

49. Darwin BondGraham, "BART Is Planning a System-Wide Surveillance Network," *East Bay Express*, August 6, 2018, www.eastbayexpress.com.

50. Tanvi Misra, "When Transit Agencies Spy on Riders," *CityLab*, September 18, 2018, www.citylab.com.

51. "Board Approves Safe Transit Policy," Bay Area Rapid Transit, June 22, 2017, www.bart.gov.

52. Misra, "When Transit Agencies Spy."

53. Bryce Covert, "Expand Fair Fares Instead of Cops on NYC's Transit System," *City & State New York*, November 19, 2019, www.cityandstateny.com.

54. Raneem Alozzi, "GO Transit Adding Fare Inspectors, Enforcing Zero-Tolerance Policy for Fare Evasion," *Toronto Star*, May 15, 2019, www.thestar.com.

55. Ben Spurr, "TTC Ticketing Data Raises Concerns That Black Transit Users Are Being Fined at a Disproportionately High Rate," *Toronto Star*, July 2, 2019, www.thestar.com.

56. Ben Spurr, "Mayor Tory's Comments Spark Debate about TTC Fare Evasion," *Toronto Star*, November 22, 2016, www.thestar.com.

57. Kira Barrett, "Metro Transit Police Target Black Youth for Fare Evasion, Report Says," *Street Sense Media*, October 3, 2018, www.streetsensemedia.org.

58. Harold Stolper and Jeff Jones, *The Crime of Being Short $2.75: Policing Communities of Color at the Turnstile* (New York City: Community Service Society, 2017), 12, www.cssny.org.

59. Alyssa Jeong Perry, "Nine Years after Oscar Grant's Death, His Mother Continues to Speak Out," *KQED News*, January 1, 2018, www.kqed.org; Sam Levin, "Officer Punched Oscar Grant and Lied about Facts in 2009 Killing, Records Show," *Guardian*, May 2, 2019, www.theguardian.com.

60. Jonathan Goldsbie, "The Most Damning Passages from the James Forcillo Sentence," *Now*, August 4, 2016, https://nowtoronto.com.

61. Charlie Smith, "Video: Grand Chief Stewart Phillip Promises to Seek Answers in Transit Police Shooting of Naverone Woods," *Georgia Straight*, March 1, 2015, www.straight.com.

62. "'You're Choking Me': Video of Montreal Commuter's Arrest Goes Viral," *CTV News*, August 28, 2018, www.ctvnews.ca.

63. "Teen Launches Multimillion-Dollar Lawsuit after Incident with TTC Fare Inspectors, Police," *680 News*, April 5, 2018, www.680news.com.

64. David P. Ball, "Transit Police Report Riders to Immigration Nearly Every Day," *Tyee*, July 10, 2014, https://thetyee.ca.

65. Hanna Gros and Paloma van Groll, *"We Have No Rights": Arbitrary Imprisonment and Cruel Treatment of Migrants with Mental Health Issues in Canada* (Toronto: International Human Rights Program at the University of Toronto Faculty of Law, 2015), 15, https://ihrp.law.utoronto.ca.

66. Safia Samee Ali, "Minnesota Transit Cop Who Asked Man's Immigration Status Still Working as Officer," *NBC News*, June 2, 2017, www.nbcnews.com.

67. Tom Lyden, "Metro Transit Cop Who Resigned Received $50,000 Settlement," *Fox 9*, September 13, 2017, www.fox9.com.

68. Hannah Critchfield, "Transgender Woman in ICE Custody after Light-Rail Arrest May Be Released," *Phoenix New Times*, December 19, 2019, www.phoenixnewtimes.com.

69. Hannah Critchfield, "Transgender Woman Stepped onto Light Rail Platform: She Ended Up in ICE Custody," *Phoenix New Times*, August 29, 2019, www.phoenixnewtimes.com.

70. Travis Lupick, "Vigil Marking One Year since the Death of Lucia Vega Jiménez Calls for Transit Police Reforms," *Georgia Straight*, December 12, 2014, www.straight.com.

71. Tamara Baluja, "Metro Vancouver Transit Police End Controversial Agreement with CBSA," *CBC News*, February 20, 2015, www.cbc.ca.

72. Rachel Dovey, "Pittsburgh's New Transit Fare Enforcement

Methods Raise Deportation Fears," *Next City*, May 22, 2017, https://nextcity.org.

73. Cyrus Farivar, "Bay Area Transit System Approves New Surveillance-Oversight Policy," *Ars Technica*, September 15, 2018, https://arstechnica.com.

74. "BART Board's Vote on Surveillance Technology Protects the Privacy of BART Riders; Promotes Public Safety," ACLU Northern California, September 13, 2018, www.aclunc.org.

75. Caroline Haskins, "Oakland Becomes Third U.S. City to Ban Facial Recognition," *VICE*, July 17, 2019, www.vice.com.

76. Dexter Brown, "Transit Systems Have Their Eyes on You—but Surveillance Footage Isn't Always There When It Counts," *CBC News*, September 4, 2016, www.cbc.ca.

77. Spurr, "Metrolinx Continues to Share Presto Users' Data."

78. Daniel C. Vock, "Citing Racial Disparities, Cities Rethink Punishment for Transit Fare Evasion," *Governing*, December 11, 2018, www.governing.com.

79. Christopher Robbins, "NYPD Officers Arrest Churro Vendor at Broadway Junction," *Gothamist*, November 9, 2019, www.gothamist.com.

80. Kathleen Culliton, "Underground Resistance Mounts against Subway Policing in NYC," *Patch*, November 24, 2019, www.patch.com.

81. Rachel Vick, "Queens Residents Swipe It Forward to Help Commuters in a Pinch," *Queens Daily Eagle*, August 15, 2019, www.queenseagle.com; Maya Kaufman, "Guerrilla Subway Ads Urge New Yorkers to Swipe in Fareless Riders," *Patch*, September 19, 2019, www.patch.com.

82. Martine Powers, "Here's Why Some Lawmakers Are Pushing Back against Fare Evasion Crackdowns," *Washington Post*, November 12, 2017.

83. Kim Kelly, "What the Prison-Abolition Movement Wants," *Teen Vogue*, December 26, 2019, www.teenvogue.com.

CHAPTER 8 > OLD TOWN ROAD

1. "One in Five Americans Live in Rural Areas," United States Census Bureau, August 9, 2017, www.census.gov.

2. Michael Ratcliffe, Charlynn Burd, Kelly Holder, and Alison Fields, *Defining Rural at the U.S. Census Bureau: American Community Survey and Geography Brief* (Suitland: United States Census Bureau, December 2016), 6, www.census.gov.

3. *Rural America at a Glance: 2018 Edition* (Washington, DC: United States Department of Agriculture, 2018), www.ers.usda.gov;

"Disability in Rural Areas," Rural Health Information Hub, www.ruralhealthinfo.org.

4. Thirty-six percent of rural residents in Georgia are Black, and 39 percent in Mississippi. ("Race & Ethnicity in Rural America," Housing Assistance Council, April 2012, www.ruralhome.org.)

5. A 46 percent increase between 2000 and 2010. ("Race & Ethnicity in Rural America.")

6. "Focus on Geography Series, 2016 Census: Aboriginal Peoples," Statistics Canada, 2019, www12.statcan.gc.ca.

7. Eric Marr, "Assessing Transportation Disadvantage in Rural Ontario, Canada: A Case Study of Huron County," *Journal of Rural and Community Development*, 10, no. 2 (2015): 102.

8. Matthew Yglesias, "Amtrak Turns 45 Today: Here's Why American Passenger Trains Are So Bad," *Vox*, May 1, 2016, www.vox.com.

9. "2018 Traffic Data for U.S Airlines and Foreign Airlines U.S. Flights," Bureau of Transportation Statistics, www.bts.dot.gov.

10. "Reducing Emissions from Aviation," European Union, https://ec.europa.eu/clima. Twenty-two percent of global emissions may come from aviation by 2050, given decarbonization in other sectors juxtaposed with increasing demand for flying. (Magdalena Heuwieser, "The Illusion of Green Flying," Heinrich-Böll-Stiftung, September 21, 2018, www.boell.de.)

11. The comparable stats for urban residents are 10.1 percent of households that don't own a vehicle, and 17.8 that have access to three or more. (Jeremy Mattson, *Rural Transit Fact Book 2017* (Fargo: North Dakota State University, 2017), 13, www.surtc.org.)

12. In 2017, 47 percent of fatal car crashes were in rural areas, down from 61 percent in 2000. The rate of crash deaths per 100 million miles is 2.2 times higher in rural areas than urban areas, with 67 percent of all deaths involving pickups happening in rural areas and 57 percent of all SUV-related deaths. Not surprisingly, 71 percent of deaths in rural areas occurred on roads with speed limits of 55 miles per hour or higher, compared to only 29 percent in urban areas. ("Fatality Facts 2017: Urban/Rural Comparison," Insurance Institute for Highway Safety, December 2018, www.iihs.org.)

13. Daniel Gatti, "Rural Drivers Can Save the Most from Clean Vehicles," Union of Concerned Scientists, December 13, 2018, https://blog.ucsusa.org. The proliferation of personal electric vehicles in rural areas is projected to reduce considerably more emissions than for a driver in an urban county: 3.3 metric tons of greenhouse gases per year in rural counties, compared to 1.8 metric tons in the city.

14. Todd Litman, *Rural Multimodal Planning: Why and How to Improve Travel Options in Small Towns and Rural Communities* (Victoria: Victoria Transport Policy Institute, 2019), 10, www.vtpi.org.

15. Alicja Siekierska, "Rural Communities to Power Providers: How Everyone Is Prepping for Electric Vehicle Adoption," *Financial Times*, August 17, 2017.

16. Diana Martin, "Charge Towards Electric Vehicles Is Trickling into the Rural and Agriculture Landscape," Ontario Farmer, April 7, 2019, www.ontariofarmer.com.

17. Chris Mooney, "How Solar Power and Electric Cars Could Make Suburban Living Awesome Again," *Washington Post*, December 24, 2014.

18. "Lyft Is Now Live across 40 States," Lyft, August 31, 2017, https://blog.lyft.com; Sarah Buhr, "You Can Now Catch a Lyft Even in Rural Areas in 40 U.S. States," *TechCrunch*, August 31, 2017, https://techcrunch.com.

19. Jonathan Wang, "Uber in Small Towns and Cities—A Data Deep Dive," Uber, September 8, 2017, https://medium.com.

20. Andrew J. Hawkins, "Uber Covers 75 Percent of the US, but Getting to 100 Will Be Really Hard," *Verge*, October 23, 2015, www.theverge.com.

21. M.L. Schultze, "Ride Hailing in Rural America: Like Uber with a Neighborly Feel," *National Public Radio*, April 17, 2017, www.npr.org.

22. Rob Nielson, "Lawsuit Brings Liberty Mobility to a Halt," January 19, 2018, *Yankton Daily Press*, www.yankton.net.

23. Tori Weldon, "Rural Transportation Service Expands to Meet 'Overwhelming Need,'" *CBC News*, July 3, 2018, www.cbc.ca.

24. Wolfgang Bernhart, Hitoshi Kaise, Yuzuru Ohashi, Tobias Schonberg, and Laurianne Schilles, *Reconnecting the Rural: Autonomous Driving as a Solution for Non-urban Mobility* (Frankfurt: Roland Berger, 2018), www.rolandberger.com.

25. Bernhart, Kaise, Ohashi, Schonberg, and Schilles, *Reconnecting the Rural*, 2.

26. Bernhart, Kaise, Ohashi, Schonberg, and Schilles, *Reconnecting the Rural*, 6.

27. Bernhart, Kaise, Ohashi, Schonberg, and Schilles, *Reconnecting the Rural*, 17.

28. Dale Neef, "High-Speed Broadband, Autonomous Vehicles and Small-Town and Rural Communities," Smart Cities Dive, June 29, 2018, www.smartcitiesdive.com.

29. Bradley Berman, "Are Electric Cars Only for the Rich?: Sacramento Is Challenging That Notion," *New York Times*, January 24, 2019. Members of the California Air Resources Board argued in a 2018 op-ed: "Volkswagen wants us to believe that it is making substantial investments in rural and disadvantaged communities. But there's a big difference between charging stations built for these communities and charging stations built for drivers traveling long distances and

stopping along the highway."(Dean Florez and Eduardo Garcia, "Volkswagen's Obligation Is to All Californians, Not Just the Rich," *Sacramento Bee*, December 18, 2019, www.sacbee.com.)

30. "Uber available in rural areas—But for now, expect longer wait times for the expanding ride-service. Uber drivers, who work on a contractual basis, cannot charge for the drive to a passenger. In a rural town about an hour outside of downtown, the wait was about 18 minutes," *Reddit*, r/uber, 2017, www.reddit.com/r/uber.

31. Aditi Shrikant, "Transportation Experts See Uber and Lyft as the Future: But Rural Communities Still Don't Use Them," *Vox*, January 11, 2019, www.vox.com.

32. Shrikant, "Transportation Experts See Uber and Lyft."

33. Joel Hruska, "Self-Driving Cars Still Can't Handle Snow, Rain, or Heavy Weather," *ExtremeTech*, October 30, 2018, www.extremetech.com.

34. Writing about "connected and autonomous vehicles" (CAVs) in the context of the U.K., Jessica Sellick of the Rural Services Network posed a series of key unanswered questions: "What will the pattern of uptake be in rural areas? Is rural road infrastructure being taken into account in the design, development and use of CAVs? And will there be a 'rural premium' in the development and deployment of CAVs in the countryside?" (Jessica Sellick, "What Future for Rural Driverless Cars?," Rural Services Networks, July 1, 2018, www.rsnonline.org.uk.)

35. Mattson, *Rural Transit Fact Book*, 18.

36. Aubrey Byron, "Getting from Here to There in Rural America," Strong Towns, November 1, 2018, www.strongtowns.org.

37. Byron, "Getting from Here to There."

38. Mattson, *Rural Transit Fact Book*, 13, 17.

39. Marr, "Assessing Transportation Disadvantage," 101; "Economics of Transportation Research Needs for Rural Elderly and Transportation Disadvantaged Populations," U.S. Department of Agriculture, 2017, https://tti.tamu.edu. Seniors with access to a vehicle may however limit their driving at night time, rush hour, and bad weather, eventually having to stop driving altogether.

40. Scott Bogren, "Rural Transit: You Can Get There From Here," Community Transportation Association of America, 1998, www.ctaa.org.

41. "Mobility & Aging in Rural America: The Role for Innovation," Grantmakers in Aging, May 2, 2018, www.giaging.org.

42. "Economics of Transportation Research Needs," U.S. Department of Agriculture, 11.

43. Tanya Snyder, "'We're Done': Shutdown Strikes Small, Midsize and Rural Transit," *Politico*, January 24, 2019, www.politico.com.

44. *Study of Intercity Bus Service*, U.S. Department of Transportation, 2005, www.transportation.gov.

45. "Linking US Small Cities and Towns: Time for State Leadership," Human Transit, August 7, 2019, www.humantransit.org.

46. "Saskatchewan Transportation Company Comes to End of Road," *Global News*, June 1, 2017, https://globalnews.ca.

47. Jennifer Graham, "Regina Woman Files Human Rights Complaint, Alleges Discrimination after STC Closure," *Canadian Press*, June 23, 2017, www.cbc.ca.

48. Ashleigh Mattern, "New Highway of Tears: Mental Health Counsellor Fears for Northern Sask. Residents after STC Closure," *CBC News*, November 16, 2017, www.cbc.ca.

49. "Loss of STC Keeping Domestic Violence Victims from Shelters, Survey Says," *CBC News*, August 13, 2018, www.cbc.ca.

50. "'Without STC, I Am in Prison': People with Disabilities Press for Return of Sask. Bus Company," *CBC News*, May 10, 2018, www.cbc.ca.

51. Kendall Latimer, "Saskatchewan Sells STC Assets for $29M, Slightly More Than Appraised Value," *CBC News*, December 13, 2017, www.cbc.ca.

52. "Sask. Made 'Fundamental Mistake' Treating STC as Business, Not Service: Researcher," *CBC News*, May 31, 2019, www.cbc.ca.

53. Abigail Turner, "Thompson Left Without Local Transit after Greyhound Pulls Out," *Global News*, October 31, 2018, www.globalnews.ca.

54. "First Nations to Feel Brunt of Greyhound Cuts in Western Canada: AMC," *CTV Winnipeg*, July 9, 2018, https://winnipeg.ctvnews.ca.

55. "Indigenous Man's Death en Route to Hospital Prompts Call for Inquiry," *CBC News*, October 17, 2018, www.cbc.ca.

56. "Still Waiting for the Bus: The Unnatural Death of Prairie Intercity Transit," ATU Canada, 2019, www.atucanada.ca.

57. Jean Dupuis, *VIA Rail Canada Inc. and the Future of Passenger Rail in Canada* (Ottawa: Library of Parliament, November 16, 2011), http://publications.gc.ca.

58. Ernie Smith, "The Consequences of Amtrak Not Owning Its Own Tracks," *Atlas Obscura*, May 2, 2017, www.atlasobscura.com.

59. Aaron Gordon, "Hyperloop Is the Midwest's Answer to a Question No One Asked," *Jalopnik*, December 18, 2019, www.jalopnik.com.

60. Paris Marx, "China's High-Speed Train Map Puts U.S. Transportation to Shame," *Radical Urbanist*, January 22, 2018, https://medium.com.

61. Brad Plumer, "Amtrak's $151 Billion High-Speed Rail Plan:

Are There Cheaper Options?," *Washington Post*, July 16, 2012, www.washingtonpost.com.

62. George Skelton, "Capitol Journal: Newsom Is Right to Scale Back the Bullet Train, and It's Good Politics Too," *Los Angeles Times*, February 14, 2019, www.latimes.com; Roger Rudick, "Skirmish Over High-Speed Rail Funds," *StreetsBlog SF*, December 3, 2019, www.sf.streetsblog.org.

63. Kate Sullivan, "US Dept. of Transportation Cancels Nearly $1 Billion Grant for California's High-Speed Rail Project," *CNN*, February 20, 2019, www.cnn.com.

64. Mick Akers, "Start of High-Speed Rail Construction Likely Delayed 2 Years," *Las Vegas Review-Journal*, May 30, 2019, www.reviewjournal.com.

65. Paul Langan, "List of All Ontario-Quebec High Speed Rail Studies," High Speed Rail Canada, May 21, 2018, www.highspeedrailcanada.com.

66. "Rural and Small Town Public Transit Ridership Increased Nearly 8% since 2007," American Public Transportation Association, October 5, 2017, www.apta.com.

67. "Future of Transportation National Survey (2010)," Transportation for America, http://t4america.org.

68. Kalena Thomhave, "Revving Up Rural Public Transit," *American Prospect*, November 15, 2017, www.prospect.org.

69. Peter Shokeir, "County Enters Agreement for Rural Transit," *Daily Herald Tribune*, October 29, 2018, www.dailyheraldtribune.com; "Rural Transit Service Rolled Out," *Red Deer Advocate*, December 18, 2018, www.reddeeradvocate.com.

70. Todd Litman, *Public Transportation's Impact on Rural and Small Towns* (Washington, DC: American Public Transportation Association, 2017), 31; Jayme Fraser, "More and More Montanans Depending on Rural Public Transit," *Billings Gazette*, July 26, 2016, www.billingsgazette.com.

71. Sue Woodrow and Day Soriano, "Transportation Partnership Offers Economic Hope in North Central Montana," Federal Reserve Bank of Minneapolis, January 1, 2011, www.minneapolisfed.org.

72. Woodrow and Soriano, "Transportation Partnership Offers Economic Hope."

73. Briar Stewart, "'Safe, Reliable and Affordable': New Bus Service Aims to Make Notorious Highway of Tears Less Dangerous," *CBC News*, September 21, 2017, www.cbc.ca.

74. "5,000 People Have Used Highway of Tears Buses in First Year of Service," *Canadian Press*, February 2, 2018, www.cbc.ca.

75. For example, the thirty-minute trip from Smithers to

Moricetown costs five dollars, about one-tenth of the cost Greyhound had charged. (Stewart, "'Safe, Reliable and Affordable.'")

76. "Bulkley Nechako Regional Transit System: Rider's Guide," BC Transit, November 6, 2017, www.bctransit.com.

77. Quinn Bender, "Highway of Tears Public Transit Plan Wins Safety and Security Awards," *Terrace Standard*, November 30, 2018, www.terracestandard.com.

78. "Transit Department," Spokane Tribe of Indians, www. spokanetribe.com.

79. "Iqaluit Cuts $17-a-Ride Bus Service," *CBC News*, December 14, 2004, www.cbc.ca.

80. Rajnesh Sharma, "Hoping for a Public Transport System," *Nunavut News*, December 14, 2019, www.nunavutnews.com.

81. Ben Adler, "Even Rural America Can Have Good Public Transportation," *Grist*, July 23, 2014, www.grist.org.

82. Kalena Thomhave, "Revving Up Rural Public Transit," *American Prospect*, November 15, 2017, www.prospect.org.

83. Mark Mather, Paola Scommegna, and Lillian Kilduff, "Fact Sheet: Aging in the United States," Population Reference Bureau, July 15, 2019, www.prb.org.

84. Thomhave, "Revving Up Rural Public Transit."

CHAPTER 9 › WALMART ON WHEELS

1. "US Unemployment Rate Falls to 50-Year Low of 3.5%," *BBC News*, October 4, 2019, www.bbc.com; Micah Uetricht, "Just How Precarious Is the US Economy?," *Jacobin*, March 18, 2019, www. jacobinmag.com.

2. Michael Lewis, "One in 10 Toronto Workers Is Now a Gig Economy Worker, StatCan Says," *Toronto Star*, December 16, 2019, www.thestar.com.

3. "New Study Suggests Automation Will Not Wipe Out Truck-Driving Jobs," SAGE Publications, June 18, 2019, www.phys.org; Maury Gittleman and Kristen Monaco, "Automation Isn't About to Make Truckers Obsolete," *Harvard Business Review*, September 18, 2019, https://hbr.org; Parix Marx, "Self-Driving Trucks Won't Kill Millions of Jobs," *OneZero*, August 19, 2019, https://onezero.medium.com.

4. "Get Started," Uber, www.uber.com.

5. "Drive with Lyft," Lyft, www.lyft.com.

6. Jonathan V. Hall and Alan B. Krueger, "An Analysis of the Labor Market for Uber's Driver-Partners in the United States," *ILR Review* 71, no. 3 (2018): 705–32.

7. "Drive for Money: 9 Reasons It's Easy to Make Money with Uber," Uber, www.uber.com.

8. "How Many Uber Drivers Are There?," *Ridester*, January 29, 2019, www.ridester.com; Iqbal, "Uber Revenue and Usage Statistics."

9. Lyft Impact, www.lyftimpact.com.

10. "How to Drive for Uber and Lyft (at the Same Time)," *Ridester*, April 9, 2019, www.ridester.com.

11. Alicia Adamczyk, "Here's Why Uber Is Testing Self-Driving Cars," *Money*, May 19, 2016, https://money.com.

12. Harry Campbell, "What's the Real Commission That Uber Takes from Its Drivers?," *Rideshare Guy*, July 25, 2016, https://therideshareguy.com.

13. Jillian D'Onfro, "Uber Says Its Drivers Are Making $75,000–$90,000 a Year," *Business Insider*, May 27, 2014, www.businessinsider.com.

14. Ryan Lawler, "Uber Study Shows Its Drivers Make More per Hour and Work Fewer Hours Than Taxi Drivers," *TechCrunch*, January 22, 2015, https://techcrunch.com.

15. Hubert Horan, "Can Uber Ever Deliver? Part Thirteen: Even After 4Q Cost Cuts, Uber Lost $4.5 Billion in 2017," *Naked Capitalism*, February 16, 2018, www.nakedcapitalism.com; Horan, "Uber's Path of Destruction."

16. Lawrence Mishel, *Uber and the Labor Market: Uber Drivers' Compensation, Wages, and the Scale of Uber and the Gig Economy* (Washington, DC: Economic Policy Institute, 2018), 2, www.epi.org.

17. Caroline O'Donovan and Jeremy Singer-Vine, "How Much Uber Drivers Actually Make per Hour," *Buzzfeed News*, June 22, 2016, www.buzzfeednews.com; Tracey Lindeman, "After 'Flawed' MIT Paper, Uber Drivers Can't Agree on How Poorly They're Paid," *Motherboard*, March 6, 2018, www.vice.com; Noah Smith, "Uber Better Not Be the Future of Work," *Bloomberg Opinion*, March 8, 2018, www.bloomberg.com.

18. "Ways Female Uber Drivers Can Stay Safe," *Ridester*, April 2, 2018, www.ridester.com.

19. Selina Wang, "The Dark Realities Women Face Driving for Uber and Lyft," *Bloomberg*, December 18, 2018, www.bloomberg.com.

20. Jaden Urbi, "Some Transgender Drivers Are Being Kicked Off Uber's App," *CNBC*, August 8, 2018, www.cnbc.com.

21. Wells et al., "The Work Lives of Uber Drivers: Worse Than You Think," *Working-Class Perspectives*, July 10, 2017, https://workingclassstudies.wordpress.com.

22. "Fired from Uber: Why Drivers Get Deactivated, and How to Get Reactivated," *Ridesharing Driver*, February 7, 2018, www.ridesharingdriver.com.

23. Ngai Keung Chan, "The Rating Game: The Discipline of Uber's User-Generated Ratings," *Surveillance & Society* 17, vol. 1/2 (2019): 1477–87.

24. Luke Stark, "Recognizing the Role of Emotional Labor in the On-Demand Economy," *Harvard Business Review*, August 29, 2016, https://hbr.org.

25. Stark, "Recognizing the Role of Emotional Labor"; Andrew J. Hawkins, "Uber Is Now Offering a 'Quiet Mode' Option for Its Luxury Service," *Verge*, May 14, 2019, www.theverge.com.

26. Noam Scheiber, "How Uber Uses Psychological Tricks to Push Its Drivers' Buttons," *New York Times*, April 2, 2017, www.nytimes.com.

27. "Can I (the Driver) Be Deactivated or Lose Uber Account for Having a Low Acceptance Rate?," *RideGuru*, January 24, 2018, https://ride.guru; "Fired from Uber," *Ridesharing Driver*.

28. "Have You Been Sidelined by Uber?," *Ridester*, January 29, 2018, www.ridester.com.

29. Jason Koebler, "Why Everyone Hates UberPOOL," *Motherboard*, May 23, 2016, www.vice.com; Harry Campbell, "2017 Uber Driver Survey Results: Earnings, Satisfaction, and Demographics," *Rideshare Guy*, January 17, 2017, https://therideshareguy.com; Harry Campbell, "7 Reasons Why I Hate Uberpool and Lyftline," *Rideshare Guy*, April 17, 2017, https://therideshareguy.com.

30. Jennifer Calfas, "Uber Just Admitted That Its Pay Policy Will Make Drivers Even More Unhappy: Here's How That Could Affect Your Future Rides," *Money*, April 15, 2019, http://money.com.

31. Johana Bhuiyan, "Lower Pay and Higher Costs: The Downside of Lyft's Car Rental Program," *Los Angeles Times*, May 20, 2019, www.latimes.com.

32. Aaron Gordon, "Uber Launches New Program to Get Drivers Who Can't Afford Cars to Drive Cars for Them," *Jalopnik*, May 30, 2019, https://jalopnik.com.

33. Noam Scheiber, "Uber Drivers Are Contractors, Not Employees, Labor Board Says," *New York Times*, May 14, 2019, www.nytimes.com.

34. Jordan Golson, "Uber Is Using In-App Podcasts to Dissuade Seattle Drivers from Unionizing," *Verge*, March 14, 2017, www.theverge.com.

35. Carmel DeAmicis, "The Flop of Uber Drivers' National Protest Shows How Hard It Is for Them to Organize," *Vox*, October 18, 2015, www.vox.com; Andrew J. Hawkins, "'Shame on Uber': Hundreds of Drivers Demand More Pay at NYC Protest," *Verge*, February 1, 2016, www.theverge.com.

36. Christian Perea, "Will Uber Rates Ever Go Up Again?," *Rideshare Guy*, April 3, 2017, https://therideshareguy.com.

37. Will Sabel Courtney, "96 Percent of Uber Drivers Ditch the Company within a Year," *Drive*, April 20, 2017, www.thedrive.com.

38. David Bush, "Automation: Will Robots Take Our Jobs?," *Socialist.ca*, February 27, 2018, www.socialist.ca.

39. Schaller, *The New Automobility*; David Z. Morris, "6th New York City Cab Driver Takes His Life in Crisis Blamed on Uber," *Fortune*, June 16, 2018, https://fortune.com; Jessica Bruder, "Driven to Despair," *New York*, May 2018, http://nymag.com; Elizabeth Chuck, "'Something Has to Change': Taxi Workers Alliance Pleads for Regulation after Sixth Cabbie Death," *NBC News*, June 18, 2018, www.nbcnews.com; Brian M. Rosenthal, "'They Were Conned': How Reckless Loans Devastated a Generation of Taxi Drivers," *New York Times*, May 19, 2019, www.nytimes.com.

40. Andrew J. Hawkins, "JFK Airport Roiled by Protests against Trump's Immigration Ban," *Verge*, January 28, 2017, www.theverge.com; German Lopez, "Why People Are Deleting Uber from Their Phones after Trump's Executive Order," *Vox*, January 29, 2017, www.vox.com; Biz Carson, "Over 200,000 People Deleted Uber after the Company Operated Its Service at JFK Airport during the Trump Strike," *Business Insider*, February 2, 2017, www.businessinsider.com; Jordan Pearson, "Lyft Accused of Helping People Cross a Workers' Picket Line in Toronto," *Motherboard*, August 28, 2018, www.vice.com.

41. Dana Hull, "Tesla Is a 'Hotbed for Racist Behavior,' Worker Claims in Suit," *Bloomberg*, November 13, 2017, www.bloomberg.com; Richard Lawler, "Tesla: Racial Harassment Lawsuit Is a 'Hotbed of Misinformation,'" *Engadget*, November 15, 2017, www.engadget.com; Ethan Baron, "Tesla Fails in Bid to Push Racism Lawsuit into Arbitration," *Mercury News*, June 4, 2018, www.mercurynews.com; Josh Eidelson, "Tesla Workers Claim Racial Bias and Abuse at Electric Car Factory," *Bloomberg*, April 12, 2018, www.bloomberg.com; Sam Levin, "Tesla Email Reveals Company's Effort to Silence an Alleged Victim with Cash," *Guardian*, April 13, 2018, www.theguardian.com.

42. Julia Carrie Wong, "Tesla Factory Workers Reveal Pain, Injury and Stress: 'Everything Feels Like the Future but Us,'" *Guardian*, May 18, 2017, www.theguardian.com.

43. Will Evans and Alyssa Jeong Perry, "Tesla Says Its Factory Is Safer: But It Left Injuries off the Books," *Reveal*, April 16, 2018, www.revealnews.org.

44. Josh Eidelson and Dana Hall, "Tesla Staff's Lost Workdays Triple on Factory Injuries, Illness," *Bloomberg*, March 19, 2019, www.bloomberg.com.

45. Caroline O'Donovan, "Workers Involved in Union Activities Say Tesla Is Illegally Intimidating Them," *Buzzfeed News*, April 25, 2017, www.cnbc.com.

46. Daniel Wiessner, "UAW Accuses Musk of Threatening Tesla Workers over Unionization," *Reuters*, May 24, 2018, www.reuters.com.

47. "U.S. Labor Judge Rules That Tesla Broke Labor Law," *Reuters*, September 27, 2019, www.reuters.com; Alexia Fernandez Campbell, "Elon Musk Broke US Labor Laws on Twitter," *Vox*, September 30, 2019, www.vox.com.

48. Michael Sainato, "Tesla Workers Speak Out: 'Anything Pro-union Is Shut Down Really Fast,'" *Guardian*, September 10, 2018, www.theguardian.com.

49. Fred Lambert, "Tesla Is Not Going to Buy GM Factory Because of Union Employees, Says GM CEO," *Electrek*, January 11, 2019, https://electrek.co.

50. Michael Hiltzik, "Why Is Tesla Fighting a Rule That Would Force Electric-Car Manufacturers to Treat Their Workers Well?," *Los Angeles Times*, June 15, 2018, www.latimes.com.

51. Susan Fowler, "Reflecting on One Very, Very Strange Year at Uber," Susan Fowler, February 19, 2017, www.susanjfowler.com.

52. Joseph Menn and Heather Somerville, "Uber Fires 20 Employees after Harassment Probe," *Reuters*, June 6, 2017, www.reuters.com.

53. Elizabeth Weise, "Uber Agrees to Pay $10 Million in Class Action Discrimination Suit," *USA Today*, March 27, 2018, www.usatoday.com; Johana Bhuiyan, "A Former Uber Engineer Is Suing the Company for Discrimination and Sexual Harassment," *Vox*, May 21, 2018, www.vox.com.

54. Andrew J. Hawkins, "Uber Senior Executive Resigns after Racial Discrimination Allegations," *Verge*, July 11, 2018, www.theverge.com.

55. Mike Isaac and Katie Benner, "At Uber, New Questions Arise about Executive Behavior," *New York Times*, July 13, 2018; Chris Welch, "Uber's Chief Operating and Marketing Officers Are Both Leaving the Company," *Verge*, June 7, 2019, www.theverge.com.

56. Biz Carson, "Travis Kalanick on Uber's Bet on Self-Driving Cars: 'I Can't Be Wrong,'" *Business Insider*, August 18, 2016, www.businessinsider.com.

57. Bernhart, Kaise, Ohashi, Schonberg, and Schilles, *Reconnecting the Rural*, 17.

58. Veena Dubal, "Why the Uber Strike Was a Triumph," *Slate*, May 10, 2019, https://slate.com.

59. Andrew J. Hawkins, "Uber and Lyft Face an Existential Threat in California—and They're Losing," *Verge*, September 2, 2019, www.theverge.com.

60. Andrew J. Hawkins, "Uber Argues Its Drivers Aren't Core to Its Business, Won't Reclassify Them as Employees," *Verge*, September 11, 2019, www.theverge.com.

61. Megan Rose Dickey, "Uber and Lyft Are Putting $60 Million

toward Keeping Drivers Independent Contractors," *TechCrunch*, August 29, 2019, www.techcrunch.com.

62. Rachel M. Cohen, "A California Bill Could Transform the Lives of Gig Workers: Silicon Valley Wants Labor's Help to Stop It," *Intercept*, July 18, 2019, www.theintercept.com; Alexia Fernandez Campbell, "Secret Meetings between Uber and Labor Unions Are Causing an Uproar," *Recode*, July 1, 2019, www.vox.com.

63. Andrew J. Hawkins, "California Just Dropped a Bomb on the Gig Economy—What's Next?," *Verge*, September 11, 2019, www.theverge.com.

64. Dubal, "Why the Uber Strike Was a Triumph."

65. Alon Levy and Eric Goldwyn, "To Build a Better Bus System, Ask a Driver," *CityLab*, June 18, 2018, www.citylab.com.

66. Laura Bliss, "There's a Bus Driver Shortage: And No Wonder," *CityLab*, June 28, 2018, www.citylab.com.

67. Tracey Lindeman, "Human Bus Drivers Will Always Be Better Than Robot Bus Drivers," *Motherboard*, May 7, 2018, www.vice.com.

68. Alexis C. Madrigal, "How Automation Could Worsen Racial Inequality," *Atlantic*, January 16, 2018, www.theatlantic.com.

69. Algernon Austin, "Transporting Black Men to Good Jobs," Economic Policy Institute, October 5, 2012, www.epi.org.

70. Patricia Cohen, "Public-Sector Jobs Vanish, Hitting Blacks Hard," *New York Times*, May 24, 2015.

71. Dan Malouff, "Streetcar Advantages," *BeyondDC*, May 25, 2010, https://beyonddc.com.

72. Jarrett Walker, "Frequency and Freedom on Driverless Rapid Transit," *Human Transit*, February 18, 2010, https://humantransit.org.

73. Beatrice Britneff, "OC Transpo to Hand Out 345 Pink Slips by Aug. 3," *Global News*, July 25, 2018, https://globalnews.ca.

74. Megan Stacey, "Some London Transit Workers Seek Union President's Resignation," *London Free Press*, November 6, 2018, https://lfpress.com; Megan Stacey, "London Transit Union President Resigns amid Pressure from Members," *London Free Press*, November 6, 2018, https://lfpress.com.

75. Ben Spurr, "TTC Criticized in Labour Ruling over 'Abuse' of Workers on Social Media," *Toronto Star*, July 28, 2016, www.thestar.com.

76. Danielle Furfaro, Elizabeth Rosner, and Ruth Brown, "Museum of Sex Ads Driving Female MTA Bus Drivers Crazy," *New York Post*, June 15, 2018, https://nypost.com.

77. Erin Corbett, "Transit Union Refuses to Bring White Nationalists to 'Unite the Right' Rally," *Fortune*, August 4, 2018, https://fortune.com.

78. Bliss, "There's a Bus Driver Shortage"; "Ten Reasons Why

Unions Are Important," War on Want, February 12, 2018, https://waronwant.org.

79. Charlotte DiBartolomeo, "Amid Automation Trend, Here's Why We Still Need Bus Drivers," *Metro*, April 24, 2018, www.metro-magazine.com.

80. Ryan Flanagan, "Bus Driver Credited with Saving Man's Life Says He's No Hero," *CTV News*, February 12, 2019, www.ctvnews.ca.

81. Maggie Gilroy, "Quick-Thinking Bus Driver Saves Student from Speeding Car," *USA Today*, May 9, 2019, www.usatoday.com.

82. "Award for Milwaukee Bus Driver Who Saved Toddler," *BBC News*, January 11, 2019, www.bbc.com; Phil Helsel, "Bus Driver Hailed as Hero in Seattle Shooting, Carjacking," *NBC News*, March 27, 2019, www.nbcnews.com; "Sudbury Bus Driver Recognized for Saving Teen's Life," *CBC News*, January 30, 2018, www.cbc.ca.

83. "Bus Driver Saves Disabled Boy from Oncoming Traffic," *CNN*, May 31, 2019, www.cnn.com; Emily Mertz, "Edmonton Bus Driver Praised for Helping Elderly Passenger with Groceries," *Global News*, May 17, 2019, https://globalnews.ca; "Bowen Bus Driver Stopped in Vancouver Traffic to Save Eight Little Goslings," *Bowen Island Undercurrent*, May 7, 2019, www.bowenislandundercurrent.com.

84. Holly Caruk, "No Fare: Transit Drivers Offer Free Rides to Pressure City for New Contract," *CBC News*, May 14, 2019, www.cbc.ca.

85. Naomi Larsson, "No Ticket to Ride: Japanese Bus Drivers Strike by Giving Free Rides," *Guardian*, May 11, 2018, www.theguardian.com.

86. Levy and Goldwyn, "To Build a Better Bus System."

87. "Amalgamated Transit Union Assault Survey 2016," Amalgamated Transit Union, www.atu.org.

88. "Allies in Public Transit," *In Transit*, March/April 2018, www.atu.org.

89. Reka Szekely, "Labour Leaders Make the Case to Nationalize General Motors at Oshawa Event," *DurhamRegion.com*, May 1, 2019, www.durhamregion.com.

90. James Bow, "A Brief History of New Flyer Industries," Transit Toronto, April 16, 2019, www.transit.toronto.on.ca. It was NDP governments that both bought the bus company in 1971 and then sold it in 1986.

91. Caroline Haskins, "Alexandria Ocasio-Cortez's Green New Deal Should Nationalize Utilities," *Motherboard*, February 7, 2019, www.vice.com.

CHAPTER 10 › MONEY AND THE POWER

1. Mike Konczal, "Socialize Uber," *Nation*, December 10, 2014, www.thenation.com.

2. Ben Fredericks, "California Gig Workers Win Historic Victory: Now It's Time to Nationalize Big Tech," *Left Voice*, September 18, 2019, www.leftvoice.org.

3. Lawrence Blincoe, Ted R. Miller, Eduard Zaloshnja, and Bruce A. Lawrence, *The Economic and Societal Impact of Motor Vehicle Crashes, 2010* (Revised) (Washington, DC: National Center for Statistics and Analysis, 2015), 1, https://crashstats.nhtsa.dot.gov.

4. Tanvi Misra, "The Social Costs of Driving in Vancouver, in 1 Chart," *CityLab*, April 7, 2015, www.citylab.com.

5. A 2012 study of automobile impacts on European Union countries—including the costs of crashes, climate change, and air pollution—estimated that driving costs 373 billion euros per year, equivalent to 3 percent of the EU's GDP. (Udo J. Becker, Thilo Becker, and Julia Gerlach, *The True Costs of Automobility: External Costs of Cars Overview on Existing Estimates in EU-27* (Dresden: Technische Universität Dresden, 2012), 33, www.stopclimatechange.net.) A more recent study increased that estimate to 500 billion euros per year, noting that cycling came with *benefits* of 24 billion euros and walking another 66 billion euros. (Stefan Gossling, Andy Choi, Kaely Dekker, and Daniel Metzler, "The Social Cost of Automobility, Cycling and Walking in the European Union," *Ecological Economics*, 158 (2019): 65–74.)

6. Laura Bliss, "Americans Are Spending Billions on Bad Highway Expansions," *CityLab*, June 24, 2019, www.citylab.com.

7. Ben Welle, Guillermo Petzhold, and Francisco Minella Pasqual, "Cities Are Taxing Ride-Hailing Services Like Uber and Lyft: Is This a Good Thing?," World Resources Institute, August 8, 2018, www.wri.org.

8. Liz Farmer, "Governments Increasingly Tax Uber and Lyft for Transit Revenue," Truth in Accounting, April 4, 2018, www.truthinaccounting.org; "Uber, Lyft Agree to San Francisco Ride-Hail Tax," *CBS SF*, July 31, 2018, https://sanfrancisco.cbslocal.com.

9. Nicole Badstuber, "London Congestion Charge: Why It's Time to Reconsider One of the City's Great Successes," *Conversation*, April 11, 2019, http://theconversation.com; "First Congestion Fines to Go Out," *BBC News*, February 18, 2003, http://news.bbc.co.uk.

10. Paris Marx, "London and Oslo Took On Cars, but the Key Was Investing in Alternatives," *Radical Urbanist*, June 3, 2019, https://medium.com/radical-urbanist.

11. Stockholm has implemented a successful system of congestion pricing that is significantly larger than London's and charges based on time of day (rather than a flat fee between certain hours).

12. Mees, *Transport for Suburbia*, 46–48.

13. James Wilt, "The Leftist's Case against the Carbon Tax," *Briarpatch*, December 20, 2018, www.briarpatchmagazine.com.

14. Craig Raborn, *Transportation Emissions Response to Carbon Pricing Programs* (Durham: Duke University, September 2009), 5, www.nicholasinstitute.duke.edu.

15. Feargus O'Sullivan, "Madrid Takes Its Car Ban to the Next Level," *CityLab*, May 24, 2018, www.citylab.com.

16. Athlyn Cathcart-Keays, "Oslo's Car Ban Sounded Simple Enough: Then the Backlash Began," *Guardian*, June 13, 2017, www.theguardian.com; Marx, "London and Oslo Took On Cars."

17. Estelle Sommeiller and Mark Price, "The New Gilded Age: Income Inequality in the U.S. by State, Metropolitan Area, and County," Economic Policy Institute, July 19, 2018, www.epi.org.

18. Rupert Neate, "Bill Gates, Jeff Bezos and Warren Buffett Are Wealthier Than Poorest Half of US," *Guardian*, November 8, 2017, www.theguardian.com.

19. Joel Shannon, "Amazon Pays No Federal Income Tax for 2018, Despite Soaring Profits, Report Says," *USA Today*, February 15, 2019, www.usatoday.com.

20. "2 Richest Canadians Have More Money Than 11 Million Combined," *Canadian Press*, January 15, 2017, www.cbc.ca.

21. Matt Kwong, "The Winners and Losers of Trump's Big Tax Overhaul," *CBC News*, December 21, 2017, www.cbc.ca.

22. David Rogers, "Politico Analysis: At $2.3 Trillion Cost, Trump Tax Cuts Leave Big Gap," *Politico*, February 28, 2018, www.politico.com.

23. Steve Liesman, "Most of the Tax Cut Windfall Will Boost Buybacks and Dividends, Not Workers' Pockets, Survey Predicts," *CNBC*, January 30, 2018, www.cnbc.com.

24. Jeff Cox, "Companies Set to Buy Back $1 Trillion Worth of Shares This Year, and That Should Keep Market Afloat, Goldman Says," *CNBC*, August 6, 2018, www.cnbc.com.

25. Lucas Powers, "Panama Papers Only a Glimpse into 'Astonishing' Wealth Stashed Offshore," *CBC News*, April 6, 2016, www.cbc.ca.

26. "Mass Incarceration Costs $182 Billion Every Year, without Adding Much to Public Safety," Equal Justice Initiative, February 6, 2017, https://egi.org.

27. Dave Colon, "MTA Will Spend $249M on New Cops to Save $200M on Fare Evasion," *StreetsBlog NYC*, November 14, 2019, www.nyc.streetsblog.org.

28. There's widespread support for community-based efforts: in the U.K., polling indicates that 56 percent of people supported the plan for renationalizing the railways as proposed by Jeremy Corbyn's

Labour Party, while only 15 percent opposed it. (Joe Lo, "Poll Shows Huge Support for Rail Nationalisation—Even from Tory Voters," Left Foot Forward, January 4, 2019, https://leftfootforward.org.)

29. Janie Velencia, "Alexandria Ocasio-Cortez Wants to Raise Taxes on the Rich—and Americans Agree," January 17, 2019, *FiveThirtyEight*, www.fivethirtyeight.com.

30. Jolson Lim, "Federal Poll Finds Few Canadians Believe Wealthy and Corporations Pay Fair Share of Taxes," *iPolitics*, August 21, 2019, www.ipolitics.ca.

31. Matt T. Huber, "Ecological Politics for the Working Class," *Catalyst* 3, no. 1 (2019).

32. Huber, "Ecological Politics for the Working Class."

33. Jane McAlevey, "Organizing to Win a Green New Deal," *Jacobin*, March 26, 2019, www.jacobinmag.com.

34. Toronto's CUPE Local 2, representing the TTC's electrical workers, called for these measures in mid-2019. (Kayla Gladysz, "TTC Electrical Employees Calling for Mass Strikes and Free Transit to 'Bring Down' Doug Ford," *Daily Hive,* July 30, 2019, https://dailyhive.com.)

35. Huber, "Ecological Politics for the Working Class."

36. "Victory for Public Education!," United Teachers Los Angeles, 2019, www.utla.net.

37. Higashide, *Better Buses, Better Cities*, 12.

38. "The STM Invites Owners of Older Cars to Join the Movement," STM, April 18, 2011, www.stm.info; "SCRAP-IT," 2019, https://scrapit.ca.

39. "Questions Raised about New Zealand's Gun Buyback Scheme as Amnesty Ends," *Guardian*, December 20, 2019, www.theguardian.com.

40. Krystal Yee, "Why Not Retire Your Ride and Get $500," *Toronto Star*, March 3, 2011, www.thestar.com.

41. "Green New Deal + Transit," TransitCenter, April 1, 2019, www.transitcenter.org.

42. Linda McQuaig, "Take It Over: The Struggle for Green Production in Oshawa," *Bullet*, September 16, 2019, www.socialistproject.ca.

43. Erick Trickey, "'They're Bold and Fresh': The Millennials Disrupting Boston's Transit System," *Politico*, October 25, 2018, www.politico.com.

44. Steve Palonis, Laura Wiens, and Tom Hoffman, "In Honor of Rosa Parks: an Appeal for Transit Equity," *Pittsburgh Post-Gazette*, February 4, 2018, www.post-gazette.com.

45. Mark Byrnes, "Why the Jane Jacobs vs. Robert Moses Battle Still Matters," *CityLab*, April 19, 2017, www.citylab.com; Linda Poon,

"Mapping the Effects of the Great 1960s 'Freeway Revolts," *CityLab*, July 23, 2019, www.citylab.com; Reft, "From Bus Riders Union to Bus Rapid Transit"; Cadie Thompson, "Protesters in San Francisco Form Blockade around Google Bus," *CNBC*, December 9, 2013, www.cnbc. com; Sarah Emerson, "'Techsploitation' Demonstrators Blocked Google and Apple Buses with Scooters," *Motherboard*, May 31, 2018, www.vice.com.

46. Patrick Sisson, "Climate Strike: Why Transportation Is Key for These Student Activists," *Curbed*, September 20, 2019, www. curbed.com.

47. "Doug Ford Is Trying to 'Steal' the TTC's Subways, Public Transit Activists Charge," *CBC News*, November 29, 2018, www.cbc. ca; Abigal Turner, "Winnipeg Transit Union Not Enforcing Fares amidst Second Job Action," *Global News*, June 26, 2019, https:// globalnews.ca.

48. Emily Riddle, "Cutting Greyhound Service in Western Canada Puts Indigenous Women at Risk," *Globe and Mail*, July 10, 2018, www. theglobeandmail.com.

Index

accessibility, 9, 78, 90, 198, 200; barriers to, 81-82; cost of, 73; for gender non-conforming people, 9, 35, 125-26, 131, 157, 187, 193; for marginalized people, 112-31; for people with disabilities, 9, 13, 35, 47, 90, 112-15, 121-24, 126, 128, 131, 187, 193, 202-4; for seniors, 9, 35, 79, 112, 113, 117, 122, 124-26, 131, 187, 193; of subway stations, 123; three revolutions and, 113-22; for trans people, 9, 35, 125-26, 131, 157, 187, 193; for women, 9, 35, 125-26, 131, 187, 193

"accidental environmentalists," 152

active transportation, 4, 83, 108; funding for, 177; promotion of, 106

activism: anti-carceral, 15; public, 85–90; transit, 16, 198-201

ADAPT (American Disabled for Attendant Programs Today), 127, 205; "Gang of 19," 127

adaptation urbanism, 108

affordability, 30–31, 33, 38

age: accessibility and, 112, 121; and driving, 152

Airbnb, 84

air pollution, 35, 37–38, 53, 54, 56, 61, 64-67, 70, 190, 201, 206

Albert, Dan: *Are We There Yet?*, 21

Albuquerque: electric buses in, 68

alcohol use, 92-93

all-door boarding, 8, 35, 66, 141

Altamonte Springs (Florida): Uber in, 46–47

alternative financing and procurement (AFP), 27

Amalgamated Transit Union

(ATU), 160, 169, 182; *In Transit*, 182; in London (Ontario), 180

Amazon, 40, 138, 194

American Automobile Association, 22, 94

American Civil Liberties Union (ACLU), 145

American Network of Community Options and Resources (ANCOR), 115

American Public Transit Association, 107

Americans with Disabilities Act (ADA), 116

Amsterdam: cycle paths in, 4

Amtrak: stagnation and decline of, 160-61; train derailments, 106-7

anonymous online reporting, 129

anti-carceral demands, 199

anti-discrimination policies, 181

anti-eviction measures, 84, 111

anti-gentrification measures, 90

anti-labour practices, 174, 177-80, 184

anti-migrant policy, 144, 204

anti-poor discrimination, 81

anti-poor policing, 147

anti-racism training, 189, 203

anti-racist struggles, 144

anti-transit sentiment, 20, 30, 109; and three revolutions, 36–49

anti-unionism, 173

Argentina, 56

Arlington (Texas): Via vanpooling in, 47

Aspen (Colorado): bus system in, 164-65

asylum seekers, 143

Atlanta: transit in, 32

Attoh, Kafui, 46, 72; *Rights in Transit*, 46, 196

Audi: Immersive In-Car Entertainment, 133

austerity, 6, 8, 15, 31, 34, 36, 47, 65, 69, 150, 153, 158, 177, 179-80, 189

Australia: crash test authority in, 94; sexual harassment and assault in, 125

automobiles: 3–4; attitudes toward, 21; banning of from downtowns, 192-93; as capital assets, 60; clean, 54-55; connected, 135, 147; as consumption choice, 197; cost of, 73, 189-90; culture of, 20, 48, 90, 108, 166; daily use of, 92; dangers of, 21, 92-93, 94 (*see also* safety); dependence on, 22, 25; dominance of: brief history of, 19–35; expansion of, 46; gas-guzzling, 24; institutionalization of, 92; loans for, 73; "love affair" with, 20; new: sales of, 36; phasing out of, 14, 190-91, 193, 200; political infatuation with, 36; private ownership of, 23, 36, 66, 95, 115, 134-35, 195; as rolling listening posts, 135; in rural areas, 150-51; single-passenger, 94; size of, 93, 94; technological upgrades to, 94-96; as threat, 21; turnover of, 59; violence of, 21; weight of, 57

automobility, 6, 8, 13–14, 20, 22; mandated, 110-11; manufacturing of, 36–49; next-generation, 9, 11, 15, 35, 38–39, 40–41, 94–95, 104, 111, 113, 132-33, 156, 167, 174, 176; transition from, 88. *See also* "three revolutions"

automotive industry, 22–25; propaganda campaign by, 22

autonomous technologies, 94, 97-102

autonomous vehicles (AVs), 5, 7, 9, 12, 15, 37, 39–45, 53, 55, 60-61, 79-80, 95-102, 103, 111, 114-15, 117-18, 131, 134-35, 147-48, 168-69, 173-74, 175-77, 183, 195, 202, 205; and accessibility, 76-77, 121; and disabilities, 117-18, 121-22; fatalities from, 96, 99; future of, 138-39; hybrid/electric, 61-62; mixing of human driving and computer control in, 99; platooning of, 65; and price control, 182; and racial inequality, 101; in rural areas, 153-56; "safe exit strategies" for, 115; safety of, 44, 97-101, 126; shared, 74; testing of, 99-100; weight of, 58

Avis, 38

AV START Act (2018), 44, 115

Bailey, Derek, 181

Baltimore: bus system redesign in, 34–35; light rail in, 34; transit reliability in, 31

Barra, Mary, 174-75

Bay Area Rapid Transit (BART), 2, 85, 140-42, 145; Safe Transit policy, 141

BC Transit, 128

Bear, Marlene, 159

Beaton, Connor, 219n25

Beauceron Security, 140

Beijing: trolleybuses in, 69

Bezos, Jeff, 194

Bhuttar, Shahid, 141

Bird, 123-24

Birnel, Alex, 78, 117

Black people: and disability, 112; discrimination against, 129; and fare enforcement, 141-43; harassment and incarceration of, 33; impacts on, 190; and pedestrian deaths, 93; and police violence, 140, 142-43, 147; in rural areas, 150; transit access for, 13; as transit drivers, 178-79; underrepresentation of in MPOs and transit agency boards, 82; in U.S. South, 150;

Spain: high-speed rail in, 161;
 sexual harassment and assault
 in, 125
Sparrow, Jeff, 21, 48
Speed, 1
speed limits, 11, 14, 92-93, 154
Spiderman 2, 2
Spokane Tribe: Moccasin
 Express, 163
Spotify, 80
Standard Oil of California, 20
Star Wars, 1
Stein, Samuel: *Capital City*, 84
Stimpson, Alexander, 117
Stranger Than Fiction, 2
streetcars, 22, 105-6, 141; electric,
 20, 69-70
Strickfaden, Megan, 117-18
Strickland, David, 41–42
strikes, 15, 181, 198–99, 204; fare,
 15, 182, 205; by ride-hailing
 services, 173, 176–77
Strong Towns, 157
substance use, 147
suburbanization, 20, 22–23, 102;
 and poverty, 110
suburbs: automobile, 109;
 expansion of transit systems
 into, 109; "last mile" problem,
 152; living in, as consumption
 choice, 197
subways, 69-70, 179, 189, 201;
 deaths in, 107; platform edge
 barriers, 107. *See also under
 individual city names*
suicide: in subways, 107
SumOfUs, 42
Sunrise Movement, 15
surge pricing, 78, 168, 173
surveillance, 112, 132-48, 174,
 187, 195-96, 206
SUVs: sales of, 57, 59
Sydney (Australia): fare strikes
 in, 182

Tait, Amelia, 120
Tampa: free fares in, 87-88
tax credits: for commuter

parking, 92, 190; for electric
 vehicles, 77, 190
Tax Cuts and Jobs Act (2017), 194
taxes, 24, 29, 43, 194–95; carbon,
 6, 192; on diesel, 103, 246n77;
 "fair," 197; to fund transit,
 30; on gasoline, 23, 103,
 156, 246n77; on ride-hailing
 services, 191
tax haven hoarding, 195
taxis, 41, 75, 79, 97, 122, 136, 138,
 152, 157, 167, 169, 182-83, 192,
 204; and congestion pricing,
 183; drivers of, 174; medallion
 system, 183; "pink," 121;
 robotaxis, 101
Tax Justice Network, 195
telecommuting, 6
tenants' unions, 15
Tesla, 37, 39, 63, 67, 99, 132-
 33, 169, 174-75, 188, 202;
 Autopilot, 99; Cybertruck,
 93-94; factory in Fremont, 174-
 75; Model S, 55, 57, 77, 94; and
 racism, 174; and unfair labour
 practices, 174
Thatcher, Margaret, 26
Thompson (Manitoba), 160
Thomson, David, 194
"three revolutions," 5, 9, 11,
 16, 35, 53, 177, 187; and
 access, 113-22; anti-transit
 underpinnings of, 36–49;
 effects of on poverty, 74-80;
 environmental impacts of,
 54-64; impact on labour, 168-
 77; and privacy, 133-39; rural
 impact of, 151-56
time-based transfers, 130
Toronto: access to transit
 service in, 81-82, 83-84, 86-87;
 commuting in, 4; Eglinton
 Crosstown LRT line, 27, 33;
 fare enforcement in, 141-42;
 female transit workers in, 130;
 GO Transit, 66, 140-41; King
 Street streetcar project, 105-6;
 light rail transit in, 27, 84;

James Wilt is a freelance journalist based in Winnipeg, Manitoba. He regularly contributes to *The Narwhal,* and has also written for *VICE Canada, National Observer, CBC Calgary, Alberta Oil, Canadian Dimension* and *Briarpatch.*